WHEALTHSPAN™

More Years
More Moments
More Money

For Everyday Mortals, Proven by Millions

Scott B. Fulton

TESTIMONIALS

"Scott Fulton's commingling of health and wealth, longevity and vitality- is novel, compelling, and wise. With great insight about the 'prizes' that truly enrich our lives, Scott lays out remarkably thorough, actionable guidance for reaching them."

David L. Katz, MD, MPH, FACPM, FACP, FACLM,
Past President, American College of Lifestyle Medicine

"Plenty of books give you advice towards better health or better health, but this one will help you build and preserve your wealth, health and your lifespan by showing you how to create a Whealthspan mindset. Scott Fulton mixes the latest research with his keen insights to help you change your health habits and make smarter financial choices for your health. The likely result: a longer life and more financial security."

Richard Eisenberg,
"The View From Unretirement" columnist, MarketWatch

"Scott Fulton's Whealthspan workshops and his accompanying book have been transformative for my family, my clients, and myself. Scott's unparalleled knowledge and passion for the subject shine through in every session and page. His research-based recommendations offer practical steps that have empowered us to lead longer, healthier lives. A must read!"

Patrick Gilmour, Senior Wealth Advisor, CFP, BA(ECON),
President and managing partner at Stone House Financial Partners,
Branch Owner at Assante Financial

"Scott Fulton and his ideas meet today's moment. A systems thinker, Scott identifies the key elements, including the role of environment, that drive not just a longer life but a better one. Reading Whealthspan and acting upon its insights are energies well spent. Your future self will thank you."

Ryan Frederick, Author of Right Place, Right Time:
The Ultimate Guide to Choosing a Home for the Second Half of Life
and Founder & CEO of Here

"Scott Fulton has an exceptional understanding and respect for healthy aging and the ability to distill complex science into language that anyone can understand and easily apply to their own life."

Dan Zeman, M.S.,
Author of You're Too Old to Die Young

Scott brings a light-hearted approach to getting started with successful aging.

Gordo Byrn,
Coach / Author / Athlete

"As an advocate for proactive (strength-based) dementia care, I highly recommend Scott Fulton's 'Whealthspan.' Scott's proactive approach equips us all to enjoy elderhood with vitality and resilience."

Judy Cornish JD, Founder, Dementia & Alzheimer's
Wellbeing Network® (the DAWN Method®)

"In a world where longevity pursuits often overshadow quality of life, Scott Fulton's expertise shines through. He offers a refreshing, comprehensive, evidence-based approach to promoting vitality, prosperity, and health. Whealthspan is an innovative and valuable resource for healthcare professionals and individuals alike."

Melissa, Sundermann, DO, DipABLM, FACLM,
Lifespan Medicine

"Scott Fulton's 'Whealthspan' is a must-read for anyone concerned about the effects of agricultural chemicals on our health and longevity. His expertise on this critical issue provides valuable insights for a healthier future."

Kelly Ryerson, MBA,
Founder, Glyphosate Facts

"Whealthspan is a book, had I read it at age 40, I could have saved myself from an immense amount of heartache, lived with greater peace-of-mind, and yes, more financial stability in my later years. Don't miss your opportunity, at any age, pick up a copy.

Patrick Roden PhD,
aginginplace.com

"As someone who intends to "die young at an old age," I know that Scott's book can literally save your life—not just in years but in quality of life."

Paul Long,
Founder, New Way Forward

"Scott takes a deep dive into health, wealth and longevity. Don't want life to pass you by? Then stop and read this book to be an informed consumer of the game of life."

Ankit B. Shah, MD, MPH, FACC,
Assistant Professor, Georgetown University School of Medicine,
President, Sports & Performance Cardiology

Copyright ©2024 by Scott Fulton
Published by: Home Ideations, LLC
All rights reserved.
First Edition
Whealthspan™ is a registered trademark of Home ideations, LLC

ISBN: 979-8-9902759-0-4

This book is a work of nonfiction.
Cover Artwork: marphotography-stock.adobe.com

Dedicated to my eternal inspirations,
Frances, and Larry

To Cindy, thank you for your love, wisdom,
compassion, and curiosity. This project is evidence
that they know no limits.

TABLE OF CONTENTS

INTRODUCTION

THE OPERATING ROOM is flooded with light. Four walls of nothing but the latest in technology and life-saving equipment. A persistent beep-beep, beep-beep from the ECG reminds the surgical team that the patient's heart is still alive and beating. Three computer monitors hover above the patient, as the surgeon watches intently, carefully threading the 42-inch catheter into the arteries that supply heart muscles with blood. Beep-beep, beep-beep. The surgeon releases a few drops of dye from the catheter tip. The blood flow into the arteries is instantly captured on X-ray video, perfusing out into the capillaries embedded in the heart muscles. Beep-beep, beep-beep. The patient lies motionless. In sharp contrast, the heart arteries appear to be riding a wild bull. Every second, fresh oxygen-rich blood pulses, as the heart thunders like a concert bass drum in a symphony. Beep-beep, beep-beep.

The surgeon and I are in constant conversation, interrupted only by terse instructions to the medical team standing at the ready. He has them turn the screens in my direction so that we can both see the blood spurting into the arteries. Beep-beep, beep-beep. He gets another cardiologist on the phone, familiar with the case, and the three of us have a brief but decisive meeting. Consensus is quick. Beep-beep, beep-beep. There's only one hitch: I am the patient.

Two hours pass. The surgeon and I resume our conversation; this time, we're both standing in a hallway outside the operating room. I'm cleared to get back to an active lifestyle. A near-miss. It's a good day for the medical team and the patient. If only more procedures were like this one. Beep-beep, beep-beep.

I teach heart function as part of my healthspan and longevity classes, and I am comfortable talking medical jargon, but I hadn't planned to be on the operating room table, never having experienced a single symptom. Life is unpredictable, and a lot goes on inside the body that we can't see or predict with ease. It was only through proactive testing that we gained the upper hand, enabling us to take full advantage. Knowing early always offers better options.

I'm not a doctor. I don't even play one on social media. Like several physician colleagues, I come from an engineering background. We tend to think in systems mindsets. When we're talking about the body, we're talking about many systems, with each action triggering multiple reactions. The body's innate drive to rebalance and heal itself is nothing short of remarkable. We are a fascinating species, with rare thought and memory capabilities, yet we've only scratched the surface of tapping into our potential.

My views on aging were etched years before any conscious awareness. In her 1967 cherry red, two-door, soft-top Chevrolet Impala SS 327, Grandma embodied what life could be like in our advancing years. I loved spending weekends with her, helping with odd jobs, and taking road trips together. The world was ours to explore.

Midlife found me immersed in endurance triathlon and reconnecting with my childhood love of cycling. Athletics presented massive new challenges and opportunities. As a researcher and athlete, it shed light on healthspan possibilities I'd never imagined.

We are living in unprecedented times. Some of us are living longer than imagined, while many more are falling decades short of their potential. It's reminiscent of a mining town: abundant opportunity for wealth, but so much of it being thrown away on the vices that exploit our weaknesses and bring us pain and suffering. Given the headlines, it's no surprise that people like to *think* they're tracking toward longevity, but there's a big difference between *knowing*.

This book is about capturing opportunities before they slip through our fingers. It places a flashlight in our hands to help guide us through the noise-filled darkness of media hype, outdated myths, and a medical system designed for purposes other than our proactive health and longevity. Life's distractions are daunting and unrelenting, but as knowledge sometimes does, it helps separate the chaff from the wheat.

At the core, our life stories are about connections with our physical, biological, emotional, and cognitive selves and, most certainly, connections with others and our life experiences. We'll explore what goes into supporting those connections, including the signaling between our cells, and even with themselves. If human longevity could be distilled down to just one simple thing, it would be preserving our connections.

My students are mostly adult professionals; smart people looking to get up the learning curve of health and aging. Our adult habits are deeply entrenched around many things, but few more than lifestyle. Whether it's a milestone or a major life event, at some point, we all come up against difficult decisions that demand significant change. Inertia is stubborn. Change is hard. Oftentimes, we know the key elements needed for change; we're just lacking the right questions to bring the answers into view.

At the time of writing this, there are over 178 million U.S. Deaths on record since 1933, which speaks to mortality patterns in given years and emerging patterns within birth years. Data is always subject to interpretation, but data of this magnitude are the foundations of trusted regional, national, and international trends. It is these data, and large population study data, that I look to for knowledge, avoiding the confusion and contradictions that small studies inevitably create. While the focus is U.S. data, the underlying principles of wealth, health, and lifespan know no borders.

Data from across the globe, and here in the U.S., inform us that there are millions of ways to age well in hundreds of locations. Longevity is happening right under our noses, in places we might not expect, and for reasons we probably discount. It comes down to foundation and framework; simple things that compound into impressive outcomes.

The second half of life comes at us quickly. There's no question that our best odds of extended health begin with the foundations laid in our childhood, but 25 years ago, few of us would have bet that smokers could turn their health around and live into their nineties. It's one of many examples of the body's innate drive to heal and regenerate. All it asks of us is to give it a chance. Longevity is not the default, regardless of all that we hear. Longevity is like a game of poker, and chance will always be seated at the table. The difference is knowing what cards we're holding and how to play them. Sure, the house always wins in the end, but staying in the game of life has never been more within reach than it is today.

The Whealthspan framework brings everyone into the game: young and not-so-young, rich and not-so-rich. Staying in the game means preserving our financial equity, large or small. The biggest threats to our equity aren't the stock markets, politics, or recessions. It is our health and housing that will have a far greater impact on achieving the outcomes we desire, and they are intimately coupled.

Whealthspan is the fusion of wealth, health, and lifespan. How can we build and preserve them all? It comes down to a relatively simple balancing act of Mind, Environment, Diet, Activity, and Community (M.E.D.A.C). They are interdependent in surprising ways, and, when in balance, provide us with amazing and lasting resilience. The foundation is a composite of clinical practice and thousands of scientific studies, distilled into knowledge we can all apply.

This book is not another diet and lifestyle prescription. Rather, it frequently weaves in and around the MEDAC principles and health underpinnings we wish we'd been offered earlier in life. It focuses on building a foundation of wealth, health, and lifespan, providing a framework for continuous learning. Each of us comes with our own set of strengths and weaknesses, offering chances for validation and growth beyond our comfort zones. With a reliable framework anchored on a solid foundation, we are presented with abundant opportunities to look forward to the rest of our lives with renewed hope and optimism, our way and on our terms.

Scott, age-64, at his rolling office on the Blue Ridge Parkway

Chapter 1

TIME, THE UNSOLVED MYSTERY

**I'm so old I've stopped worrying about time.
It is incredibly freeing.**

THE LIST OF THINGS more precious than life is short, very short. In the second half of life, time arguably tops the list for most of us. Time enables the experiences of living one's life and is both magnificent and abstract. Our construct of time is foundational to our perspective on life and can shift dramatically across one's lifespan. Longevity is rather meaningless without an informed sense of time beyond some arbitrary age pulled out of a hat. The earlier we can sort this out, the more doors open to better understanding ourselves and our journey. Ironically, wisdom beyond our years isn't reserved just for the young. Many of those who live long possess a heightened awareness of time that seems to go even beyond their many years – wisdom on a whole other level.

We can measure a trip around the sun as a chronological year, a rotation of the earth as a day, the beat of a heart in a second, and the blink of an eye in a hundred milliseconds. These are helpful constructs for relative measurements of motion, but do they relate to the human sense of time over a lifespan? Not really. I propose that time, in a human context, is abstract. Our sense of relative time, even of short duration, is surprisingly weak. At rest, a 50-year-old's mean heart rate is about 74 beats per minute. It pulses within us like a metronome, synchronizing our perception of time. As our heart rate

7

shifts, so does our perception of time. As seconds compile into minutes and minutes into hours, human-time becomes more and more abstract. Days, years, and even decades become blurred, but within the blur are moments etched into our memory that leaves us craving for more moments. The anticipation of more moments is at the core of our desire for longevity. More chronological time allows us more opportunities to both experience and retain life's memorable moments. The gaps in between quickly slip away, preserving space in our brains for the next memorable moment. It is the illusiveness of special moments that add to the magic of life, never knowing when the next one will present itself to us.

Despite all our calendars and clocks, humans are far more attuned to "moments" than the rigid constructs we commonly refer to as "time." Moments in conversation with a new love can occupy every corner of thought. Music moments can captivate and envelope us, carrying us off on a mental magic carpet. Major achievement moments remind us of the importance of the hours and years of struggle. The hours of labor fade into the shadows when a newborn's foggy gaze appears before a mother's eyes. The last touch of a loved one now departed. These are moments we cling to, pushing back thoughts that inevitably close in and bring precious moments to a close as fast as they appear.

The memories we carry for decades define us and form our understanding of how and why we fit into the world. The exact date and time may grow hazy, but emotions of the moment hold power over us for a lifetime.

While we sleep, our brains decide which emotions of the day matter most and assign them a priority ranking in the library we know as memory. We unconsciously rewrite and merge memories, but special memories remain, flawed, but largely intact and important for reasons we may not fully understand.

HOW LONG WOULD YOU LIKE TO LIVE?

This is a question I ask my students. Occasionally, someone will declare an age beyond one hundred. It's a tall order, given the odds of living to one hundred are about 1 in 1,000 for women and 1 in 3,000 for men (U.S. population basis), but those odds are still about 150,000 times better than winning the lottery. Most adults' idea of longevity is maximizing years of healthy life and limiting late-life morbidity, or what is termed healthspan.

Living to age 100 can be an appealing goal for many of my students, but not if it involves a decade of suffering or dementia. Moments and memories are the very things that dementia steals from us. For good reason, we don't relish the idea of being a burden to our loved ones or the idea of living in a memory care facility, but nothing compares with the notion of losing our moments and memories. To lose them feels like ceasing to be human. It scares us more than anything imaginable, and for good reason. If our lifespan happens to be a nice round number of age 100, that's great, but arriving at our final moment with clarity of mind and thought means considerably more than counting trips around the sun.

I have the rare gift of a university history professor and archeologist for a son with remarkable insights into prehistory and ancient humans. Are ancient humans different from humans today? Not in terms of genetics, physiology, biology, affective neuroscience, or emotional psychology. We'd be more accurate to think of them as ancestors living a couple of thousand miles away, living a simpler life with fewer modern conveniences and different life experiences.

Longevity, in a societal context, has been realized by mitigating deaths from childbirth, infection, dehydration, starvation, and accidents. Medical science isn't creating longevity. Rather, it is discovering the root causes of health and longevity by learning from what's gone wrong and focusing on finding interventions. Longevity is personal to the people I encounter daily. They seek to understand their longevity potential and what stands in the way of them achieving their potential. And that's who this book is written for.

The language around longevity, lifespan, and life expectancy can be used carelessly and taken out of context frequently, but for clarity, my focus will be on personal longevity, personal life expectancy, and personal lifespan. Population longevity statistics serve as mileposts to understand where we, as individuals, fit into the bigger picture, but at the end of the day, my objective is to help you, the reader, objectively assess where you are today, and your potential. Part of serving that goal will be to try and help sort out the things that matter most from the things that content writers and advertisers pump out every day.

There is no substantive genetic evidence to suggest we've made step-change progress on lifespan potential since humans began forming societies well over 10,000 years ago. That might sound like a long time, but it is only about 0.2% of the time since the first evidence of bipedal hominins began walking upright over four million years ago. Human genetic evolution has largely been in response to environmental influences, adaptations to disease, and natural selection, most of which is believed to have taken place during the preceding Pleistocene epoch, which began about 2.5 million years earlier. There are anecdotal reports of people living into their nineties in ancient Greece and in Roman times, but vital statistics weren't gathered until the 19th century in Europe, and the early 20th century in the U.S.

Headlines can lead us to think that blue zones hold the secrets to living to 100. These are some positive examples, but they tell a very small part of a much bigger and more compelling story. Communities in Vilcabamba, Ecuador; Campodimele, Italy; Crete, Greece; Loma de Montija and Campillo de Ranas, Spain; Héviz, Hungary; Bama County, China; and hundreds more are rich with longevity and offer insights to guide us. Even within the U.S., there are over 60 longevity communities with secrets in plain view, but lost in the noise and media machinery.

Reflecting on the longevity of others is one thing, but envisioning ourselves in the future, decades from today isn't an innate strength. Most of us feel just like we did decades ago. Both conscious and subconscious factors contribute to the perception of life and feeling youthful in older age. While conscious efforts can help promote a positive outlook and behaviors conducive to healthy aging, subconscious influences may also shape our attitudes and perceptions about aging.

Our brains developed with a strong bias toward near-term survival needs, accounting for temporal discounting — a discounting of future time and future opportunities. Thankfully, we have clinical experts in our midst who can help us. Gerontologists, physicians, and caregivers see our future every day in the unique age spectrum of those they serve. They are a wealth of clinical knowledge that I am fortunate to lean on frequently.

THE MISSING DECADES

As children, we were surrounded by an adult demographic, and marketing focused on young adults, which made it relatively easy to place ourselves in their shoes. In contrast, we know far less about the older adult demographic, partly because we don't interact with them in our daily lives, and what little marketing focus they receive, is dominated by pharmaceuticals for age-related diseases.

Whether it is out of cultural fear and discomfort associated with aging, the absence of positive marketing to seniors, older adults consciously choosing not to spend time with younger adults, apparent differences in values and priorities between generations, or the absence of multigenerational housing, perceptions of life between ages 60 and 90 can appear surprisingly cloudy to younger adults. For many, years of anticipation met with a lost sense of purpose and identity upon retirement. Words like *old* and *aging* can be taboo because of what they presume to infer. It can easily amount to a black hole, and it is difficult to envision aging objectively or as the best years of life.

And so, looking across the patchwork spectrum of a lifespan, what if our time means many things? Perhaps it's more about small buckets of time, an accumulation of important memories, and the rest just temporary placeholders. We line the memorable moments up over the course of a life. Some we keep close, others we empty and refill, never knowing until later, if this moment will go into the bucket as a keeper. The buckets can accumulate into clutter, or they can be the foundation blocks of things bigger than us. Hopefully, with practice, we get better at recognizing the difference. The better job we've done at managing our foundations, the easier it will be to see patterns in our lives, patterns that can help to predict and guide us toward the vision of our future self that we hope to foster over many years.

An exercise that I have found helpful is to take a moment to create an image of the final days and weeks of life. My students always seem receptive to the thought of an engaging week that leads up to our 100th Birthday. Maybe it is nine holes of golf in the morning, lunch with friends on the patio, followed by a nice afternoon nap while a warm, gentle breeze sifts through an open window. Family and friends gather for dinner, and everyone joins in a loud and lively chorus of Happy Birthday. We've grown accustomed to hugging each one, young and old, like it might be our last. We retire to bed, reflecting on how proud we are of the family we've helped guide, and grateful for experiencing so much love in our life. We pass peacefully in the night, ready and accepting of whatever awaits us on the other side.

If one could script it to be our penultimate year, how might it look? Chances are there are family and friends at the forefront, and most likely, we are active and engaged. Perhaps several scenarios hold appeal. Envisioning these moments helps to shed anxiety and open us up to positive visions. With appealing outcomes awaiting us down our journey, we are better able to imagine paths to get there, and one can more easily lean into the idea of influencing our outcomes.

This is the exercise of reverse engineering. We tend to think of reverse engineering as remaking something physical, but the same process applies to creating life outcomes. We design things all the time, simply by imagining how something will work. Imagine if we could fly, or see each other on our telephones, or send a tiny camera to look inside our bodies? These are examples of things we have today because someone imagined them. No doubt, none of them turned out exactly as envisioned, but that matters little. It was the willingness to let go of the constraints of the moment and shift to a future state that made it possible.

So, how do we begin this process of reverse engineering our lives? We could rush out and buy 100 candles for the cake, but there are a million things we can and need to do in advance of that. We start with setting some milestones as guideposts to lead us there. Who is involved? How much time do we have to prepare? What are the risks we need to mitigate? What can we do to optimize our odds of success? And how do we ensure that we remain engaged in the journey and able to maintain focus? Slowly, an appealing future takes shape, and life becomes a journey that leads somewhere.

If our time mostly comes down to opportunities for moments, and we view moments as the measures of one's life, then a purposeful investment in personal longevity helps create the time and space for more moments. Living in moments that lead us somewhere is at the essence of human life. Letting our creative minds out to play allows the child in us a safe and purposeful place to explore. The disciplines that we refer to as *lifestyle* begin aligning in support of our bigger purpose. Time shifts from scarcity to friendship, and time becomes a companion on our journey, something we can leverage with intention. We become ageless opportunity-seekers, and we all know that the odds favor those who make their own luck.

As we move forward, holding these thoughts of an intentional journey toward a desirable outcome will be helpful, as the details will inevitably threaten to cloud our vision. It is this alternative concept of time that is the foundation of the intentions and purpose we seek to build.

Chapter 2

A RESILIENT WHY

**The only thing certain in life is death,
but the journey is negotiable.**

FREEDOM 55 WAS THE marketing brainchild of the financial industry, to set young investors up for early retirement at age 55. *Work the fewest years as possible and get the heck out,* was what my 22-year-old brain heard at the time. Put another way, expect 33 years of drudgery, and then retire. To do what? It would be a lot too late to start my pro golf career and a lot too early to park myself in a rocker on the front veranda. I loved my work, had an amazing boss, was well compensated, and had a future with immense career possibilities. I understood the retirement investment concept, but the destination he was selling was for another audience. Traditional retirement didn't hold much appeal then and still doesn't today. I see others thriving on that path. It's just never been mine, or maybe I'm just a really slow learner.

For all the effort placed on careers and retirement, eventually, most come to learn that neither was ever really their "Why." They were frameworks to support their Why(s).

Why would anyone care about extending their health and longevity? It's not like the end is in question, and it seems like a lot of work just to get a photo attempting to blow out 100 birthday candles. Western culture paints an unappealing picture of aging, a burden on society and serving no purpose. It is little wonder people expend great effort and expense to avoid the perceived embarrassment of aging, accelerating the very process they are trying so hard to elude.

15

Start up a conversation with an older adult and pay attention to how long it takes before they volunteer their age. Most are proud to have made it to elderhood and delighted to discover that it can be a terrific time of life. They likely had many of the same anxieties around aging as adults do today, and they've likely grown to appreciate the body and mind that got them there. They may have a few replacement parts and some bodywork, but they're excited to have their aging fears behind them. Most report feeling as young as ever and happier than the general public. Many choose to move slower, not so much because of their age, but because it allows more time to enjoy the journey. Isn't that what it's all about anyway?

SOBERING FACTS

Before going any further, we need to get grounded on a few key facts. A Why based on myths isn't of much value.

Globally, life expectancy has risen significantly but not uniformly over the last 50 years. Once ranked among the top countries, the U.S. has been in a steady freefall from 10th in world rankings in 1940 to 58th at last check (Figure 1), despite spending twice per capita on healthcare than the closest country (Germany) in 2021. Clearly, the issue is not a lack of healthcare spending or cost efficiency. U.S. life expectancy flatlined in 2010, and the COVID pandemic underscored the already vulnerable state of U.S. public health. Well into the second year of the pandemic, I witnessed a senior CDC leader stand before the news cameras, parroting the familiar message that we're all living a lot longer. It's little wonder why the public is so confused about basic facts when our health leaders feel compelled to choose false narratives over facts. Or maybe she didn't know, and that's even more unsettling, given her leadership role.

Figure 1: Life Expectancy (1975-2022) USA, Canada, France, Italy, Japan

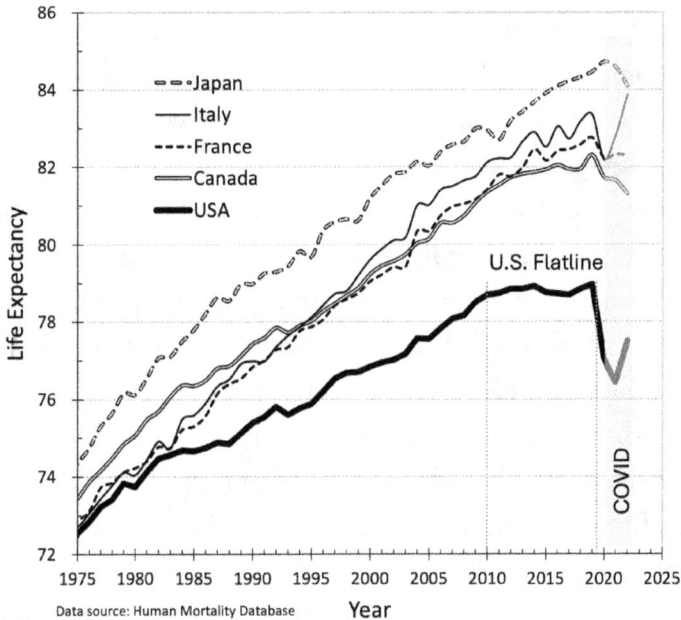

By 1980, the U.S. life expectancy lost pace with global peers, flatlining 2010-2019, and experienced far greater setbacks during the 2020-22 COVID pandemic.

Reasons for the U.S. Life Expectancy freefall in the world ranking are many, but there's a more important takeaway from this that has direct implications for longevity seekers. The fact that 48 countries passed us in life expectancy, none of whom have better access to healthcare or food, says that a longer, healthier life isn't tied to our healthcare spend or where we live. What are these other countries doing that we can learn from?

I'm inundated with people who claim to know the secret to living better longer. It comes with the turf. Beliefs are important, even if a bit misguided and simplistic. We all have our biases.

"Never let a good crisis go to waste." **Winston Churchill**

U.S. GOLD ZONES

Every coin has two sides. If more than 50 countries can have a better life expectancy than the U.S., then why can't we? Much has been made about a handful of cultures around the world, thanks to National Geographic's 2005 cover story: The Secrets of Living Longer. We've been lulled into thinking that healthy longevity happens in other places and involves lifestyle sacrifices that would never be acceptable in the West. Yet, right here under our noses are over 60 communities with life expectancies over age 90. They represent about a quarter million people. These communities are part of my research into inspiring model communities that I refer to affectionately as the U.S. Gold Zones. They are distributed among 22 states across the country, from small towns to communities within big cities like New York and Los Angeles. They have access to the same food, water, and healthcare, yet outperform our average life expectancy by more than 15%. An extra decade or two of healthy living might not sound like much at age 20, but to a 65-year-old, the opportunity to double our remaining years and fill them with remarkable moments is an unrivaled investment opportunity deserving of our attention.

MY LIFE EXPECTANCY

It's important to recognize that Life Expectancy (LE) headlines relate to the median expected lifespan of children born this year. The inputs are based on the median death age of the current population, so it's really a hybrid term with limited value for adults. Actuarial Life Expectancy (ALE), on the other hand, is a statistical prediction that can be applied at any age and takes several factors into account, including gender, race, socioeconomics, health, location, and lifestyle habits. It's what life insurance companies use to calculate our premiums and is based on our mathematically predicted death-age risk relative to peers. The way the statistics play out, the older we live, the longer we're expected to live, steadily advancing our expected lifespan. Even upon reaching our 100th birthday, 50% of us would be expected to see age 102, and a third of us see age 104. That's well and good for benchmarking populations, but at the end of the day, there's only one number that really matters, our own ("n=1"), and that's proven to be significantly influenceable.

The n=1 concept is important and will pop up from time to time in upcoming chapters. It is an important concept because we are all unique. Otherwise, we would all live to a much closer lifespan than the 24-year median lifespan spread we see today. In 2019, half of the population passed away between the ages of 62 and 86. Twenty-five percent of the population died before reaching age 62, while another 25% lived beyond age 86. This underlines just how much potential there is for living well significantly longer, no matter where we are today.

The upsides of extending a healthy life for adults are many: economic independence, individual sovereignty, and years to contribute and experience life – "more years to our life and more life to our years." We all have our own list of high-value things we'd like to extend.

Any investment consideration begs the question, what return on investment (ROI) can we expect? It's not to suggest that life is all about numbers, but certain numbers matter a lot. Just as in the financial industry, past performance doesn't guarantee future performance, but it does provide us with a framework to predict our future. The Human Mortality Database is a goldmine for those of us who enjoy swimming in millions of data. These data include a view into the statistical opportunity for longevity. The charts in Figure 2 are for female and male lifespans. The lower line represents the median lifespan for a female of a given age (X-axis). Let's assume we're building toward a lifespan investment that places us at the 90th percentile for life expectancy (LE). That's not an outrageous goal. For a woman aged 60, that would increase her LE from 87.1 to 98.0 for an extra 11 bonus years. At age 75, that moves her LE from 89.1 to 98.6. for an extra 9.5 more years. For a man, it's 11 bonus years at age 60 and an extra 9.9 bonus years at age 75. That's a lot more living!

Figure 2: Lifespan Median and 90th Percentile

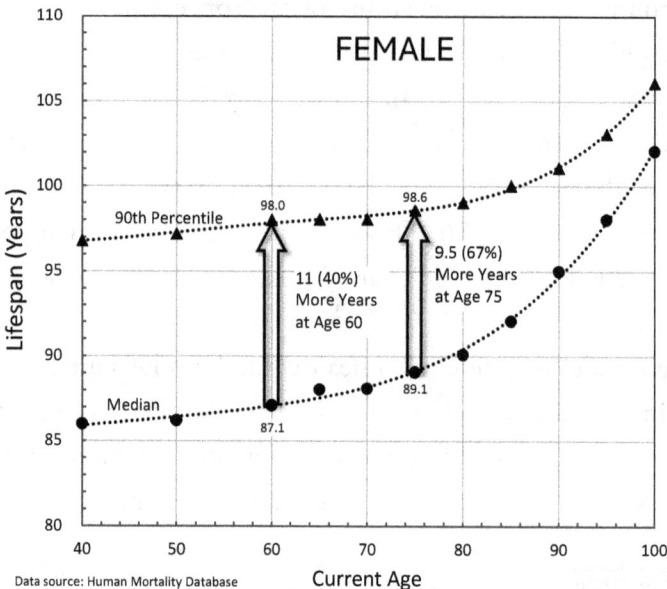

Data source: Human Mortality Database

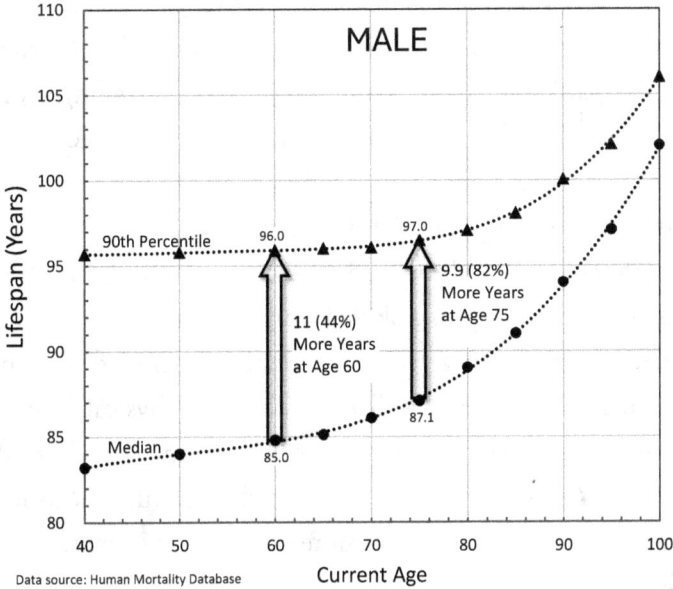

The opportunity to outperform U.S. median life expectancy is significant.
These charts illustrate female and male life expectancy (Y-axis) at a given age (X-axis).
Reaching the 90th percentile is well within reach for many.

HEALTHSPAN

Healthspan can also be described as healthy life expectancy. It is the number of years we can continue to live an active life unimpeded by disabling illnesses or injuries. The routine activities of daily living (ADLs) might take a bit longer, and we might be managing some common diseases, but we've got them in check and remain competent, cognizant, and actively living and loving life.

The key to living longer and shortening morbidity is sustaining health.

Understandably, many people ask: "Doesn't extending lifespan just add on years of suffering to the end of life?" Thankfully, the answer is no. The New England Centenarian Study, which started back in 1974, continues to observe that disability and morbidity shorten with a longer lifespan. The key to living longer and shortening morbidity is sustained health. We've all heard stories of people locked away in a nursing facility for several years, kept alive on life support seemingly indefinitely. Such stories are rich fodder for eye-catching news head-lines, but that's not how death and dying is managed. Only about 5% of adults over 65 end up in a skilled nursing facility.

The more concerning risk is premature cognitive dysfunction, when brain health declines well in advance of physical health. Ear-ly-onset dementias have become more common, and these disease states are complicated by patients' diminished communication skills. These situations are significantly more challenging to manage, partic-ularly for families, as all are impacted.

KNOWING OUR WHY

An optimal Whealthspan might seem part of our *Why*, but it requires more than just an aspiration. For many, Whealthspan might be es-sential to keeping medical and housing costs within a limited bud-get. (After age 55, nothing impacts economics more than health and housing.) Our Why may be more about purpose, impacting people or the environment, or helping a big project get to the next level. There are no right or wrong Whys, only that they are big hairy audacious goals (BHAGS). Most inspiring longevity success stories commonly revolve around service to goals bigger than self and often beyond our lifetime. Ultimately, our Why involves unfinished business, and that requires consciously investing energy toward securing more healthy years to do whatever it is that gets us out of bed in the morning.

Knowing our Why is core to setting priorities and long-range plans. It enables us to quickly know when to say yes and when to say no, helping shed stress and uncertainty from daily life. Self-doubt and second-guessing are paralyzing and stressful. For many of us, building clarity and certainty around our Why is often our biggest lever to reducing chronic stress because it makes decisions easier and keeps our focus looking far ahead.

GETTING A GRIP ON COMPOUNDING BALANCE

For decades, we've been exposed to a barrage of siloed messaging from disparate disease-centric entities advising us what to do and what not to do, and often not knowing why. It's no surprise that the messaging has been largely ignored by the general population, given how frequently it has changed and how much of it is fear-based. It might have been well-intentioned, but the public health data would say it's been ineffective. A look at the polarizing views within both the diet and exercise communities also informs us that there are some fundamental flaws in interpreting the science and applying the logic.

In the same way that the financial industry learned how to design for positive long-term financial outcomes, we've finally seen health and longevity data clustering around a series of inputs that collectively contribute to significantly influencing the odds of positive health outcomes. As more studies emerge, scientists now find themselves with a lot more data to analyze with the emergence of meta-analysis science. (A meta-analysis is a statistical tool for assimilating research findings from individual studies, quantifying the combined observed effects to get a more accurate idea of the true effect in a population.) A clear trend began appearing around a decade ago from across unrelated clinical studies. Many of the same things that contribute to cognitive health, also contribute to heart health, and reduced risks of cancer, stroke, and dementia, because they share several common root causes. Single lifestyle upgrades can help, but when coupled with several upgrades over time, the compounding benefits work cooperatively to help shield us from multiple physical and cognitive threats.

Let's look at a simple but novel analog. Our hands can do amazing things. Individually, they have unique traits and capabilities, and it is the cooperative effort of our fingers and thumb that creates grip strength, which ironically is one of the strongest correlations with physical, biological, genetic, and cognitive health outcomes. The thumb is important as it is the only opposing digit, but on its own, it has limited capabilities. The thumb needs the four digits as much as the digits need the thumb. The middle and ring fingers provide strength, while the index and little fingers provide fine motor control. It is the compounding effect of all five fingers working together that enables our hands to do amazing tasks like play music, write, type, play golf, and a lot more. This is a convenient analog for the five elements foundational to Whealthspan: Mind, Environment, Diet, Activity, and Community, or what I refer to as "MEDAC." We'll go into MEDAC more as we progress through upcoming chapters. Getting our *Why* into the palm of our hands helps make actionable lifestyle upgrades more attainable and actionable by being right in front of us and always within reach.

Figure 3: MEDAC Whealthspan Principles

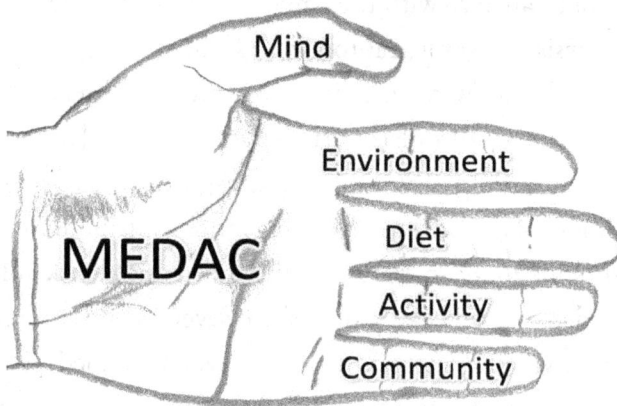

Interestingly, grip strength is a strong predictor of longevity.

24

FINDING CENTER

Finding our *Why* is more than just finding purpose. Our *Why* is a statement of our approach to life, how we interact with the world, and how we allow the world to interact with us. Achieving our optimal self is evidenced by tracking along a sustainable path that supports resilience and the ability to pursue our Why well into our future. A sustainable Why cannot exist outside of our biological, mental, and spiritual selves. These need to be in balance and resilient for our Why to receive the sustained support required for our life journey. I like to think of our biological, mental, and spiritual selves as being held together by springs, creating a necessary healthy tension. Neglect any one of them, and the system goes out of balance, and our Why is likely to get caught in the crossfire and ejected. The better we keep our biological, mental, and spiritual selves in a healthy tension (Figure 4), the better our Why can resist the inevitable earthquakes of a long, productive life.

Figure 4: A Resilient Why

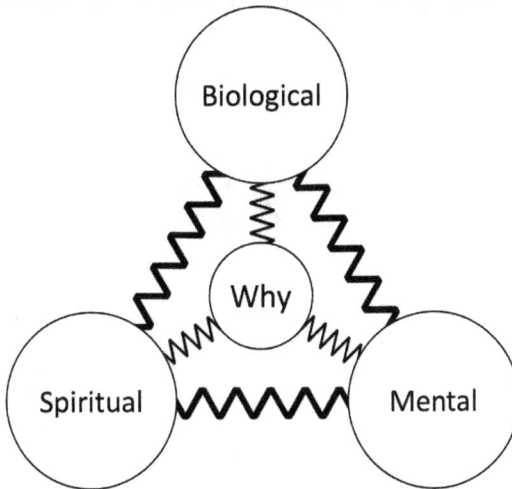

Tension is healthy. The key is getting it into balance.

A visual analog of this is being centered in our lane while driving a vehicle. Our speed isn't too high or too low, and we're not following other drivers too close or jumping lanes. We're alert and attentive to what's going on around us, and our journey fits into a bigger plan. Getting there safely is our overriding priority despite threats and temptations happening all around us. We're positioned for success and able to enjoy the journey in the community of drivers that we're sharing the road with. Some unexpected events will no doubt occur, but we'll have the time and space to react without a major setback. It's our journey, resilient and minimally affected by other drivers and changing road conditions.

Ikigai is a Japanese concept formed by "iki," which means life, and "gai," which means worth or value that many have found useful. When our *Why* is in alignment, we are keen to get up and go each morning because we can do the things we love, that we're good at, that are needed, and for which we are somehow rewarded. Reward might be financial, being recognized for contributions to our community, or feeling a sense of belonging to a community. Taking inventory using this Ikigai is a good investment for all of us from time to time.

Figure 5: Sandi's Ikigai

What I Love

Passion   Mission

What I'm   IKIGAI   My
Good At   Community
                                 Needs

Profession   Vocation

What I'm
Rewarded For

Ikigai is the alignment of purpose, passion, talents, and needs.

Sandi had volunteered at a local seniors' community center, hopeful that they would hire her on as staff, once they got to see how hard she worked and how much she loved being with older adults. Over the following months, she found herself picking up and dropping off a few of the daily visitors. It was on her way, and they genuinely enjoyed spending time together. No jobs had materialized at the center, and Sandi was now barely scraping by on the wages from her part-time retail job. On one of the trips home, David, one of the seniors, mentioned that he'd learned that a local seniors transportation company had a job opening and wrote down the name for her. "Good luck, and be sure to mention my name," he said as he got out and said goodbye. A week later, she'd landed the job and was shuttling adults *all around town for more than she was making in her old job, meeting and making new friends, while filling an important need in her community. Sarah's new employer, Marilyn, used to work for David, and a glowing recommendation from David was golden. She'd discovered her Ikigai by moving toward it with intention, and eventually, fate smiled on her. She'd made her own luck.*

Finding our Why is rarely a eureka moment. It's more likely discovered over contemplative time and may require testing and validation. The more disparate and pressured our lives, the more fragmented our Why is inclined to be. Taking note of unexpected moments, good and bad, can be a simple and effective means of learning to listen for our Why. Pausing to listen with intention is powerful and leverages across all aspects of life. This also creates mental space to assess if our Why is the right Why for us. Write it down. Post it on a computer screen or a mirror. Discuss it with those whom we trust the most. The impact will cascade.

Chapter 3

WHEALTH – AVOIDING THE CLIFF

SHE WELCOMED THE COOL washcloth pressed to her forehead as she gazed through her bedroom window, envying the older man dancing carefree in the street. His tattered hat and shoes, both softened by time, spoke of years delighting audiences. As he moved, his jacket floated lightly behind. Passersby were unable to resist the attraction, each one reflecting the old man's infectious smile back into the quiet street. It felt as if an angel had sent him to lift her from her bed and carry her out to take his hand in the dance. The woman's money had bought her the best in life, and now the best in private care, but she'd trade it all away to join in the dance. If only one last time, just one more moment to feel her body move, freed of the relentless pain that had shut her in for so many long months.

Wealth and whealth; subtle differences in language that speak to profoundly different journeys. Money can indeed be helpful, but a wealth-centric pursuit too often brings stress and threats that come with a price. Money is a valuable tool but offers no guarantees, and falls short of delivering the things we value most. The momentary endorphin flood of driving off the dealer lot in a new car is pleasing but doesn't stand up to the test of time when stacked against intimate connections, the first time standing up in front of an audience, or the sustained happiness that comes with being part of a supportive community. Whealth possesses far more intrinsic and extrinsic value than financial wealth.

AGING ECONOMICS

There are many ways to make long-term personal economics work. Health and housing are cornerstones to sustained fiscal health. Even those who retired in 2009, at the worst financial market collapse in recent decades, witnessed their investments rebound within months. Stock market bubbles and corrections will continue to get a lot of press, but there are many new protective measures in place since the great depression. Health and housing continue to be the two big levers.

Longevity Risk is something financial advisors like to raise up. It's a way of alerting clients that their annual spending is too high relative to their income and equity reserve. Aging exposes vulnerabilities in our planning and execution around health and money management. Running out of money is no fun at any age, but it's much worse if it occurs in our later years. A life planned and managed well alleviates fears of living too long.

The upsides of quality planning and execution are abundant, but few illustrate our potential like Dorothy Hoffner.

Jump!

On a clear October day in 2023 in Chicago, IL, 104-year-old Dorothy Hoffner decided to go visit the local airport. She'd celebrated her 100th birthday there by trying skydiving for the first time, while also setting the record for the oldest skydiver in recorded history. It was time to go back.

There's only one outcome from stepping out of the plane; it's only a matter of how long it takes to hit the ground. She indeed broke her own world record by an impressive four years. The many photos of her smile in flight and walking off the grassy field after the jump under her own power had everyone in tears of joy. Just days later, Dorothy passed peacefully in her sleep.

There's likely no more clear example of amazing healthspan and longevity than Dorothy. She executed a late-life plan with unrivaled passion and adventure, surpassing everyone's expectations. It's hard to say what might have motivated her first skydive, but there seems little doubt that her second was to inspire us and turn a firehose on ageism.

OUR PIGGY BANKS

At age 65, the median net worth of Americans currently sits at about $250,000. That means half the population has more, half has less. Meanwhile, the *average* net worth sits at over $1,000,000, multiples higher. Why? The top 1% of U.S. households hold 32.3% of the country's wealth, while the bottom 50% holds just 2.6%, according to the Federal Reserve. The distinction matters because news feeds are careless in the use of "average." Median and average values are rarely so different.

Retirement investment accounts, stocks, bonds, etc., are the key yardsticks for upper-income earners, but it's home equity that accounts for 67% of the net worth of Americans aged 65 and above. Of this demographic, only 36% have at least $100,000 saved for retirement. Understanding our financial situation involves some upfront work, but once organized, the value of having done it only increases over time. Thankfully, it's relatively easy to update annually once we've done the hard work at the front end.

BUDGETING FOR RETIREMENT

In my twenties, I didn't have any clue how much equity I'd need to accumulate for retirement, but I quickly recognized that was one of the values of working with a financial planner. As retirement grows ever nearer, time diminishes a lot of the uncertainty. For any given equity, three key factors still apply:

- Standard of living (annual spending rate)

- Housing (fixed and variable costs of rental or ownership)
- Medical-related costs (insurance and out-of-pocket treatment, drugs, care, housing)

Discovering our current standard of living should be relatively straightforward. It's something most of us enjoy as much as preparing tax returns, but given the seniors' economic tsunami that's brewing, blindly hoping for the best is inviting disaster. Health is a huge financial shield, but there are many more smart decisions we can make once we understand our finances.

What follows is a very simple outline. Whether we use a financial planner or not, these are the same things a planner needs to be able to help, so the exercise is of value to anyone not already on top of their finances.

There are two distinct views to understanding financial health: budget and balance sheet. A budget informs us of how well our financial lifestyle and income are aligned, while a balance sheet provides a view into our equity, aka net worth.

A Budget can quickly get into a lot of detail, but a simple start is to compare bank statements for the previous two years. That can be as simple as pulling the December 31st statement for the last three years. Has the balance increased, decreased, or held steady? Looking over the statements for the months in between, make adjustments for one-time unusual cash outflows or unexpected windfalls. Have there been any transfers to/from investment accounts? This short exercise provides a quick budget snapshot of whether we're living with a surplus or a deficit.

A more detailed budget approach is to list annual income from all sources in an Income column, as shown in Figure 6. Next, we can add up fixed costs like housing, utilities, taxes, insurance, groceries, communications, loans, etc. Then, we can add up the discretionary and variable costs like clothing, medical, dining out, personal care, clubs, entertainment, travel, etc. Some credit card companies provide monthly or annual expense summaries, which can save a lot of time. The final step is to add up the three columns and subtract the costs from the income to arrive at a net gain or loss. If the Gain or Loss doesn't align approximately with the bank statement, that indicates there are some income and/or expenses missing. It might require adding a Miscellaneous Expense item to make up the differences. These are often creeping discretionary spending that seems insignificant at the time but add up over a year. View them as opportunities.

The Balance Sheet is usually a much simpler exercise. This time, we add up investments, assets, and liabilities (what we owe) to arrive at a net worth. Estimated home values can be found on Zillow.com. In the end, we arrive at a Net Equity, which provides an insight into how much money we may have access to. It is normal to draw down on this during retirement years, but that can be a slippery slope if not well planned.

Ignoring inflation, we can look forward and add in some extra line item costs for health and housing in future years. Once the money's all spent, that's our Healthy Financial Lifespan (HFL). Life never plays out so simply or predictably, but like any plan, the real value is in the thought process and guidance these data provide. Learning today, for example, that our equity isn't going to get us to age 95 means we have time to assess options, like working longer, sharing housing, having more homemade meals, etc. Projections get more challenging when we overlay our future health of ourselves and loved ones, so let's take a look at that.

Figure 6: Simple Budget and Balance Sheet

BUDGET

Income	Fixed Costs	Discretionary & Var. Costs
Employment	Rent	Clothing
Pension	Utilities	Medical
Investment	Taxes	Meals out
Other	Insurance	Personal care
...	...	...
TOTAL	TOTAL	TOTAL

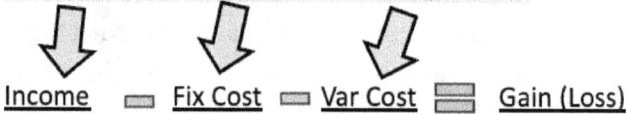

Income ▭ Fix Cost ▭ Var Cost ▭ Gain (Loss)

BALANCE SHEET

Investments	Assets	Liabilities
Cash in bank	Home	Mortgage
401k	Vehicle	Loans
IRA	Furniture	Credit Cards
Stock	Valuables	Other
...	...	...
TOTAL	TOTAL	TOTAL

Investments ➕ Assets ▭ Liabilities ▭ Net Equity

TARNISHED HEALTH COSTS

Our golden years are likely to get a little dented and tarnished along the way. While there's no crystal ball that we can gaze into for any individual's answers, there are several benchmarks beyond the usual things we hear about that can help put some economic motivators in place early. Since 2000, the medical care service costs have risen 40% higher than the cost of all goods and services, with no end in sight. The causes are many, but without question, healthcare costs are far outpacing rates of income growth, and that should be especially concerning for anyone living on a fixed income.

Most of us have no concept of how big healthcare and homecare numbers get. Years of saving to build equity flow out of our hands in just a few months as we fall off a financial cliff. (More on the financial cliff later.) It explains why medical expenses account for over 60% of bankruptcies.

For one-time surgeries, such as heart bypass (CABG), patient costs are commonly a significant portion of the $40,000 surgery, depending on insurance. If the heart attack doesn't kill us, the medical costs just might. One-and-done treatments like these are significant in cost, but it's often the chronic disease care costs that erode one's equity over time. Focus shifts steadily toward care and away from personal finances.

The idea of long-term care insurance (LTC) is appealing but out of reach for most of us. A 65-year-old couple should expect to pay between $4,700 annually for LTC insurance they hope to never need. Patient costs accumulate quickly and tend to rise as more acute care is required.

A colleague shared a recent case of a woman in her sixties with Parkinson's Disease in a care facility who had a $3,000 cash monthly shortfall. Long-term insurers demanded about $490,000 of the couple's equity to cover her care costs for the duration of her life.

Searching, they found an insurer who wanted $165,000. That's still a lot of money but a bargain compared with the other insurers. Numbers like this would wipe out at least half the population when faced with such a challenge and leave nothing for the surviving spouse or heirs. A typical $10,000 annual out-of-pocket for diseases like Parkinson's and Alzheimer's will wipe out most families' savings.

These numbers likely evoked some sticker price shock. While costs will vary based on individual circumstances, it doesn't take an accountant to see that the investment in one's health can have massive economic returns by avoiding the need for medical treatment, in addition to the years not lost to decline and medical care. Chronic diseases like hypertension, type 2 diabetes, and heart disease have become commonplace, but these are the canaries in the coal mine. These are diseases to get out in front of and rein in early, as slowing their progress can quickly earn us another decade or more of health and defer or prevent the diseases that tend to follow them.

Someone turning age 65 today has almost a 70% chance of needing some type of long-term care services and support in their remaining years. Women need care longer than men, 3.7 vs 2.2 years, according to the Federal Administration for Community Living. Women usually need longer care than men because women typically provide care for a male partner and outlive their male partner. Let's put some dollar numbers to that.

Assuming the final year of life requires full-time care (44 hours per week), the period leading up to that requires about a third of that. Genworth reported the annual cost in 2021 for a Home Health Aide to be $61,776 for a 44-hour per week (in-home or in a senior living community). The total caregiving spend comes out to $217,000 for a man and $365,000 for a woman, totaling $582,000 for a couple. Direct medical costs would be on top of these costs. Depending on insurance, some or none of this may be covered. The cost of professional caregiving is escalating (Figure 7) due to several factors, but none more than an increasing demand juxtaposed by a low birth rate in recent decades that has resulted in a severe staffing shortage. There are no solutions to this on the horizon, so we'll need to be very intentional about limiting our care needs by investing in our health and making our homes more livable in our later years.

Figure 7: Home Health Aide Cost

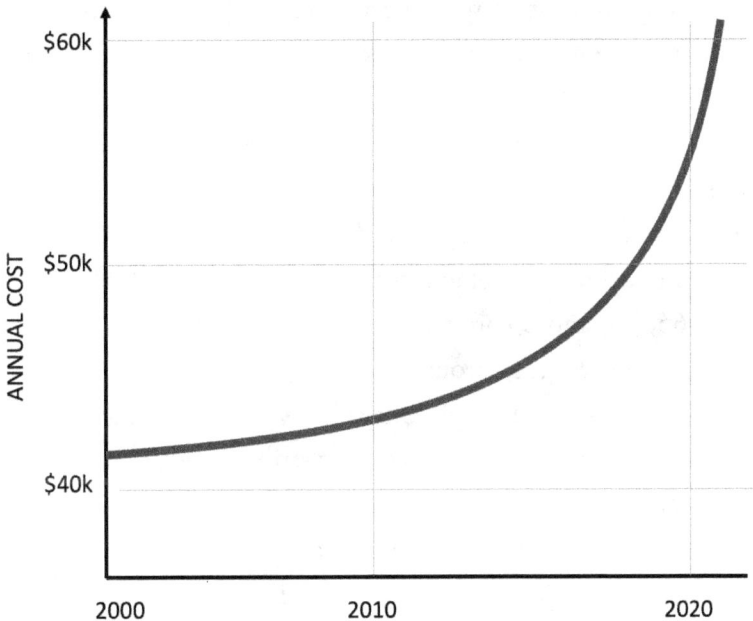

Source: Genworth Financial, inc.

Aging-related costs are rising sharply, but none more than service costs.

SHIRLEY'S ROI

Every investment consideration is weighed against our expected Return on Investment (ROI), risk exposure, and timing. Let's assume our subject is a 50-year-old single female we'll call Shirley, whose career has her juggling the pressures of work and travel, while trying to meet the needs of teenage children and pay 100% of her housing and living expenses. Many days leave her feeling like she's on the ragged edge. She's making good money but 26% less than her male peers, and she feels the pressure of having to outperform her counterparts just to maintain her place at the table. She tries to get to the gym a couple of times a week, but travel and routine are always at odds. Weekends are about playing catch-up on work, kids, house, and sleep. It's all slowly taking a toll, and Shirley is 38 pounds north of her varsity athletics self, despite several attempts to drop the extra weight. She's feeling like her health is a ticking timebomb and beginning to dread visits to the doctor.

We've all met several Shirleys over the years. There are no easy answers, and almost certainly, no one is coming to their rescue. The Shirleys of the world will be forced to work more years than their male peers to achieve retirement security, whatever that looks like! But ages like 65, 75, and 85 are far beyond Shirley's capacity to imagine. She's focused on getting through today.

"I just need to get through today." We've all found ourselves there at the loss of a loved one, an illness that strips away all our energy, or a child that pushes our buttons, leaving us paralyzed and consumed in feelings of failure. When "getting through the day" becomes a recurring event, it's a sign that we are sacrificing beyond our safe limits. Our body is signaling hopelessly against the overwhelming external and self-induced pressures that compel us to do more.

It's typically not until midlife, when children are older, that we finally get a chance to breathe. This is a pivotal moment to take stock of our whealth priorities. Making time for health at this stage is paramount. If not now, when? There is unlikely to be another opportunity because it can be a surprisingly short break between caring for children and caring for adults. The sandwich generation is learning this firsthand, and it's only getting more common as the Baby Boomers age.

Changing lifestyle patterns is almost always associated with a life event, the most common being a medical event. Life affords us with very few clear opportunities to change our patterns and rebalance our priorities. Choosing to proactively make real change before a health event is hard but is always incredibly empowering.

"*I regret taking better care of my health*," said no one ever.

Caring for parents places unexpected demands on adult children, evidenced by the frequency that adult children, most often women, exit their careers early to care for parents. So many of us find ourselves waiting for a break to focus on our own health, but the break never comes, and pressures just continue to mount. If we miss the midlife opportunity to reset our whealth balance, the chances of finding it later only get harder. Habits become too entrenched, the climb back to health looks too daunting, and depression becomes a close companion, further adding to the inertia. No one wins when we sacrifice our health, not an aging parent, a child, a spouse, or an employer. We know it, but holding ourselves accountable to it is easier said than done. There's no way to put a ribbon on it; it sucks! Investing in our MEDAC foundation will help us navigate these immensely challenging life events.

HOUSE & HOME

It's easy to get complacent and miss out on some of the best opportunities to promote whealthspan at home. Location matters even more when we start assessing housing priorities for our future. We can explore many options to make a home function well for us in the right location, but there is never a right home in the wrong place. Ryan Fredrick's book, Right Place, Right Time, is an excellent resource to explore this important and complex topic.

Wherever we are located, we need to be putting things in place for our future selves. More than 90% of adults over age 60 want to remain in their homes as long as possible, but only about 10% of them are in homes that support their objective. One could reasonably argue that none of the other financial discussions matter much until we get aligned on putting in place what's going to be needed in future years. The separate discussion around our aging brains will underscore this, but from a financial perspective, setting our homes up for success is one of the easiest and most obvious actions within our control. The urge to put lipstick on a pig and say *we're done* is compelling, but optimal outcomes demand optimal inputs.

Figure 8: Optimal Outcomes Demand Optimal Inputs

Cosmetic upgrades that don't address home functions are expensive mistakes.

Housing costs can skyrocket, even for homeowners without a mortgage. A planned move to an adult child's home or into shared housing can be a win-win for families that prepare early. One client put a lovely addition on for an aging parent, with the plan to use it as an art studio later. The forethought resulted in a flexible design and a smart investment.

Homeownership can be cost-effective and help build equity over decades of ownership. For many, the market value has increased and contributed to significant home equity. The reverse mortgage market has undergone a significant overhaul and is a viable option for many homeowners looking to access their home equity. It enables them to remain in their homes with safeguards that are not possible with other funding options.

Rental is another viable alternative. Multiunit buildings will have several building code accessibility features in place and provide an instant community within close proximity. They are also likely to be close to public transit. Rental cost increases are common and need to be factored into the plan.

If the move is to a seniors' life plan community, we can expect annual housing costs anywhere from $48,000 to well over $100,000, depending upon location, services, and amenities. In several circumstances, this can be a financial win once we objectively factor in the financial and social costs of remaining at home. Either way, it's a big number and a big decision that deserves some solid research. Catherine L. Owens, *Be Your Own Hero* is a great resource book for uncovering how to do this well.

The National Aging in Place Council is a rich talent pool of people who see how real life plays out every day. Let's look at four housing scenarios.

Scenario A: Leave it to Luck

By far the most common strategy, this appeals to a reactive mindset coupled with a weak awareness of the magnitude of the financial risks. Over time, the homeowners cease making updates, followed by a decline in maintenance and general upkeep. The upkeep gets harder with age, and they don't secure adequate help. They're convinced they're saving money for the potential medical costs their friends are constantly harping on about. Their health is in slow decline, and the medical costs are outpacing their ability to save. Their gait slows, and while retrieving the mail, the crack in the sidewalk, left unattended for over a decade, suddenly catches a toe, resulting in a broken hip and elbow. The injuries prevent climbing the three steps up into the home, and the flight of stairs to the bedroom might as well be Mount Everest. Even simple routine tasks like washing dishes and bathing become physically impossible.

They need to find immediate community-based housing on a few hours' notice. The family steps in, and they're forced to sell the house in its current condition, far below market value, kissing away the added equity they'd been thinking was as good as in the bank. The lack of mobility resulting from the fall and feeling booted out of their own home leaves them physically and emotionally defeated. The rehabilitation exercises seem pointless, and they'd rather just sit and watch TV. The grandchildren get dragged in monthly, quick to offer a hug, and quick to make an escape. Their health spirals downward, evidenced by more than 20 prescription drugs prominently on display.

In the background, the personal finances are in freefall, (Figure 9). No one thinks to get working on a Medicaid strategy, and by the time an elder law attorney gets brought in to help them through the 5-year lookback audit process, another $50,000 of family money has gone up in smoke. Recognizing the resident's inability to make monthly room and board, an eviction notice is filed, and the senior becomes a ward of the state. When the estate finally settles, it's a $170,000 debt on paper. Seniors in this situation are often judgment-proof, meaning the family thankfully isn't saddled with the debt, but that's little consolation. Not every plan-A scenario ends this way, but it's a fast-growing common middle-class outcome. Thirty percent of seniors can't meet their financial obligations due to housing and medical costs, and that number is rising annually.

Scenario B: Get Lucky

We like to imagine that if we get lucky and can manage our health, we'll do well enough. This scenario is identical to Scenario A, but health is amazingly good, reducing health spending by 50% — a windfall in savings. The reality, however, is that it is still a reactive mindset and brings all the same risks. Good health doesn't prevent falls, and events play out the same way as in scenario A. Relying on luck is not a strategy for success. It had many ways to fail and carries tremendous consequences.

Scenario C: Get Smart

This is the proactive mindset that addresses both health and home and pays off big time. It starts out the same as above; they keep on top of their health, and at age 70, the homeowner makes a $30,000 investment to support longer life and improve home equity. The health trajectory is good, and the catastrophic fall and collateral issues are averted. Care can be delivered at home in the later years, and the time in a seniors' care community is cut in half. Medicaid is avoided, and there's about $100,000 left in the estate.

Scenario D: Smart Centenarian

This scenario follows Scenario C, but healthspan comes into play, and unsurprisingly, the homeowner lives to the age of 100. It's the ultimate Whealthspan outcome, made possible by proactive decisions over several years.

These basic example scenarios help bring focus to the big levers: health and home. There are many more variables in practice, with everyone starting at a different place, but the trends follow the same patterns. Health and housing overshadow everything else in the second half of life, so setting intentions and addressing them are essential to achieving our desired outcomes.

Figure 9: Wealth Preservation Requires Proactive Investment

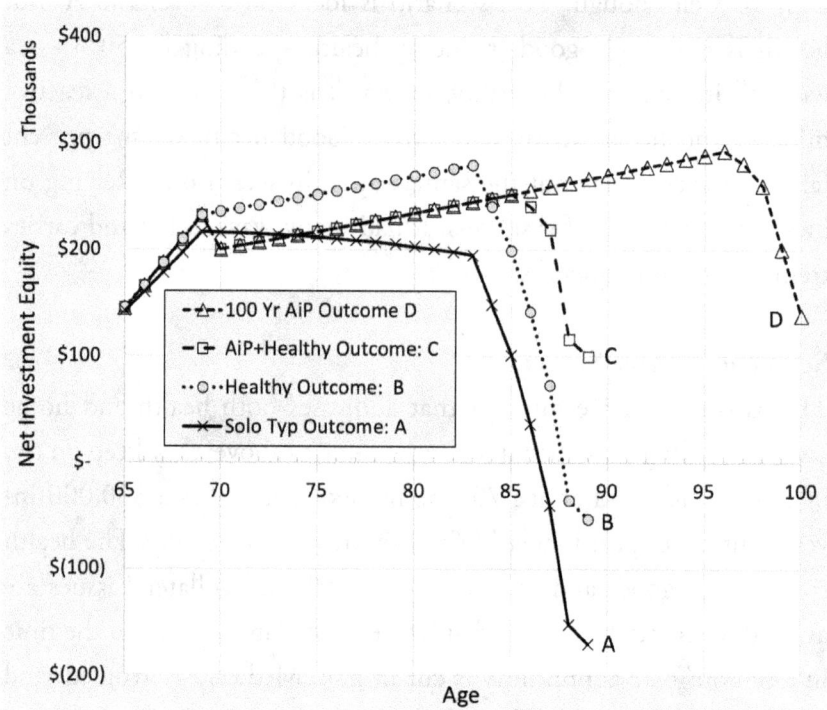

A comprehensive housing and health strategy will mitigate the impact of many common risks.

FINANCIAL CLIFF

It's shocking how easy it is to burn through $1,000,000 in retirement savings and home equity, but one only needs to ask a few people in the industry how the costs suddenly pile up and money flows out. It is possible to live very well within a modest, realistic plan, provided we take proactive measures to mitigate the impact of life associated with later years. Luck always plays a role in our outcomes, but as we all know, luck happens to those who make it happen for themselves.

There are many potential scenarios, but the message here is to appreciate the value of investing in living at home longer. Late-life decisions get made very quickly, and often, we're just passengers at that point. Our only options are early options.

The same principles apply to a couple's model, (Figure 10) with two important adds. 1. When all the equity is spent caring for the first-to-die, the surviving spouse is effectively left with nothing. 2. Where one of the partners needs to be relocated into an assisted living facility, and the other remains at home, housing costs skyrocket. A couple might assume they have plenty of funds, relative to their peers, but that's not a meaningful financial benchmark.

I describe many of these scenarios as falling off a financial cliff. Ideally, our plans equip us with a parachute to slow the financial descent, but many aren't so lucky. Once in freefall, all the usual strategies and tactics go out the window. All available energy is consumed getting through another day and yet another difficult conversation. Long-term plans can go up in smoke. Emotions run high and tug at us in ways we've never experienced. Adult children are forced into difficult decisions on behalf of their parents and sibling tensions escalate. Circumstances don't permit clear thinking, and obvious decisions are clouded with doubt, leaving us paralyzed and unable to think rationally. Higher cash outflows are to be expected toward the end of life, but it's the decisions we make decades earlier that shield our loved ones from dealing with the mess at the bottom of the cliff. Forget plan A and focus on realistic scenarios. Then, involve others in the discussion and set about giving ourselves and loved ones the best chance for success.

Figure 10: Wealth Preservation, Million Dollar Couple

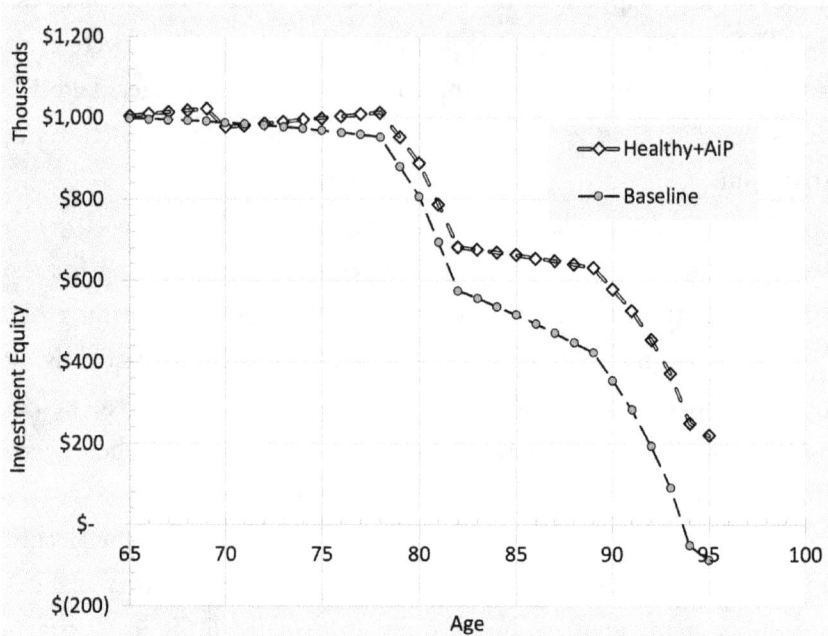

It's hard to appreciate how fast money flows out,
especially when couples face separate housing costs.

GROWTH STARTS NOW

Mom did me a huge favor by taking me to the bank to open a savings account when I was seven years old. My eyes barely reached the counter height if I stood on my toes and clung to the marble counter by my fingertips. Back then, a teller updated a passbook manually by writing in every deposit and withdrawal, along with his/her initial in the margin. Deposit accounts paid meaningful interest and I was able to see the balance grow as interest accumulated. By age 12, I started working Saturdays at my dad's manufacturing company, where I was introduced to the two handles that would make me the wealthiest 12-year-old I knew: a broom and a toilet brush. The more my bank account balance grew, the more inspired I was to work. By age 16, I was working full-time during the summers with no ambition to give up the cleaning tasks. I knew others tended to look down on cleaners and caretakers, but to me, it's always been honorable work. I was able to pay my way through college and graduate debt-free.

The big return-on-investment discipline is personal sovereignty: to be the authority over one's own mind, body, direction, and destiny.

Everything meaningful in life requires constant investment, whether it's family, faith, friendships, career, athletics, or health. They all compound in response to persistent investment over time.

FINAL THOUGHTS

Many of my adult students offer stories of their experience cleaning up after their parents: *"I wouldn't leave that mess to my worst enemy"* is a common one. The urge to wait until the cliff is in sight is at least a decade too late. We don't even realize we're in freefall until the bills start coming in, and by then, we have little choice in altering its course.

It's a little late to start checking for a parachute after we've already stepped out of the plane.

Takeaways:
- Investing in personal health can reduce future costs significantly
- A supportive home environment enables living at home longer
- Expect the financial cliff. Have a plan to mitigate its impact
- Real life happens. Real planning helps keep everyone whole

Chapter 4

JUST BETWEEN US NEURONS

JOHN LAY IN HIS skilled nursing facility bed, relaxed, drifting in and out of sleep. Jane, an old family friend, had arrived to pay him a visit. Having been forewarned that John's dementia was advancing, Jane took John's hand in hers and leaned in close. "Hi, John. Do you know who it is?" He turned his head towards hers, cracked his famous smile, and replied, "Why, don't you know?"

The present and the past got harder to differentiate, but John's sense of humor, honed over many decades, was still razor-sharp. Once a vice president of a top-10 Fortune 500 company, John had been reduced to needing help with the most basic of human activities, but his spirit was undaunted.

The human brain might give the impression of a static organ, but there are parties going on up there 24/7. It's a dynamic marketplace, actively responding to what our eyes are importing, the food we tasted just minutes ago, the sounds from the next room, and the thoughts consuming us. It processes all of this and more, while managing multiple organs and functional systems without even breaking a sweat. The brain is nothing short of miraculous. Nearly impossible to access, it holds functional secrets we're only beginning to appreciate. Unlike other body organs, the brain shares many functions across regions, creating redundancy and distributing resources that enable it to function, even when some sites within the brain are failing. Its 100 billion neurons are in constant communication, consuming oxygen and glucose at disproportionately high rates compared with other organs. It is truly a constant hub of activity while we are awake, asleep, and even seemingly distant.

HOW NEURONS COMMUNICATE

Neurons communicate with each other, relaying messages and thoughts and eliciting actions. They talk with one another using electrical and chemical signals. Electrical signals are sent down a neuron by what's termed an action potential. When the signal reaches the gap between two neurons, it is transformed instantaneously into a chemical message to cross the synapse (the gap between 2 neurons.) The adjacent neuron senses the chemical change, triggering an action potential on the receiving side of the synapse. Important messages get amplified and repeated. Unimportant messages are quieted. The repeating pattern is how the brain learns and adapts to important information and filters out information that doesn't require a response.

Most novel engineering ideas are based on observations in nature. Benjamin Franklin proved a couple of key theories in his famous 1752 balloon experiment: 1) that lightning and static electricity were the same phenomena occurring at very different scales, and 2) that electrical energy can travel through various media, including air. Both principles apply at a much smaller scale, between the neurons inside our brain and in the microchips that allow our electronic devices to process information quickly.

There are two hemispheres, four main regions of the brain: frontal, parietal, temporal, and occipital lobes, and 360 distinct regions, according to recent brain mapping. We can think of the brain as a city, divided in half by a river, with many neighborhoods, roadways, and sidewalks. Within the many buildings are people in conversation, exchanging information on millions of topics. During the day, a certain amount of information is dedicated to the activities of the day. At night, when the traffic is lighter, there are more opportunities to focus attention on cleaning and repairs. As the city ages, some of the old infrastructure starts showing signs of age, and additional repairs are needed to keep the city running. Eventually, potholes begin forming, and eventually, some minor roads become difficult to pass. Some small roads become closed to traffic. Lots of communications still happen, just not as smoothly as they once did, and keeping track of all the historical information is an ever-increasing challenge. All of this we can imagine as normal aging.

Vascular and neurodegenerative diseases, like dementia, Parkinson's, and Huntington's diseases, can be thought of as failures in the infrastructure that advance quicker than usual, perhaps because of trauma (like a damaging storm), genetics (inherently weaker building materials or faulty design), or weak immune and endocrine systems (inadequate resources to repair and maintain integrity). Consequently, some main roadways get blocked, and traffic must be rerouted. Given the fine balance needed to keep things running smoothly, these major pathway failures begin having increasingly noticeable effects on communications and the normal functions of the city.

THE AGING BRAIN

If there's an organ to get proactive around, it's the brain. There is a natural aging process in the brain, but many live to age 100 and remain cognitively sharp with intact memories. Unlike other organ diseases, options to restore brain health are rare. Brain health relies heavily on our lifestyle habits. It's the most devastating of organs to experience the loss of function, but thankfully, it's also malleable and responds to positive influences.

While there are still massive amounts of information that medical science has yet to discover, some of the major knowledge building blocks are falling into place. It isn't quite as dark and mysterious as it once was. Today, we have access to computed tomography (CT), magnetic resonance imaging (MRI), computed angiography (EEG/CTA), positron emission tomography (PET), and single-photon emission computed tomography (SPECT). These are just some of the diagnostic tools in use for research and patient care. Each has unique capabilities and applications for medical investigations.

The naturally aging brain finds it harder to retrieve proper names, like people, street, and restaurant names, partly due to the constantly accumulating data that memory must sort through over so many years of input (more conversations, more knowledge, and more aging infrastructure), as well as some natural signal decay (a lot more potholes).

Another analogy that is helpful is: Try to imagine having to recall an ingredient in a recipe. When we're young, all we might care about is chocolate chip cookies – one recipe, eight items. Not too difficult. Now insert a few million miles and several decades. That chocolate chip cookie recipe is now in a large recipe book, on a bookshelf with 100 other recipe books, in a library with several aisles and racks containing over 100,000 books. The competition for memory storage is infinitely greater, and unlike our computers, we don't have the option to pay $19.99 to plug in another terabyte of memory. These are normal changes with age.

Conversely, confusing apples for oranges, cookbooks for romance novels, not realizing where we are or how we got here, unexplained mood changes, or changes in gait are potential signs of accelerated brain aging.

SHRINKING BRAINS

During childhood, our brain and skull grow together at a pace that keeps the brain secure in a space that is not too big, not too small. At about age 35, peak brain growth is achieved. Beyond age 35, our brains slowly begin shrinking by about 0.2% per year, doubling to 0.5% per year by age 60, and increasing to over 2% per year at age 80.

At this age, studies indicate that our gray matter will have atrophied by 14% and our white matter by about 24% (Figure 11). Meanwhile, our skull remains fixed, so the voids left by the shrinking brain become filled with fluid, causing the brain and skull to be less intimately coupled. The implications of this are significant when kinetics gets involved.

Figure 11: Shrinking of the Aging Brain

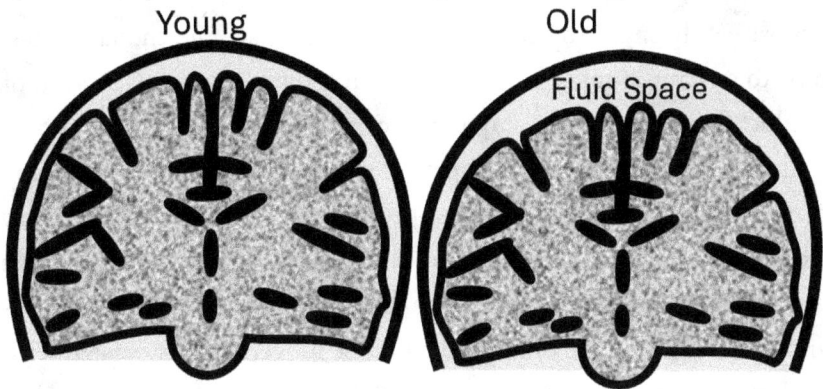

By age 80, the brain's gray matter will have atrophied by 14% and white matter by about 24%.

When we're young, our brain and skull pretty much move as one, but in adult years, that brain-skull relationship begins to decouple due to the decreasing brain volume. Innocent slips and falls in later years play out differently inside the skull. The brain continues accelerating, even though the skull has come to an abrupt stop. The delay results in increased g-force stress to the brain when it collides with the skull, leading to age-related trauma. Additionally, the excess movement can stretch the connections between the brain's hemispheres and the connection between the cerebrum and the brain stem. These accelerate the degradation of our brain's infrastructure.

Most falls don't cause a loss of consciousness, but that doesn't mean there isn't permanent damage to brain tissues and the neural network. Each minor occurrence triggers a series of reactions within the brain, depending on the nature and scale of impact. Unless severe, the damage is challenging to measure with a CT or MRI scan.

The frequency of falls increases for all of us as we age, and we shouldn't kid ourselves on that unfortunate reality. Thinking we outsmart falling is tricky business. Anyone who has consciously thought about taking each step on a staircase is likely to report that it was almost paralyzing. Proprioception, also known as kinesthesia, is coupled to our autonomic nervous system and refers to our perception of the location, movement, and action of parts of the body. Our motor skills rely on a complex network of physical sensations that come from signals of sensory receptors, primarily in our muscles and skin. The brain issues the order to move, and from there, it's largely just along for the ride, providing course direction and general spatial guidance. Try engaging the brain in the precise movements associated with walking to experience it firsthand. Do NOT try this on a staircase.

The best intellectual and practical defense against falls, and every reasonable health risk, is a strong offense. The adage, an ounce of prevention is worth a pound of cure, could not be more apt. Avoiding falls is as important for the brain as it is for the body.

DEMENTIA IQ

In studies around aging, dementia continues to occupy a lot of attention. Alzheimer's is the most familiar and most researched, but it is just one of four common dementias:

- Alzheimer's disease
- Vascular dementia
- Lewy Body disease
- Frontotemporal dementia

There are physiological and behavioral traits associated with each dementia type, but in practice, it is common to have multiple dementias, with one considered the primary dementia. One of the complications in understanding dementias is that symptoms vary depending on where the damage or dysfunction is located. Unlike a broken leg, which is a fracture of the femur or tibia bones, dementias can occur in any of the 360 regions of the brain, each resulting in different symptoms or groups of outcomes, such as memory, thinking, confusion, mood changes, balance, and speech.

The primary risk factor for dementia is age, but dementia is not inevitable. The longer we live, the greater the odds. Just like the tires on our vehicle, time exposes every system to wear. Research indicates that about 40% of dementias are associated with modifiable risk factors. From an investment approach, several small healthy lifestyle habits have an estimated worth of about ten additional healthy brain years.

One of the unsettling aspects of dementia is how long it goes undiagnosed. The individual might be noticing signs, but they're subtle, spread over long durations, and our instinctive response is to discount them. Like so many diseases, our medical system is built around response, not early detection. There's also little medical incentive to detect something that's viewed as untreatable. If symptoms progress, eventually, a patient will get a cognitive assessment. By this stage, however, most patients will have already passed through the preclinical phase and reached the Mild Cognitive Impairment (MCI). This is the physically advanced state before reaching dementia. It's a difficult road from there, trying to find medications that ease symptoms and comfort both the patient and his/her family. Most dementia patients can remain living at home for many years, depending upon severity and support systems, but sometimes, behaviors and personal situations require memory care residency.

I interviewed Judy Cornish, founder of The Dawn Method®, on the topic of living with dementia, and was fascinated by the unique approach she had developed while working with families caring for loved ones at home, as well as with people living at home alone with dementia. It remains one of the most profound and inspiring interviews I've had the privilege to host. We all tend to focus on what dementia steals away from its victims. The Dawn Method is a kind, strength-based, person-centered approach to dementia care that trains families and caregivers to capitalize on the skills dementia does not take away. Find the interview with Judy Cornish on the Whealthspan Longevity YouTube channel.

Judy and her amazing team have gone on to train thousands of families in the DAWN Method in the U.S., and it's now being studied in Brazil, and practiced in countries such as Denmark, South Africa, India, and Malaysia.

A primary risk factor across all dementias is reduced blood supply to the brain. The brain is a major blood consumer, demanding up to a quarter of the body's blood supply. Without sufficient oxygen, glucose, and nutrients, the brain finds itself on the losing end of an ever-increasing damage rate. It is helpful to keep cardiovascular health front of mind when thinking about dementia. Dementia risk increases significantly with heart disease, type 2 diabetes (T2DM), and high blood pressure (over 120/80).

ALZHEIMER'S

Thus far, about 70 regions of the brain have been identified as factors associated with AD and are the focus of current research.

In an Alzheimer's Disease (AD) patient, amyloid plaques and tau proteins form adjacent to neurons, interfering with communications and weakening or modifying neuron signaling. It is well known that amyloid plaques and tau proteins inhibit signaling, and for several years, much of the AD research focused on trying to remove them. It's now viewed that amyloid plaques and tau proteins are more likely formed in response to the body's protective mechanism and not the root cause of AD. A rough analogy is the swelling and pain associated with a sprained ankle. The swelling and pain make it hard to function, but they aren't the root cause. Hyperextended and torn ligaments are the physical root cause. Pain and swelling are provided by the body to help stabilize the area and prevent further damage while it works on healing the ligaments. Unfortunately, the brain isn't nearly as simple or as accessible to analyze.

Genetics play both protective and risk roles, depending on subtle differences. Scientists have been working for several years to understand the many alleles (versions) of the APOE gene, which is well known to be associated with AD. The APOE-e2 allele version is somewhat protective and appears to help defer AD onset. Recent work led by Michael Greicius, MD, professor of neurology at Stanford Medicine, has identified a gene variant, R251G, that is also protective against AD. The mutation is rare but may provide insights that scientists can leverage against the disease. There are many other different research programs going on in parallel that are likely to reveal other protective gene variants.

The APOE-e4 allele, however, present in about 25% of the population, doubles the risk of AD versus those without this allele, and is associated with early AD onset. About 2-3% of the population inherited two copies of the variant (one from each parent), escalating AD risk roughly about 8 to 10 times. As with all these diseases, the presence of the APOE-e4 is not an AD sentence. Rather, it is a higher risk and adds motivation to be vigilant with lifestyle habits that help offset the genetic predisposition.

Promising clinical studies are being led by Dr. Dale Bredesen, CSO at Apollo Health. Dr. Bredesen first published findings in 2014 showing the reversal of AD. The team subsequently received funding for a 72-person trial expected to be completed in 2025. These trials are very tightly controlled and monitored lifestyle and environment protocols, with patients managed directly by physicians. Bredesen protocol training is available under a program named ReCODE 2.0, focusing on seven lifestyle areas: nutrition, exercise, sleep, stress, stimulation, detoxification, and supplements.

OTHER DEMENTIAS

Vascular Dementia is the second most frequent dementia, followed by Lewy Body Disease and Frontal Temporal Dementia.

Vascular issues are frequently underlying contributing factors in all forms of dementia. Vascular Dementia, specifically, is typically associated with a stroke. Strokes can be major events or a series of ministrokes that fail to cause noticeable symptoms.

STROKE

Ischemic strokes occur following a critical reduction or blockage of blood to a region of the brain. It can also be due to atrial fibrillation (AFIB), when heart pumping malfunctions and sends coagulated blood to the brain. Strokes can be localized or affect an entire brain hemisphere if the blockage occurs in a carotid artery. In the case of heart failure, a stroke can affect the entire brain. About 85% of strokes are ischemic strokes.

Less common are hemorrhagic strokes, where an artery inside the brain ruptures, sending blood into the brain. This depletes blood delivery downstream and adds external pressure to other brain arteries, causing further reduction in blood supply. It's not unlike a garden hose that loses flow when there are holes that result in water escaping prematurely. Vascular dementia causes include high blood pressure, high cholesterol, and diabetes. It is mostly found in older adults due to the slow, steady breakdown of the micro blood vessels deep within the brain, a condition known as Cerebral Small Vessel Disease.

PARKINSON'S DISEASE

Parkinson's Disease (PD) is a neurodegenerative disease that is rising at an alarming rate. A large study looking at over 5 million PD patients revealed that the disease has increased by over 50% since two 2010 studies. Michael J. Fox is perhaps the most recognized individual with PD and has been instrumental in helping fund research. The average diagnosis is age 60, but Fox was diagnosed at age 29. Victims of PD suffer from tremors, stiffness, movement, memory, sleep, and pain issues, as well as anxiety and depression.

Doctor Will

Will is a primary physician, fit and strong in his forties. We sat down to discuss his Parkinson's Disease. "The year following my diagnosis was really tough," he said. "But I have a young family and patients counting on me, so I needed to find a way to deal with a disease that affects almost everything I do." As we talked, he exhibited the classic symptoms of Parkinson's, including resting tremors in his head, arms, and legs. Everyday activities like sipping hot coffee require his full attention.

Will's medical training hadn't prepared him to treat his condition, and his own healthcare system offered very little. It sounded like there was little they could offer, that his fate was inevitable, and they would just track its progression.

Part of PD is toxicity sensitivity. It is unclear which toxins trigger the disease in which people, but that actually simplifies the approach – clean up all food sources and limit/remove potential environmental toxins. A clean diet, a natural environment, and daily exercise are the three legs of early treatment. As a bonus, Will dropped some excess weight. Best of all, the disease progression was arrested, and he felt back in control of his life.

In addition to the neuromuscular system, Parkinson's is also strongly associated with the endocrine system, which is responsible for balancing hormones- signaling chemicals the body produces naturally. Patients with PD typically have low levels of dopamine, a neurotransmitter hormone associated most often with exercise. Dopamine is synthesized primarily in the brain and in the gut. It's not yet clear why these patients do not produce sufficient dopamine, but several studies link PD to environmental toxins exposures from industry and agricultural chemicals like Paraquat, Roundup (Glyphosate), Dicofol, Endosulfan, Naled, Propargite, Diquat, Endothall, Trifluralin, copper sulfate Folpet, Simazine, Lindane, and Atrazine. Patients are eventually treated with a precursor drug that aids the body in producing dopamine. For now, it remains an incurable disease that requires close management to slow progression and address its symptoms.

DEMENTIA — TOP SIX FOCUS AREAS
At this stage of published research and clinical observations, four clear focus areas benefit cognitive outcomes:
1. High cardiovascular health (fitness)
2. Clean environment, including limited exposure to toxins in food, air, and water.
3. Quality sleep: 7-8 hours per night
4. Hearing protection and use of hearing aids as soon as recommended
5. Protective eyewear and keeping vision prescriptions up to date

6. Dental hygiene: brushing for two minutes, twice daily, flossing daily, and professional cleaning every six months

We'll go more into items #1-3, but proximity to the brain is common among items #4-6. While not well understood, location matters. Hearing and vision loss place added stress on the brain to try and fill in the gaps coming from dirty signal inputs. Oral bacteria easily find their way into the brain, where they can prey on brain tissue.

NEURONAL THOUGHTS

The neuronal network is nothing short of fascinating and ridiculously complex. The challenge to understand how it works in the brain is made even more difficult by the skull that protects it. What we know with some certainty:

- The brain needs blood, lots and lots of blood to maintain normal function
- Brain and heart health are intimately connected
- Simple falls impact the brain more in later years as it shrinks in size
- Chemical toxins and residues in food affect some people more than others

Chapter 5

CONNECTIONS ON MANY LEVELS

THE SWEET SCENT OF lilies and carnations fills the air. "Amazing Grace" plays in the background of a room filled with somber faces dressed all in black. Children look lost and out of place. They should be at school or outside playing amid screams of excitement, but they're here. In the corner, a woman sits, comforted by the gentle, caring strokes of a friend. All have been drawn together by an invisible life force that defies explanation. Sisters and brothers, fathers and mothers, daughters and sons, grandparents and grandchildren, friends and neighbors have all come together to reconnect. They are fulfilling a need to be reminded of where they fit into the world, now that it has changed. They are beginning the process of remapping connections in a world now absent of one they lost. Our need to connect is primal. Death reminds us that life is about connection.

What's the first thing that comes to mind when we think of *connection*? There are many possible responses because *connection* takes on many forms and has so much to do with being human. Human connection can be about relationships, being on the same wavelength, physical touch, cellular and neural biological signaling, spiritual connectedness, and many more. Connections are the essence of life. They awaken us and make us feel alive, supported by a healthy dopamine release that reminds us that connections are essential for life.

Unfortunately, our desire for connection is how some technologies prey on our vulnerabilities. Surrounded by technology that pings us day and night, we now avoid answering phones, doorbells, and emails. The invasion has pushed us into putting up barriers to the very things that make us feel truly connected. Digital connectedness is one of the great fallacies of the 21st century we've yet to come to terms with. The result? Isolation and a sense of loneliness are escalating, confounding dementia challenges even further.

Connection takes on even greater significance within our bodies. The 100 trillion cells in our body aren't just along for the ride; they are in constant communication as well, even while we sleep. Our signaling systems all determine how we grow, how we maintain health, and how quickly we age.

Imagine sitting on a park bench with a loved one, holding hands and talking. As each person speaks, the words are simultaneously heard in our ears, confirming our sound signals are being broadcast. Body language overlays the words, adding depth, verification, and meaning to the exchange. The time comes to leave, and we agree to continue the conversation via cell phones. That goes well until one of us starts to lose the phone signal. Parts of words start getting clipped, and soon, entire words start getting skipped, and we find ourselves filling in the blanks and guessing at the missing words. The weaker the signal, the more we are guessing, and the more likely we are to misinterpret what the other is saying. The gaps grow longer, but we are reluctant to hang up on a valued discussion. We wait, eagerly hoping for the signal to return, but soon we're both looking at our phones – no signal, no words, not even static.

The signaling within our bodies isn't without challenges either. Human cells age, weaken, and eventually die as part of the normal lifecycle. It is one of the reasons cells replace themselves multiple times over a lifetime, through the process of mitosis. Signaling grows increasingly problematic with age, as old cells begin accumulating, failing to get cleared away by the apoptosis process. These become senescent "zombie cells" that clutter the signal pathways and trigger inflammation. Senescence interferes with our ability to fend off threats as we age and accelerates the aging process even more, which is why it is one of the Hallmarks of Aging.

If we had to choose one root cause of health, it would be communication. Effective communication only happens when there is a connection. From the trillions of messages sent through the body in a single blink of an eye, to the words of a child saying, "I love you," to the touch of a hand at the bedside comforting a dying parent, communication is another word for life. Sustaining our communication networks is at the core of everything we discuss in healthy aging. It's by supporting healthy signaling that we leverage the most advanced system known to science: the human body.

NOTHING IN HEALTH IS BINARY

Other than life or death, almost nothing in health is binary. Thousands of headlines tease us with notions of simple answers, but health isn't conveniently simple. It is its complexity that enables the human species to do so many amazing things.

It is helpful to remind ourselves that aging is a continuum. Each season of the year presents its own beauty and challenges, and it is the flow and progression that provide dimension and evolving perspective. Kneel down and take a closer look at the grass, a forest floor, or even an exposed pile of soil, and there is abundant life unfolding in perfect balance. Underneath the things we see are trillions of bacteria and fungi going about their business, completely out of sight, but essential to everything going on at the surface. The microbial life beneath our feet is a drop in the ocean compared with the complex life and communication systems within us, each one influenced by our lifestyle choices, which is why they matter so much.

CONNECTING WITH THE FUTURE

We are all at some *place* in our lives today, focused on the moment and allocating small portions of our attention to the future. The future shifts between minutes, hours, or days from now and, occasionally, years down the road. The farther we try to envision, the harder it gets. Evolution designed it that way because survival is, and always has been, our primary goal. Make it through today and hopefully wake up tomorrow with opportunities to do it all over again, and possibly make a few new connections that will enhance our sense of belonging and support.

Earlier, I offered the idea of envisioning our optimal late stage in life as a means of reverse engineering our lives. We certainly don't need to dwell too long on the idea, but it can help us reach forward into life and use it to help define our values and build the framework needed to get us from here to there.

In this visioning thought exercise, we can hold our heads high, having done a lot of things right and inspired a few others along the way. Our vision likely points to a life that was active, full, and long. Suffering was short. Let the mind wander to notions of the hours, days, weeks, and months leading up to the end of a well-lived life. Imagine the faces, places, and activities. Imagine the conversations, the deep connections, and reconnections with those from our past. Imagine the celebrations, the laughter, and the smiles, and yes, some tender tears.

This exercise grows more comfortable with occasional practice. It helps to connect us with the choices we make today with a destination worth building toward. It's less about certainty of specific outcomes but rather about building awareness and belief around the possibilities – making our own luck. Most of us aspire to leave a legacy, just as others have done for us. Our legacy is unlikely to be about the size of our house, our golf handicap, or the number of social media followers.

People will remember how we made them feel, how much we enjoyed sharing a game or event with them, how often we smiled, and how the thought of us makes them smile. With that imagery far off in the distance, it offers a target to align our thoughts, values, priorities, and choices to build a bridge to span the distance of time. Daily choices become clearer when values and priorities become obvious. Temptation, emotions, and life events don't magically vanish, but practicing alignment helps us get back on track quicker and easier.

The Verrazzano-Narrows Bridge is a double-decker 13,700 ft (2.6 miles) long bridge that connects Staten Island with Brooklyn, New York. It took forty years to plan and another ten years to build. The legacy of bridges built earlier provided the belief that it was possible. Tens of thousands of components and over one million fasteners went into its construction. Each one supported the next, until it was finally completed in 1969. Most of the bridge is repeating groups of the same parts over and over, one by one, with precision and purpose. Its designers started with two defined endpoints and began breaking it down into manageable repeating parts and assembly patterns until it eventually all came together. Whealthspan applies these same proven concepts. It begins with a vision worth planning and building toward, and adopting small, simple behavior patterns that support the next.

One Flew Over the Cuckoo's Nest

Dad was the ultimate Whealthspan Cinderella story. A product of the early 20th century, his life was consumed by events surrounding two world wars and families getting back on their feet in the decades that followed. Farming and lumberjacking were his roots, and given the option, outdoors was always his preference. Life was a struggle. Health was a luxury. Almost half the population smoked, and none of them wanted to hear about the health risks. He spent more than half his adult life managing heart disease and recurring rounds of cancer but fought back every time.

For his 75ᵗʰ birthday, he asked me to take him waterskiing, something he'd introduced me to at age 5. Mom sat waiting on the dock, shaking her head at his foolish behavior, seemingly inviting a heart attack. Pulling him around the lake was an honor I'd been given many times, and he announced that this would be the last, as they were leaving the lake to move into town. Most times, he'd ski slalom, but not this time. I suspect he wanted his waterskiing farewell to be unblemished, and a fond reminder of how far he'd come from life on the farm.

The boat sliced through the calm water, like a surgeon's scalpel. His trademark infectious smile and windblown hair spoke of his delight, as his skis skipped across the glassy waters. I gently steered the boat on the final turn back toward the dock. Like an airplane on its final approach, Dad let go of the tow rope, coasting smoothly back into the dock. A perfect landing. The operation had been a success. Mom breathed a sigh of relief.

Fifteen years later, I sat with Dad in hospice. Another cancer had arrived, and his days were quickly counting down. We'd had a challenging night. The painkillers and the strange surroundings left him disoriented and anxious. He'd never been shut in for so long, ever!

Morning came, and the fall colors were ablaze under a spectacular blue sky. He'd asked me to get outside several times through the night, and it was time for a Cuckoo's Nest-inspired breakout. The nurse and I got him into a wheelchair, bundled him up in my parka, and we headed outside through a backdoor. The crisp air slapped our faces. He squinted, blinded by the piercing sunlight. He loved it. Family members arrived as we rounded toward the front door, startled to see him outside. Busted!

It was short, but such a delight to see him smile that trademark smile one last time. We'd reconnected in the place he knew best, nature.

Photo: Dad, waterskiing at 75

MINDSET MATTERS

Lists are helpful when buying groceries, and completing project tasks, but less powerful in promoting longevity. That's because our outcomes are the result of millions of little things we do out of habit. The smoker doesn't need a list to tell them it's time for a cigarette, and the daily walker doesn't need a list to remind them of what's waiting for them on the other side of the door. Habits and outcomes are influenced more by mindsets and desires than lists.

Mindset breeds strength and resilience. In my field of work, stories of super-seniors come across my desk almost daily. What's common is their willingness to do hard things, and they are exceptional survivors. Some take up fitness in their sixties and go on to do amazing things in their nineties. Today's centenarians are all survivors of World War II. Many survived multiple wars, loss of children, poverty, separation from family to escape hardship, limited schooling, physical abuse as children, pandemics, and on and on. A 2022 report cited over 1,000 Holocaust survivors living in Israel over the age of 100. That survival rate far exceeds the U.S. rate of living to age 100.

"My father was strong and healthy. … They lined up the working men, and they shot them all." Among the miracles Fanny Krasner Lebovits shared in her book *Memories, Miracles & Meaning: Insights of a Holocaust Survivor*, was surviving on a bare minimum of supplies, floating on a barge for 9 days with nothing but a piece of bread, a bowl of water, and potato peels.

I don't suggest for a second that subjecting children to horrific experiences is the key to longevity. Rather, it speaks to deficiencies of modern life. These centenarians learned how to cope with life's challenges early on, skills that no doubt served them throughout their lifetime. They adopted healthy survivor mindsets with clear values and priorities. They learned not to sweat the small stuff at a young age, and it stuck with them. We pay a price by shielding ourselves too much and hiding safely inside our comfort zones. Wrapping ourselves in bubble wrap doesn't extend healthspan; it shortens it.

I was studying aging decades before I realized it. My parents spoke praises of respected elders who had served their communities for so many years. There was a societal expectation that older adults were deserving of our respect. It was easy to point to examples of how elders had invested themselves in our future, many paying the ultimate sacrifice. It wasn't just those who served in the military, but all older adults. They all paid a price in their own way and put a lot on the line for our future. Their investment in making life better wasn't a single event; rather, it was often several pivots over a lifetime. Without the demands that major world events place on us, it's easy to overlook the needs and opportunities to invest in our personal aging future.

As I began studying aging with more intention, my researcher's appetite for data drew me deeper to understand the challenges today's age 50+ adults are facing. Most of the population appears to be blindly sailing toward the Silver Tsunami, as many like call it. By several measures, we're headed for possibly the biggest challenge in over a century.

SILVER SUPER-TSUNAMI

The Silver Super Tsunami is a confluence of 10 identifiable factors that started unfolding decades ago. The physics term for this is Constructive Interference – when two or more waves combine to reinforce each other, increasing a wave's amplitude. We're all heading for a ride that no one in history has ever experienced.

Silver Super-Tsunami Factors:

1. The Baby Boomer generation (1946-1964) has resulted in an unprecedented surge in the older adult population.
2. A global population surge from 2.5B in 1950 to a projected 8.6B in 2030.
3. A 31% increase in the U.S. median population age, rising from an age of 30.2 in 1950 to a projected age of 39.7 in 2030.
4. A steadily declining birth rate has led to an inversion of the older/younger demographic distribution, with fewer caregivers and many more needing care.
5. Adults aged 65-74 have median retirement savings of $266,400, well short of the anticipated need, placing millions of seniors in crisis.

6. The rising healthcare cost will further limit access for older adults, placing even more burden on families and taxpayers.

7. Healthcare and social services are already struggling to find workers, and demand will continue to increasingly outpace supply for another 10+ years.

8. Retirement communities continue to focus on serving the wealthiest, leaving the middle class with few alternatives.

9. Economic pressure will force governments to change priorities.

10. Steadily declining public health places yet more stress on healthcare systems.

The social forces are too big and too many to expect it will be life as usual. Our retirement will be significantly different than our parents' retirement. We have yet to see any serious action by governments or consumers. A plan to get far ahead of the curve, be far more proactive than most people, and have a robust and well-connected support network will pay big dividends.

INVESTMENT MINDSET

Proven principles and mindsets of the financial planning community apply equally well for successful Whealthspan outcomes. The value of investing early, compounding interest, and diversification all apply. If there's a gap, it's that financial planners focus too little on wealth preservation. This is one of the subtle distinctions between a financial planner and a wealth manager. In fairness, they have few financial products to offer, so often, it is the planner who wants to go above and beyond for their clients that helps them plan for indirect or non-financial matters.

The objective of a typical financial plan is to create a mountain of funds that's big enough to draw from in our later years. Ideally, there are some funds left over to pass along to heirs and charities. Today, those with more than *$2,000,000* in investments are likely in a favorable position, assuming they live within budget. The other 98% of people have less margin for error and will need to proactively guard against avoidable expenditures. Most of those will be planning to age at home, which means they need to prepare their homes for aging well into their nineties. Mindset mistakes are almost always a combination of health and home oversights. We'll get into that more when we discuss the home environment.

Sitting Pretty

Bill and Mary were sitting pretty. At the end of long careers, they'd raised three great children, two daughters on the opposite coast, and a son close to home. They were proud to have saved up and acquired almost $1,000,000 in net equity and had opted to retire a couple of years early. They were cautious with their money but spent more than planned on trips to take their beautiful grandchildren on vacations during the early years. It was money well spent. Their son needed financial support from time to time. That wasn't in the budget they'd discussed with their financial planner, but they didn't know how else to help.

At age 70, Bill was diagnosed with early-onset Alzheimer's Disease, eventually needing more care than Mary could manage. Mary arranged for home care but needed to place Bill in a memory care facility for his final years. The homecare, five years of Bill's memory care, and mounting medical expenses totaling $8,500 per month had burned through their savings. Mary had to take a loan against their home to cover the last year of care and pay for a modest funeral. Bill's dementia had sent everything into chaos. Mary had been treading water for a decade, taking care of Bill, taking care of the house, and trying to be a good grandmother.

Mary was a healthy, young 74-year-old when Bill passed. Ten years ago, she thought they were sitting pretty, but now found herself with no partner, no local family support, no money to keep the home, and twenty years of uncertainty in front of her.

Bill and Mary's story has become increasingly common. The details vary, but the outcomes are surprisingly similar, largely attributed to our general lack of preparedness and low awareness of our vulnerabilities until fate plays its hand. Sure, Bill and Mary could have done several things differently, but once a life event gets its teeth into us, options slip away before we even get a chance to consider them.

Consumed with anxiety around our own fate, we also have a habit of forgetting to think about life after one of us is gone. Life still goes on for the surviving partner. That fate usually falls to women, who outnumber male solo-agers about 2 to 1. Women, Aging, and Myths is a must-read, offering a seasoned perspective on the unique challenges and opportunities for women. Having worked on the front lines and cared for several family members, author Patrick Roden, PhD, is an especially insightful gerontologist and trusted mentor.

Financial advisors specialize in managing money, not life. That's our job, and it's not something we are trained for. Recent years have seen a growth in retirement coaches looking at non-financial matters. These are people who help us sort out what we'd like to do with our lives after the traditional career winds down and navigate the next phase of life. More are coming to the market, but very few are skilled in age-related health issues.

SACRIFICE NOTHING

Aging has been caught in tangled perceptions of sacrifice and loss. Science and society have embraced notions of anti-aging. What is anti-aging? It was a delightful plotline for the Back to the Future movie, but the term is used to play on our vulnerabilities and reinforce that aging is a negative experience. There's no question that some aspects of death and aging are negative, but positive opportunities far outweigh the negative, as healthy agers soon discover.

We've known for thousands of years that we don't all age at the same rate. Genetics plays a role that we'll address later, but thanks to recent science, it's clear that lifestyle habits are what dominate our rate of aging. The question is how best to integrate positive habits into daily life.

We all arrived at where we are right now for many reasons, most of them inconsequential. Good or bad, it really doesn't matter. Whether we're sitting alone in a small apartment or on a million-dollar yacht, we are where we are. The past is the past; this is now, and the future awaits. We are in a place of shelter and well-shielded from the threats our ancestors faced not so many years ago. Our opportunities dwarf anything they could have imagined. We are surrounded by abundance. Part of the abundance includes temptations that serve no value beyond immediate pleasure and gratification, but almost all of us can spot obvious differences between health-promoting and disease-promoting lifestyle habits. Yet, knowing the difference, temptation doesn't conveniently vanish. It isn't going anywhere… ever. Temptation tugs at us every moment of the day.

If temptation can't be squashed, our only viable option is to overpower it by stacking the odds in our favor with more appealing alternatives. Imagine that temptation was on the other end of a rope and that our future depended on a single tug-o-war showdown, winner-take-all. We'd be looking to stack our side with better, stronger options. A mindset that focuses on better, stronger, and more options is better equipped to win the contest. This is an example of when focusing on the positive holds such power. It won't win every contest, but it will win most of the important ones.

Making the connection with positivity changes the "sacrifice mindset" to a "better options" mindset. Eating better is hard until we explore new foods. Exercise gets easier when we discover new activities we truly enjoy. Stress becomes more manageable when we learn new tools to apply. Relationships improve when we intentionally move beyond our circle and form new connections. All of these actions help to identify new opportunities to upgrade, replace, and generally enjoy life more. Every micro-decision and tug-of-war victory reinforces the strength within us and empowers us to continually raise our game. As we progressively connect the micro-decisions with our values, we build a fortress of strength and resolve, overpowering the temptations that may have once ruled over us.

CONNECTING IN THE MOMENT

Somewhere along the way, living in the moment came into conflict with living for tomorrow, as though it was an either/or choice. Please excuse my directness, but what a load of crap! It's become a poor excuse to rationalize doing things in the moment we know don't align with our true values, while sabotaging our future in the process.

Moments are all we have. Moments matter in the here and now, and in our future. They come, they go, and we invite more into our lives. Some moments that grab and envelope us:

- The face of a child, excited by our return from being away on travel.
- A room filled with people we love and who love us in return.
- Music that flows into us, pulling us into complete emotional engagement.
- The look in another's eyes that says love like words never can.
- Athletes exhilarated by new levels of performance.
- Seeing the finish line of a challenge we never imagined starting.

These are feelings of connection, feelings that know no age. People over 100 years of age dream as much as they ever did. Connections happen every day, within our cells, within the environment we interact, and with others we encounter. They are not measured by the size of our investment account or the lines on our faces, but rather by our willingness to lean forward into life at all ages and experience authentic connection. The more we approach each day and each opportunity with an investment mindset that's looking for moments of connection, the more we'll have to look forward to, and the greater our inevitable Whealthspan.

Chapter 6

INCONVENIENT FACTS

At age 20, we think we've learned 80% of
what needs to be known in life.
At age 80, we think we've learned 20% of
what needs to be known in life.
The 80:20 wisdom paradox.

Think Bigger

FOUR HOURS INTO THE HIKE, the snowcapped peak glistened above against a warm July clear blue sky. The dirt trail transitioned to loose rock scree, slowing the pace significantly. Things were about to get interesting. Eventually, the rock gave way to a blanket of snow, the pitch kicked up steeper, and the snow deepened with every step. At 300 yards to the summit, the snow was above the knees, and oxygen was getting scarce. Every step took deliberate effort. The sheltering mountain walls of the valley had given way to vast emptiness. Some turned back, overcome by the sudden and unsettling sensations of altitude and vertigo.

Atop the windswept summit, it was comforting to see the rock underfoot once more. The landscape pulled me round and round in circles. Nothing but ragged mountain peaks for miles and miles, pointing toward the sky. I'd never felt so small, never experienced the world to be so powerful. How little I knew of it. So much more to learn. It exposed how easy it is to feel safe in our beliefs, tucked inside

*our comfort zones, looking at life through a window. I needed to
think bigger, much, much bigger.*

Banded Peak, Elevation 9,626 ft (2,934 m)

THE UNLEARNING

I love teaching adults. We aren't sponges like we were back in our
school-age days. We know stuff now! We're even paid for stuff we
know. Thanks to the internet, what we don't know, we can discover.
Depending on what we're searching for, some of it might even be true!

The process of academic learning is like building a house. It starts
with laying a foundation of principles and continuously building
upon them. Problems arise, however, when the foundation comes into
question. A single challenge is easy to reject, but the more we're exposed to challenges, the more we're obligated to engage in the debate.
The natural reaction is to fight with stubborn determination, to resist

admitting we got something wrong along the way, even if the battle is only waging in our mind. It's often more about the consequences of all the beliefs and habits that are built on the faulty foundation that are at stake. Apart from the chemical addiction of smoking, for example, is coming to terms with all the time and money spent on smoking for so many years. None of us feel good about feeling like we've wasted time or money, or feel like we're going to look or feel like a fool if we change course after many years. It was one thing to change our minds as children; it's quite another to change it as adults. It usually takes time, repeated exposures, and often being confronted with a dead end on the path of old beliefs before we are ready to revisit our foundational beliefs and be open to new learning. Those are the breakthrough moments that make teaching adults gratifying. Once we get unstuck, our attitude shifts, and we can move to a new level of understanding.

Puzzling

There's nothing like a big jigsaw puzzle to get used to tackling challenges that require thousands of small steps. Ari always liked to start puzzles with the outside edges, carefully searching and gathering all the straight-sided edge pieces to build the frame. With all the edge pieces gathered, all but three were connected, and though near complete, the frame refused to entirely close. There must be missing pieces, but scouring for more proved wasted time. It wasn't until Ari let go of finishing the frame and began working on the interior pieces, that the mistake suddenly became obvious. Two edge pieces that had appeared to fit together, were now plainly misfit. Going back and reorganizing the pieces, made space for the other pieces to fall into place.

As adults, we learn this same way. We gather pieces along the path of life and put them together in what appears to be a logical order.

They have more plasticity than a rigid puzzle piece, so it's far more forgiving, and mistakes are much harder to notice. Eventually, we come to terms with things not adding up like they should, and we go back and find the mistake. Just one correction can enable many pieces to suddenly fit together quickly, with very little effort. Getting unstuck requires some letting go. That's often the hardest part.

Over time, the lines get blurred between what we learned formally and what we learned through life experiences. Being street-smart can be invaluable, but it can also be a trap, particularly when it comes to lifestyle habits. Testing our beliefs from time to time is healthy. There are far worse things than unlearning, based on new knowledge, and getting a health benefit in return.

FOUNDATIONS ARE SET EARLY

By the age of seven, most of our primary lifestyle habits have been formed. In most cases, they've been shaped by our environment. Many of us learned early that conformance is praised, and following our parents' lifestyle brought us validation. It assumes, of course, that our parents knew the secrets to health and longevity. There might be a crack in our foundation!

Growing up, Friday night dinners were fish and chips from the local grease fryer, pepperoni pizza, or deep-fried KFC chicken, fries, and coleslaw. I always liked the coleslaw. It wasn't that I didn't love drowning in the fat; it was more that it was the one thing that didn't put me into a food-induced coma. Thankfully, most days, we ate much better homemade dinners, but like all families, we were a product of our era.

If grocery food purchases were driven by the lowest cost and included trips down the snacks and soda aisles, these were our norms. If sitting on the couch watching sports on Sunday afternoon versus organizing a neighborhood game of two-handed touch football, our ideas around the role of athletics would be quite different. We tend to build beliefs around established lifestyle patterns observed in our environment. We see patterns and how they fit together like a jigsaw puzzle.

Over about five years of primary school education, we learned several mathematical ways to arrive at a resultant value of 9. We likely started by adding up nine items; $1+1+1+1+1+1+1+1+1=9$, with no concept of what was to follow. That progressed to $1+8=9$, $2+7=9$, $3+6=9$, $4+5=9$, $3x3=9$, $1x9=9$, $2x4.5=9$, $3^2=9$, $\sqrt{81}=9$, etc. At its foundation, we retain a strong belief around the concept based on nine items.

If I were to suggest that $1+1+1+1+1+1+1+1+1=111,111,111$, it could reasonably be rejected, followed up with a suggestion that I go back to school and start over. I've applied a written language convention in place of a mathematical convention. A geometric convention would have resulted in a nonagon shape. We learned these things in academic settings through progressive developmental exercises, and in doing so, we also developed learning patterns to apply in the real world. It works well most of the time, so long as the foundational evidence is solid, and our convention is clear and understood. Let's look at a more relevant example.

When a calorie isn't a calorie

Let's say we have two meals, each providing 500 calories:

Meal A: Consists mostly of simple carbohydrates (sugary snacks)

Meal B: Contains a balanced mix of proteins, fats, and complex carbohydrates (lean protein, vegetables, and whole grains)

Meal A: Simple carbohydrates are relatively quick and easy to digest and absorb. Let's say the body burns 5% of the total calories to process the food, resulting in net calories absorbed of 475 (95% of 500).

Meal B: A mix of macronutrients, including proteins and complex carbohydrates, requires more energy for digestion and absorption. Let's say 20% of the total calories are burned in processing the food, resulting in net calories absorbed of 400 (80% of 500).

In this example, both meals provide the same number of calories, but the thermic effect of food (TEF) differs. (TEF is the energy consumed in breaking down and digesting foods.) Meal B has 4x the TEF, meaning the body expends more energy to process and absorb the nutrients. Even though the calories consumed are equal, Meal B results in a 16% lower net caloric intake. This is one of the foundations of why weight management is easier with eating whole foods. The presence of fiber in Meal B is significant as well, given that the fiber is consumed by our microbiome. Fiber also expands and achieves satiety (fullness) earlier, resulting in less caloric intake, making weight control even easier, but we're getting ahead of ourselves.

That's a look at calories from a nutrition convention, but let's look at calories from a physics convention. Science defines a calorie as the energy needed to raise the temperature of one gram of water by one degree Celsius, which is approximately 4.184 joules. Science doesn't care where the energy is being applied; one calorie is always 4.184 joules. Nutrition and physics may appear to be in conflict, but they aren't. The missing 75 calories went to supplying the body with an extra 314 joules of heat energy instead of glucose. Not a bad deal!

Examples like these exist across many fields of science, and so it is easy to see how much convention matters. It's not that one field is right, and the other is wrong. Often, different mechanisms have led to applying knowledge from one field slightly differently in another. Too frequently, the convention isn't even mentioned. We're just supposed to know. That's quickly sorted out in an academic setting but leads to constant confusion in the public arena.

One of the ways we all get tripped up is by mistaking common beliefs for academic truths. By academic truth, I'm referring to principles developed and tested over thousands of years, such as the earlier mathematical example. A check on cholesterol studies suggests there are over 18,000 published studies. The reason there are so many studies is because science continues to search for scientific truth. There is a strong common belief that cholesterol is bad, and we need to lower our LDL to some prescribed level. Yet it appears that isn't true for everyone, and so the search for truth around cholesterol is far from over. It's not that there aren't areas of strong evidence and consensus. Voluminous, and continuing studies convey there are still many unanswered questions. Add the confusing relationship between dietary cholesterol and blood cholesterol, and it's easy to see how we can quickly get tripped up in our understanding. We'll come back to this later.

Modern academic truths tend to be more fluid, as they are reflective of our current state of scientific understanding. Sticking with the cholesterol example, it's relatively recent that the relationship between dietary cholesterol and blood cholesterol became better understood. We can look back over the history of the federal dietary guidelines over the decades to see that it's been a moving target. Little wonder there is so much public confusion.

In our complex information world, where there are relentless attempts to influence our beliefs, we shouldn't be expected to vet them all to determine which *truths* should be embraced, yet that's precisely what we do. The need to establish core truths early in life is essential; otherwise, we'd walk around in a state of overwhelming confusion and paralysis. We're continually discovering that health and longevity depend on many new and evolving factors, each with varying degrees of certainty. It's genuinely challenging to discern whom and what to trust, making it ever more important to guard against confusion and paralysis. It's a process!

Ultimately, we are the masters of our outcomes, and no one can make the thousands of daily decisions for us. That's why it's more constructive to start with a stable foundation and objectively work on building a framework with elements and connections of high certainty. A blended view of science, clinical practice, and long cultural histories, leads to foundations of greater certainty that are less threatened or influenced by the latest opinion or published study. Small decisions become more obvious, and we're less inclined to feel threatened by information that challenges our beliefs. Equally important, we should be open to the fact that our beliefs could be misinformed and be prepared to change our minds when enveloped in compelling evidence.

The fact that we continue to read books and search for information speaks to our curious nature. But how much of our searching is to affirm or build on our current beliefs, and how much challenges them? This is where our need for tribal belonging can get us into trouble. It's important to be in supportive environments, but it's also important we challenge our viewpoints and our knowledge in safe ways that don't result in conflict, passive or otherwise. It's one of the great benefits of reading. We can do it in private and hope to learn viewpoints from alternative perspectives and experiences without finding ourselves in a heated debate.

WHAT'S OLD IS NEW AGAIN

The headlines constantly try to impress us with ideas that longevity is a new concept. Earlier, I gave some historical evidence that challenges this. Let's put it to the test in a more modern context.

The confusion stems from a numbers game and repeating something long enough until it becomes modern folklore. The numbers error goes like this: In 1900, the U.S. Life Expectancy (LE) was 47.3. Jump forward to 2019 (pre-pandemic), and U.S. LE was 78.8. That's a significant increase (31.5 years), but recognize that most of it comes from reducing the infant mortality rate from 157.1 deaths per 1,000 live births in 1900 to 5.6 deaths per 1,000 live births in 2019. The next numeric contributions come from lower communicable diseases and infection rates that resulted in many premature deaths. The popular phrase, "We're all living a lot longer," is more media and marketing than fact. A more accurate statement would be, "Fewer are dying below age 50." LE for a 50-year-old U.S. person has increased by 10.9 years since 1900. For a 65-year-old, LE has increased by 4.7 years since 1980. That's good, but nothing like the near-doubling so often pitched.

The U.S. continues to invest tremendous resources into treating chronic diseases, to the tune of about $3 trillion annually, with only incremental improvements to show for it. When it comes to longevity, the most advanced medical system in the world is losing the tug-of-war with the U.S. lifestyle, with no evidence of that changing. The other side of the coin speaks to how much power individuals have over their healthspan and longevity. We may be powerless to fix the system, but we have significant power to fix our personal healthspan trajectory.

NO ONE IS COMING TO THE RESCUE

I used to naively believe that healthcare included a strong health promotion component. Signs of change are on the horizon, but it will be painfully slow and not in time for us to benefit. The healthcare system is a massive ship in disrepair that resists change at every opportunity. The complexity of the system, too much money, and too many jobs on the line, make altering its course a daunting task. It is the Titanic of our day. Valued at 4 trillion dollars, it is deeply woven into the fabric of every government agency, making the prospect of change seem insurmountable. The political temperament appears content to "manage" the financial hemorrhaging for as long as voters are willing to tolerate it, or until national security is on the brink. Despite my typical reputation as an optimist, the U.S. is displaying signs of an addict in denial, refusing to believe there's a better way to live. If the addiction scenario holds true, meaningful change may not be embraced until everything comes crashing down, and all options have been taken away.

The U.S. health system is a labyrinth of epic proportions. In theory, the U.S. Department of Health and Human Services (HHS) should be a good place to understand government priorities. However, this optimist was disappointed to find that HHS does not prioritize rebuilding or promoting preventive public health. As of 2024, Xavier Becerra, Secretary of HHS, lists the following as top HHS priorities:

- Ending the pandemic
- Reducing health care costs
- Expanding access to care
- Tackling health disparities
- Strengthening behavioral health

The $2.98 trillion budget priorities focus on trying to plug holes in a failing public health dam versus leveraging humans' innate ability to self-heal and restore its integrity.

Here is HHS's stated Mission: *"To enhance the health and well-being of all Americans, by providing for effective health and human services and by fostering sound, sustained advances in the sciences underlying medicine, public health, and social services."*

Nowhere in the department charged with health leadership is there a goal of proactively fostering public health. It is built on the foundation of being a reactive service. I hoped the "Strengthening behavioral health" might be a glimmer of hope, but no, it's a flowery way of pointing to mental health issues. I don't presume that the responsibility for public health rests solely on the shoulders of HHS or Secretary Becerra, but they don't even appear to have a vision statement to point to where they are headed.

My disappointment led me to search deeper into the organization. Perhaps the priority I was hoping for lay in another HHS mission statement also published on their website: *"Improving the health, safety, and productivity of federal employees."* No mention of the public! HHS is indeed the department responsible for public health, raising the question: Are we all caught in a composite Hollywood version of The Wizard of Oz and Groundhog Day? The actors change, but the storyline remains the same. There is no one at the helm of promoting public health broadly, either in the departments that serve us or among our political leaders.

The last broadly recognized leader in public health was in the 1980s when Dr. C. Everett Koop served as the U.S. Surgeon General. Koop faced political interference during his tenure, particularly concerning the rising AIDS epidemic and public sentiment around homosexuality. However, there was a recognition that public health needed to rise above politics. Subsequent Surgeons General have been reduced to figureheads, brought out for brief appearances. One might ask why politicians think they are better equipped to manage public health than the thousands of trained public health experts in our midst. While spending around healthcare is undoubtedly a significant political issue, depoliticizing health priorities could benefit us all.

Even educators remain reluctant to embrace a step change in health education. According to a 2020 School Health Profiles study, 58.8% of high schools still provide unhealthy snack foods and beverages from vending machines, at the school store, canteen, or snack bar. Without a shift towards health-focused education, Western longevity is likely to continue declining against developed countries, with un-enviable long-term consequences.

The effort required to adopt the sweetened beverage tax serves as an example. Despite industry lobbying, some cities successfully implemented the tax. A 2023 study found that Oakland residents reduced their sugary drink purchases by 26.8%, signaling a potential change. Critics cite the tax penalizes low-income families and those in food deserts, yet water remains almost free across the country. Who loses by redirecting chronic healthcare spending to investing in low-income and food deserts with better health education and ensuring access to healthy foods and habits? The processed food industry and the healthcare industry. The only force big enough to go up against these powers is the public. Who will be the next Ralph Nader to rally the public?

SMOKE ON THIS

Processed foods are often compared to smoking as a health challenge of the 21st century. While smoking rates declined after 40 years of evidence highlighting the risks, the health challenges posed by processed foods are on a much larger scale. In the era of cigarette advertising, there were only a few producers and one product—cigarettes. In contrast, the processed food sector offers a multitude of products grouped into categories like minimally, basic, moderately, and ultra-processed. Twenty-five of the top food and beverage companies reported $1.8 trillion in sales, with profits exceeding $160 billion, dwarfing the tobacco challenge.

Despite regulatory requirements to ensure product safety, the complexity of assessing *actual* long-term safety over a human lifetime remains a theoretical exercise. Animal testing, typically lasting no longer than 24 months, forms the basis for determining safety for humans. It's convenient to believe that testing just 2.2% of a human lifespan on a different organism, under an ideal, controlled environment, would scale to project human safety, over a lifetime exposed to millions of uncontrolled variables, but even scientists within the chemical industry would agree that is fraught with high risk. Almost nothing scales up so conveniently. That's why the industry spends significant time and resources before building new chemical plant processes. The path to regulatory approval for billions of human and environmental exposures is trivial by comparison. The food and chemical industries are largely doing what's required; meanwhile, public and political leaders are quick to deflect responsibility.

To complicate things even more, genotoxic carcinogens add another layer of difficulty in risk assessment. Genotoxins can be found in environmental pollutants, industrial chemicals, certain pharmaceuticals, food contaminants, and naturally occurring substances that damage human and animal DNA. About 90% of the Group 1 carcinogens listed by the International Agency for Research on Cancer (IARC) are reported to be genotoxic. With exposure to thousands of toxins over a lifetime, and no reasonable means to comprehend the direct or synergistic risks, we, as individuals, face a daunting challenge. Over 350,000 synthetic chemicals are already in circulation, with 2,000 new chemicals introduced each year, projecting nearly half a million chemicals over an 80-year lifetime. These are chemicals that are not naturally occurring, yet we expect the human body to accept and assimilate them without any hiccups. Compounded chemical exposure risks to humans have become a game of Russian Roulette, grounded in a belief that this is the only path to advancement. Chemicals like PFAS and glyphosate are now found in virtually all waterways and human blood, but they represent a small fraction of our challenge. Meanwhile, billions are spent to identify and litigate culpable parties, and the system marches on, ever-resistant to change.

The Devil's Value Chain illustrates how big companies navigate various points in the value chain to mitigate risks and enhance profits. In the food industry, pharmaceutical companies move up the value chain by engineering seeds and acquiring chemical companies. This positions them to potentially treat illnesses caused or complicated by their own products, creating a shocking conflict of interest that somehow is legal and acceptable.

While public discomfort with these realities varies widely, individuals have the power to decide where to spend their money. The public, collectively, shares some responsibility for the choices made. While it may be challenging to fathom how things spiral out of control, individuals have control over many aspects of their lives. In an imperfect world, opportunities for affordable healthspan abound, but managing hidden risks becomes crucial.

While some actively challenge industries and governments, individuals can take care of themselves, influencing matters where it counts the most—at home with those who depend on them. Growing awareness is reshaping the marketplace, evidenced by the booming organic food sector that is struggling to meet consumer demand. With a compound annual growth rate (CAGR) of 12.90%, the organic food market is projected to reach $535 billion by 2032, highlighting a shift in consumer preferences and a growing focus on healthier alternatives.

NEXT STEPS

Economies drive financial markets, and nothing counts more than where we spend our dollars. Every dollar we direct toward extending our healthspan inspires others who watch us make those key choices. Every dollar also drives down the cost and makes the choice accessible to more people because of the impact of scale. It might seem hard to envision today, but we are trending toward a scenario where many organic foods will cost less than conventional foods treated with agricultural chemicals. It comes down to scale and policy. The growing trend is already evidenced by converging prices on store shelves.

At some point, health-minded organic farmers will be afforded a level playing field and not burdened with the added regulatory costs they face today. Chemical farmers get a free ride, while organic farmers are forced to pay added fees for running clean operations. Those fees hit the consumer's pocketbook, putting yet another barrier to helping people make better health choices.

FINAL THOUGHTS

Understanding the complex world of health is part of our journey. An open-minded, curious approach will serve us well over our many years. Threats are inescapable, given how many are now present in the same environment we depend on for our food and water. But, as with all threats, we can stay engaged in the discussion and apply reasonable logic, to not knowingly walk into a burning building. Part of upgrading our healthspan is limiting the exposures we can control. The small choices add up over decades. We may be able to avoid the heat, but it's essential we don't get burned.

Chapter 7

GENETICS SPEAK

It's not about the instrument.
It's how we play it that makes the music.

FEW THINGS HAVE BEEN more exciting to observe than genetics research. Although its history can be traced back to the late 1800s, it wasn't until 1990, when the Human Genome Project was launched, that genetics experienced its moonshot. Top scientists from across the globe came together to collaboratively break the code, with many people expecting that it would unlock the doors to solving cancer and several other diseases. Together, with the aid of the most advanced analytical equipment of the day, they learned a lot about human genetics in a relatively short period. However, as is often the case in science, the research raised more questions than answers. Behind the doors of genetics lay an even bigger labyrinth that quickly became the puzzle to solve, known as the epigenome. While the epigenome has been researched since the 1940s, it has proven to be complex and intensely intriguing. The Genome Project was followed by another international effort; The Human Epigenome Project, launched in 1999. The field has expanded immensely, spurring thousands of projects seeking to address unanswered questions and validate new theories.

Most of us are familiar with the heritable genetic information passed on from our parents, half of our genes from our mother, and half from our father. They are the building blocks for every cell in our body and what is known to most as our genetic ancestry, popularized by 23andMe. Collectively, all our genes are referred to as our genome, a unique composite library (with the exception of identical twins) that reveals our precise physical identity, familial relations, and regional origins.

GRAND GENOMES

At the certain risk of insulting the experts, we'll try to take a simplistic look to appreciate why lifestyle habits matter and how they interact with our genome. We'll ignore elements that aren't critical to our purpose here and leverage some analogies to help explain the concepts.

Our genome is like a personal library of books that cover all the reference materials, manuals, and instructions for our lifespan. In our library, there are many, many books with instructions covering everything we might ever want or need to do. We can think of our chromosomes like 26 pairs of cookbooks. They are organized on shelves, which we call histones, as shown in Figure 12. The pages contain words and sentences of unique information and instructions.

We express genes by taking books off the shelf and opening to the chosen page. We can't remove the books, but we can copy the page and take the copy out of the library as messenger RNA proteins.

As the pages get worn with age, that's akin to telomeres on the tips of our chromosomes wearing down and exposing the DNA.

Figure 12: Genome Library

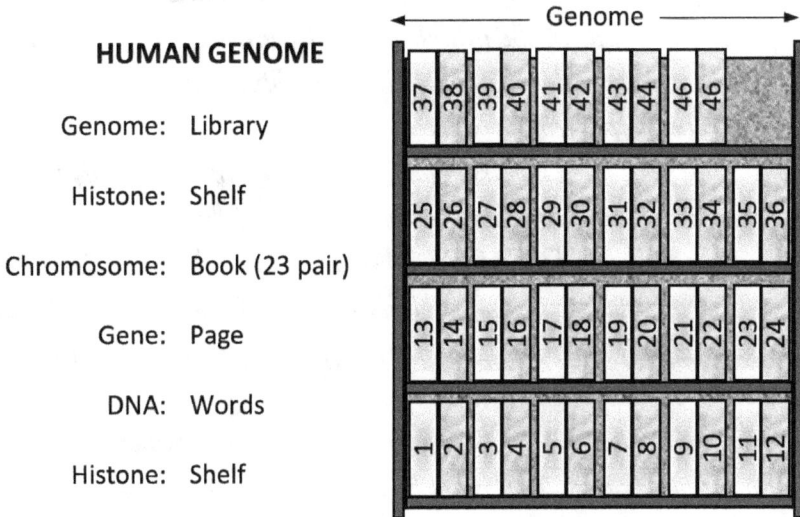

HUMAN GENOME	
Genome:	Library
Histone:	Shelf
Chromosome:	Book (23 pair)
Gene:	Page
DNA:	Words
Histone:	Shelf

To put some scale to our genomic library, we have over 20,000 unique genes, or sequences of DNA, within every 23 pairs of chromosomes. A chromosome is about 1 to >20 microns in length. If it were possible to lay all the chromosomes from a single human cell, they would measure about 6 feet (2 meters) in length. If it were possible to lay them all out in a string from our estimated 37 trillion cells, it would span over 40 billion miles.

Keeping this simplistic concept in mind, we can connect some dots regarding a few things occurring inside us over a lifetime. With over 300 billion cells replicating daily, errors are commonplace. Thankfully, the body produces molecules designed specifically to repair damaged DNA and RNA. If DNA can't be repaired, the cell is marked for disposal and put out as trash, a process known as cell apoptosis. It's a system that works masterfully in the background. With normal aging, the rate of repair declines due to a decline in the production of repair molecules. As repair capacity declines, the rate of exposed DNA rises, and we exhibit natural signs of advanced aging.

Jesse's Fleet

It was Jesse's job to maintain a fleet of 20 brand-new trucks his employer purchased. In the initial couple of years, the tasks were minimal—topping up fluids and occasional washing, followed by the start of tire and wiper replacements.

Five years later, repairs began to be needed, and it was easy to discern the crew's driving habits by the condition of their trucks. Arnold's truck appeared half the age of Darcy's. Their attitudes and habits were reflective of the condition of their trucks. As the years accumulated, Jesse gradually slowed his pace. Keeping the trucks on the road became an ever-increasing challenge.

Now, a decade since Jesse started, keeping up has become nearly impossible, exacerbating issues further. The fleet has devolved into a patchwork of scratches, dents, and rust. Arnold's truck stands out now more than ever. The paint is a bit faded, but everything still functions well. In contrast, Darcy's truck is parked out back and serves as spare parts. How much better it would have been for the staff and the business if everyone tended to their trucks like Arnold.

One way to think about genes and aging is to envision our many miles of chromosomes as billions of balls of string. When we're young and still growing, the string is wound nice and tightly, and very little string is exposed. Only the outside layer is accessible. Over the years of normal wear, the string loosens, exposing more chromosome string in the layers below, much like in Figure 13. More exposed chromosomes also mean more exposed DNA to become vulnerable to damage. The more damage, the more the string loosens, and the process keeps accelerating faster with each passing year of life. The more we can preserve the balls of string along the way, the better health is preserved.

Figure 13: Exposed DNA in Chromosomes

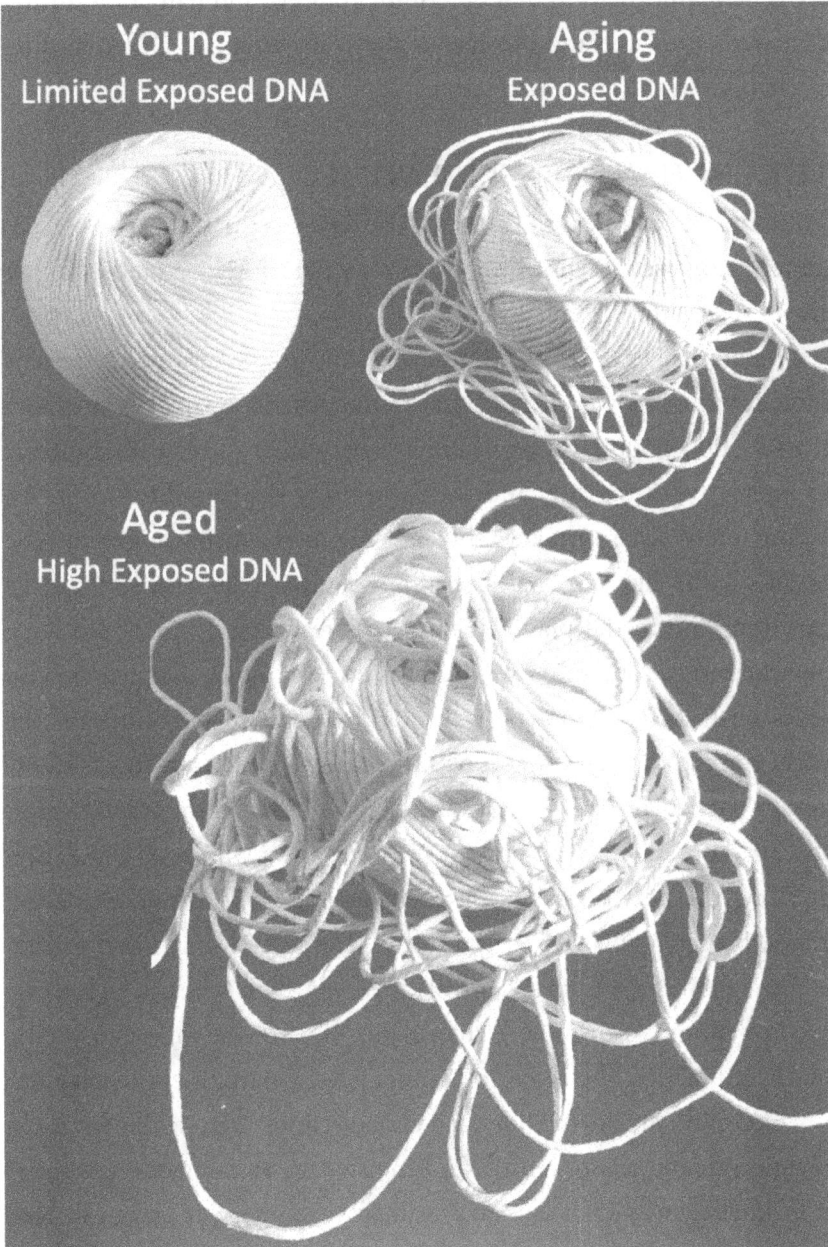

Chromosomes are coiled up like balls of string,
slowly loosening with age, exposing DNA to damage.

Hopefully, we're beginning to think of DNA as more than just the genetic information that determines our eye and hair color during development. Time and life events physically alter our DNA, leading to changes in the adult body, too.

THE ENCHANTING EPIGENOME

Thus far, we've been discussing our hardware—the things we can see under a microscope. However, that's only part of the secret to why we are all such amazing creatures.

Before us sits a beautiful grand piano, its 88 keys perfectly tensioned within its wooden skeletal frame. On its own, it is no more than a 1,000-pound, dust-gathering paperweight. It requires someone to interact with the keys and pedals to bring the sound out of it. An infant might fist some keys, but as cute as the child might be, the sounds aren't likely to be appealing. Alternatively, a skilled pianist can bring life to the piano in ways that reach inside us and change our chemistry, something we know as our emotions. The pianist also relies on music that not only details the notes to play but also the pace, emphasis, pitch, duration, and volume. With each touch of the keys, a particular note or chord can be heard. When the pianist stops, the last note fades away, and once more, the piano rests in silence, awaiting the next opportunity to enchant those in the room. Good genes, being the piano and the music, are helpful, but the musician is ultimately the one that controls the song that is heard. Think of the epigenome as all those factors that influence the musician — the hours of practice, the intention, and a good environment to play in.

Consider the smartphone—a modern tool that, while far more practical than a piano, remains reliant on human interaction to function intelligently. Like our own cellular machinery, it lacks inherent intelligence and can even make mistakes without proper guidance. Just as smartphones require software or apps to bridge the gap between hardware and user, our cellular processes rely on the epigenome to interpret and execute genetic instructions effectively. In essence, the epigenome serves as the crucial interface between our genetic hardware and the intricate workings of our cells.

Genes can't do everything on their own. It is the epigenome that interacts with our genes to switch on (express) or off (methylate). It does this through chemical reactions that influence the reactivity of the DNA. Methylation can be thought of as throwing a chemical blanket over the DNA, blocking access to trigger signals. Gene expression removes the cover and allows groups of genes to work together, like the multiple notes that make up a musical chord. The epigenome is a dynamic, living ecosystem that is the interface between the world we interact with every day and our genome. From the air we breathe in during our morning walk, to the music playing, to the idiot who just cut in front of us while we were driving home, the experiences of daily life are received and processed by our epigenome. It is the software for our genome, constantly making decisions on what chemical molecules and proteins to make and how to fold them to ensure accurate reception and interpretation at their destination.

One powerful example of our epigenome at work is our endocrine system, which is comprised of many hormones. Happy hormones like serotonin, dopamine, endorphins, oxytocin, and sex hormones like estrogen and progesterone, and stress hormones like epinephrine (adrenaline), cortisol, norepinephrine, and about 50 other messenger hormones are all produced in response to signals from our epigenome.

Think of the epigenome as the interface between our physical body and the world in which we interact. When we are exposed to a change in temperature, it is our epigenome software that automatically adjusts to help keep us from overheating or getting chilled. Our epigenome is tied to all five of our senses (sight, smell, touch, taste, and sound), helping interpret the information coming into us and signaling appropriate responses to the body. In human health, we throw the term "lifestyle" around a lot. A large part of what that means is managing our epigenomic experiences from day to day. Good or bad, it is our epigenome that is on the front line managing information in the body.

BIG DOG BACTERIA

Human genes aren't the only genes inhabiting our bodies. Far from it. Our gut microbiome boasts an estimated 2 million genes belonging to all those bacteria and other microorganisms. That's roughly 100 times more than in our human cells, and the gut microbiome *also* possesses an epigenome. As if that wasn't mind-blowing enough, our microbial and human epigenomes are in constant signaling communication with each other. The important point here is that we, as human hosts, create an environment that brings out the best or worst in these microbial passengers.

The gut constitutes approximately 75% of our total microbial cell population, but distinct microbiomes are also found in the mouth, nose, eyes, urinary tract, lungs, vagina, and skin, and each has its own epigenome. The gut microbiota is comprised of around 500 to 1,000 different species of bacteria, in addition to viruses, fungi, and other organisms. It is this vast and balanced diversity that ensures healthy gut function and the extraction of diverse nutrients required for cognition and longevity.

Many of the foods we eat contain prebiotics (non-digestible fibers, starches, and polyphenols) that promote the growth and activity of beneficial microorganisms, and contribute to a healthy gut microbial balance. A healthy balance, in turn, creates a positive environment for the growth and maintenance of beneficial bacteria. A healthy gut microbiome relies on a balanced diet. A wide variety of foods and plenty of fiber are essentials because human health is so heavily reliant on gut health. Fortunately, the activities that support healthy epigenomes, human or microbial, are well understood and supported by broad scientific consensus.

GENETIC AGING

Longevity researchers aiming to extend life beyond two centuries face the serious challenge of preserving DNA integrity. While we understand some of the chemistry involved in DNA repair, the prospect of discovering ways to supplement that chemistry or trick the body into extending it longer remains a distant possibility. For context, scientists have yet to reach a consensus on the number of hormones we have, let alone their individual and collaborative functions. Genetics is only one of several operating systems collaborating to support health and, therefore, longevity.

Experiments that attempt to tease out multiple variables are inherently complex to design and measure, and even more challenging to distill and draw verifiable conclusions. Randomized Controlled Trials (RCTs) work well in laboratory studies but are generally prohibitive for studying population healthspan and longevity. They easily lead to significant errors and incur substantial costs. That's why they are so rarely performed. Mendelian randomization studies often prove to be a more appropriate method for assessing genetic variants, as they are not confounded by dietary, lifestyle, or socioeconomic factors. Undoubtedly, Artificial Intelligence will be a powerful and necessary tool moving forward, but AI still requires much learning (quantities of reliable input data) before we can fully leverage its capabilities in this arena.

At this juncture, we can delineate optimal age ranges for fertility, physical performance, cognitive processing, and decision-making. However, determining our genetic peak is not a simple question and must be framed within the context of the aging process. Both our human and microbiome genomes and epigenomes undergo constant changes over a lifetime and never act in isolation. They operate within hypercomplex interdependent biological systems. We can simplify genomics down to an information system that we know deteriorates with age. Is it the genome itself that is deteriorating, or are changes in other molecules and chemicals contributing, such as nitric oxide, collagen, coenzyme Q10, hyaluronic acid, NAD+, neurotransmitters, mitochondria, and others known to decline naturally? Numerous proteins, enzymes, and molecules collaborate to detect and correct DNA damage, but their decline also reduces the rate and capacity of DNA repair. It quickly becomes a game of chicken and egg, and ultimately, all systems enter a state of decline.

To simplify, our rate of aging is intimately tied to our rate of DNA damage versus our DNA repair capacity—recalling Jesse's earlier story. In youth, our ability to repair is high, but this balance gradually gets challenged over decades, eventually tipping towards higher rates of damage than repair. The Lifetime DNA Damage vs Repair in Figure 14 illustrates this, showing that as the DNA damage rate rises over the years and repair capability declines, the two lines cross over each other. At this point, the rate of aging accelerates and markedly increases disease vulnerabilities.

Figure 14: Lifetime DNA Damage vs Repair

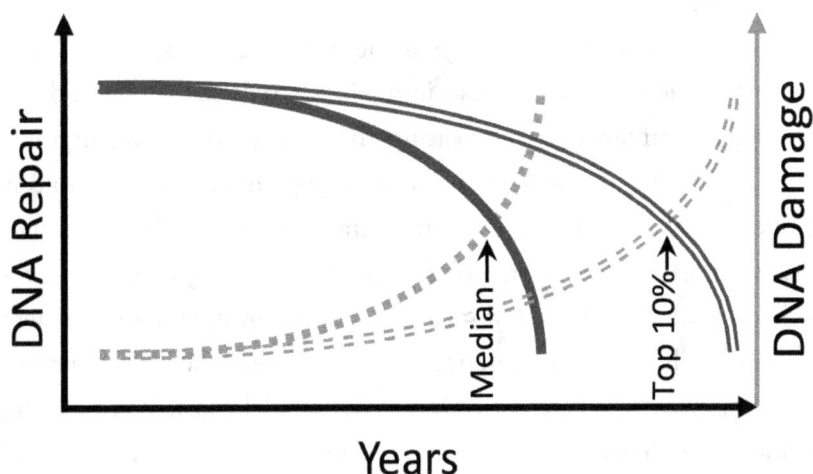

Over time, DNA repair rate declines and DNA damage rises. Reaching top 10% life expectancy involves preserving DNA repair chemistries and minimizing negative lifestyle habits.

By pushing the crossover point out several years, we can transition from median health and life expectancy to the top 10%. The damage and repair phenomena are interlinked—what's beneficial for one also benefits the other. This means that each positive daily lifestyle decision yields a double payoff. It not only reduces the daily insult to our DNA but also optimizes the levels of molecules and chemicals listed earlier that are crucial for repair. The compounding benefits explain why investing more years in proactive health habits yields high returns. Rather than attempting to outrun time, we are leveraging time.

The genetic backdrop to all of this is intriguing, but there's no need to let technical aspects be intimidating or obstruct what's important. It's most productive to think in terms of adopting lifestyle habits that help preserve our current state and potentially regain levels reminiscent of earlier years. These are dynamic chemical systems within the body that respond quickly to positive habitual stimuli.

Even for the average person, modest lifestyle investments can yield significant returns.

For those who haven't always made healthy choices, there's good news. Lifestyle interventions can immediately reduce the rate of damage while simultaneously increasing the production of repair molecules, initiating the reversal of tissue aging. A notable example is smokers who quit before age 50 and miraculously live into their nineties. With sufficient time, the body regenerates damaged cells with refreshed DNA. We observe similar phenomena in older adults, where diseases are halted and sometimes even reversed. Genetic improvements are possible at any age. Drawing a parallel to the ball of string analogy, it's akin to carefully replacing damaged sections of string and winding them back onto the ball, restoring the ball of string to a state closer to what it was a decade or two earlier.

BIOLOGICAL AGING

Realizing that genetics are intimately connected with aging, significant research has gone into understanding those relationships. This area of genetics research is generally referred to as biological aging, which has led to scientists creating mathematical models based on genetic expression. These models are referred to as biological clocks and are designed to compare a genetic profile versus an individual's chronological age. They are quite useful in evaluating individual health baseline versus population data. They are also helpful for comparing an individual's biological health improvements over time. Most who utilize these clocks proactively tend to have strong health habits, and their biological clock scores tend to reflect that.

One of the early biological clocks was developed around measuring telomere length at the tips of our chromosomes. Telomeres can be measured, categorized, and compared with large sample data to provide an estimate of one's current biological age. Blood samples are used for this test and are available from several small biotech companies.

Phenotyping using DNA methylation, an update on the Horvath Clock, is a more advanced method that looks at pro-inflammatory and interferon pathways, decreased activation of transcriptional and translational machinery (the process by which genetic information encoded in DNA is converted into functional proteins within a cell), DNA damage response, and mitochondrial signatures. As complicated as that sounds, getting a test result is easy if we have blood lab results handy. Standard blood panel lab test data typically measures Albumin, Creatinine, Glucose, C-reactive protein, Lymphocyte, Mean Cell Volume, Red Cell Distribution Width, Alkaline Phosphatase, and White Blood Cell Count. These are the individual measures that are used in the calculation. Check out a free phenotypic, biological age clock: longevityadvantage.com.

ONE BREATH

Some scientists are exploring the possibilities of modifying human genes to address genetic-based diseases and conducting blue-skies research to extend human lifespan. However, in doing so, numerous technical, ethical, and moral issues need to be addressed. My interest lies in leveraging the innate genetic capabilities already within us, eager to elicit the best of the genome we've been given, making our life's journey healthier and longer than we might have assumed possible.

A recurring theme in discussion groups is the human body's remarkable ability to adapt. Our genes are fixed at conception and persist despite countless cell replications, enduring until the end. The opportunity lies in the software we choose: clean, healthy food, movement, and human connection. The epigenome is our lever. It is a critically important, dynamic layer influenced by our environment and intentional actions.

Changing our epigenome is very much in our control, and it can happen quickly. However, we mustn't kid ourselves that we have somehow evolved to need less movement than we did 200 years ago, or evolved to metabolize all the synthetic toxins of the modern age. Much has changed in our lifetime and even more in the 250 years since the Industrial Revolution, but these are all environmental changes, not genetic. To put genetic evolution into context, the 250 years since the Industrial Revolution equate to about one breadth in a 100-year lifespan. Humans have proven a tremendous capability to influence their living and food environments, but we are still the same genetic species we were thousands of years ago. This is a valuable reminder to think about how to align our Mind, Environment, Diet, Activity, and Community to support our personal healthspan and longevity.

Chapter 8

ELEPHANT IN THE ARTERY

OF ALL THE AREAS of health and chronic disease that give me hope, it's our arteries, because gains can be realized so easily and reliably, and the leveraging is unparalleled. Arteries aren't as sexy as genetics, as mysterious as the brain, or as controversial as diets, so they remain in the shadows. And despite decades of effort and billions in research, medicine has been brought to its knees, unable to keep up with eroding Western lifestyles. It's been steadily losing the tug-o-war with lifestyle, and without a silver bullet, it seems lost and relegated to focusing on better band-aids.

This discussion will focus on the heart and brain because they're more easily recognized, but know that it's really all about the feed system: our arteries. Quality blood flow underpins functional and cognitive health, which are critical components to the healthspan and longevity of every organ in our bodies.

THE ELEPHANT

One of the most effective ways of confusing the public is to confuse the facts. Several decades ago, the CDC began reporting Cause of Death (COD) annually as a means of summarizing millions of death certificates into a condensed format that told a succinct story of mortality trending as an indicator of U.S. population health outcomes. The format (Figure 15) has remained consistent over the decades, but for a few minor changes. Half of all deaths occur above the Life Expectancy in the given year, which means that today, about half of all deaths occur over the age of about 78.8 (2019, pre-pandemic), depending on the year. Prior to that age, causes of death tend toward non-age-related accidents and diseases. If we're looking at longevity as an indicator of public health, we focus on chronic diseases for the population above age 75.

The confusion stems from the disease groupings. For decades, the trends have remained consistent, with heart disease and cancer towering over all other CODs. The question arises: do these groupings make sense? Heart disease is an organ, but cancer is a bucket list of several organs and differing mechanisms and cell types with each cancer. Lower respiratory is asthma and COPD, so that's lungs, but it doesn't include lung cancer. Stroke is the brain, but so is Alzheimer's. Influenza and pneumonia are typically viral. One doesn't have to look at it very long to realize that it's a patchwork of data that easily leads the public, investors, and medical professionals to misguided conclusions.

Figure 15: Leading Cause of Deaths in U.S., CDC, 2018/19

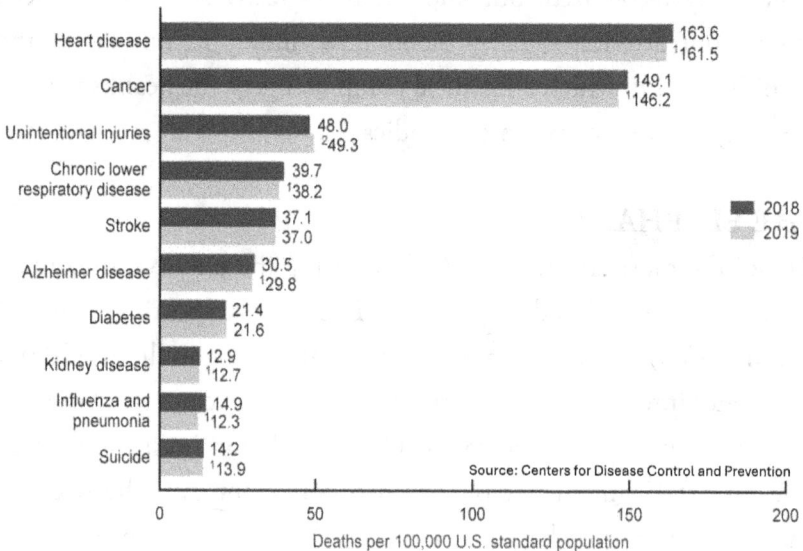

Ischemic heart and stroke deaths tower over all other causes of death, far more than suggested by how the CDC reports leading cause of death.

110

ROOT CAUSE

A more logical and consistent approach to understanding what the data is trying to tell us would be to look at the root cause. A standout example of this would be ischemia. Nowhere does it appear on the CDC's COD list, yet it is unquestionably the #1 COD disease state in the U.S. and globally. The absence from the listing is astounding, but kudos to the World Health Organization (WHO) for getting on board. It recently aligned its reporting to more accurately reflect the data, and unsurprisingly, it shows ischemic heart disease as the #1 global COD (Figure 16). It shows stroke as #2, which is interesting because 87% of all strokes are ischemic as well.

Figure 16: Leading Cause of Deaths Globally, WHO, 2019

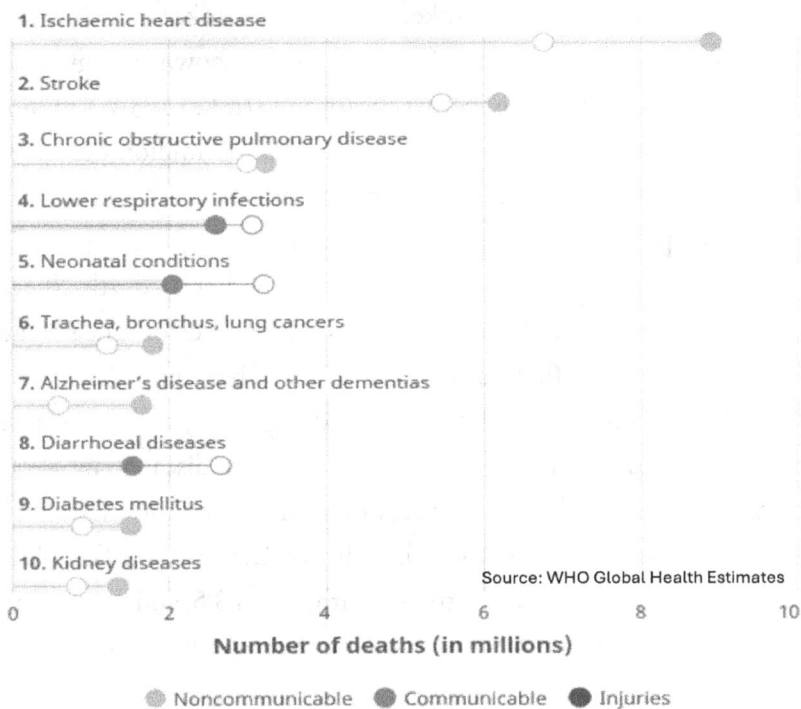

1. Ischaemic heart disease

2. Stroke

3. Chronic obstructive pulmonary disease

4. Lower respiratory infections

5. Neonatal conditions

6. Trachea, bronchus, lung cancers

7. Alzheimer's disease and other dementias

8. Diarrhoeal diseases

9. Diabetes mellitus

10. Kidney diseases

Source: WHO Global Health Estimates

| 0 | 2 | 4 | 6 | 8 | 10 |

Number of deaths (in millions)

● Noncommunicable ● Communicable ● Injuries

The World Health Organization provides a clearer illustration of the leading causes of death than CDC reporting.

What is ischemia? It is a restriction of an artery that limits blood flow, commonly the result of atherosclerosis (plaque and calcium buildup in arteries). It develops at multiple locations in the vascular system over many years. Atherosclerosis doesn't care if the artery is supplying the heart, brain, intestines, kidneys, liver, or peripheral limbs. The same blood circulates continuously throughout the body, recirculating through all our major organs every minute of every day.

Okay, so ischemia is obviously important, but what does that mean in the big picture? I mentioned above that the WHO reports ischemic heart ranking #1, at 9 million deaths. Those used to seeing the CDC reports would expect cancer to be #2, but only one cancer makes the WHO's top 10, and that is lung cancer, coming in at #6. Stroke ranks as the #2 COD, with 87% of those ischemic, as mentioned earlier. Prorate total strokes to ischemic strokes, and it comes in at 5.4 million deaths, still #2 leading COD, shown in Figure 17. That places death due to ischemia (heart and stroke) at 14.3 million globally. The next is COPD, coming in at about 3 million deaths. In other words, ischemia is 4.8 times higher than the next COD.... and most of the public has never even heard of it.

Let's take a closer look at the U.S. data. Ischemia deaths (heart + stroke) for the 75 to 84-year-old group accounted for a death rate of nearly 1,000 per 100,000 people in 2019. That jumped to nearly 4,000 deaths/100,000 for the 85 and older group. Just as shown in the WHO report, ischemia towers over all other diseases, by about 4:1 or more. It overshadows cancers on average by more than 20:1, with lung cancer being the top cancer in the U.S. as well. For added context, ischemic heart and stroke deaths are 28.5 and 38.6 times more prevalent than breast and prostate cancer deaths, respectively.

Figure 17: Leading Cause of Deaths in U.S., Root Cause, 2019

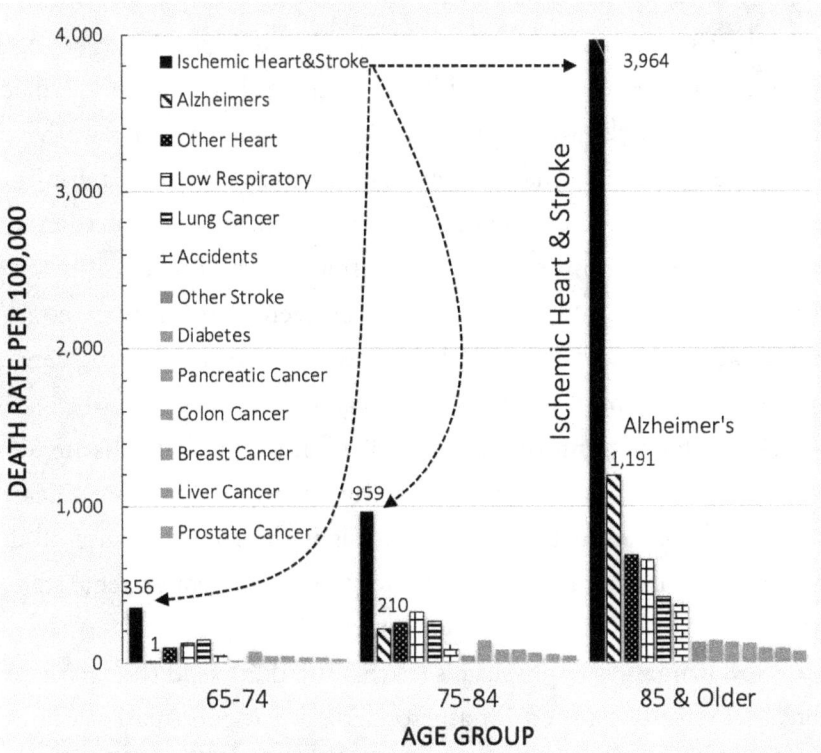

Ischemic heart and stroke consistently accounts for almost 4 times the death rate over the next leading cause for Americans age 65 and above

I sat down for an interview with respected cardiologist, Joel Kahn MD, in early 2020, just days after the publication of The Ischemia Trial that followed 5,000 patients for five years. As a couple of study nerds, we were both intrigued by the findings, most notably that invasive heart procedures proved far less effective than lifestyle upgrades at preventing heart events and deaths. The study findings were consistent with several other recent studies.

Atherosclerosis is the cause of plaque and calcium buildup. Ischemia is the term to describe the resulting physical restriction in blood flow. For our purposes, we can consider atherosclerosis and ischemia to be synonymous.

Atherosclerosis gained prominence more than 50 years ago, due to its prevalence in autopsy studies of both cardiac and non-cardiac deaths. Fortunately, we don't need to die to find out that we have atherosclerosis. A Coronary Artery Calcium (CAC) scan is a non-invasive, inexpensive screening that can be done at any age to determine how much of a deposit there is in our arteries. Atherosclerosis is now being observed in patients as early as their teens, and there are established variables associated with the disease that can affect its incidence and progression, both positively and negatively.

Death statistics inform us that 20% of heart attack deaths are under the age of 65, and the average age for a man to experience a heart attack is 64.5. Given that atherosclerosis is the #1 root cause of all premature deaths and takes decades to progress to that extreme state, why aren't we checking for it a lot earlier?

Most primary care physicians (PCPs) still don't send their patients for CAC screening to test for atherosclerosis, and most patients don't know to request this quick and highly reliable test. The PCPs that do refer their patients, typically wait until the patient is at least age 50. By then, the disease will likely have been decades in development. Another unfortunate outcome of deferring testing is that lifestyle habits become even more entrenched.

Early screening confirms a patient is at low or high risk. For those at risk, it provides them another decade to improve lifestyle habits and slow, or potentially halt disease progression.

Data is powerful. We may not always like the news, but ignorance around such a prevalent and patient-controllable condition denies them the opportunity for an extended healthspan.

DEMENTIA

Earlier, I mentioned the relationship between heart health and brain health, and it's worth revisiting. As with all diseases, there is a tendency to focus on the differences more than what they have in common. Heart disease, stroke, and dementia share a root cause - they are driven by diminished blood supply from our arteries (ischemia). The specific disease location is likely to be associated with a stenosis (artery restriction) that feeds that area, which inevitably drives dysfunction. A car with a dirty fuel filter can't deliver power if it is starved for fuel, and eventually won't even be able to idle smoothly when the flow becomes critically restricted.

Nothing, of course, is more intimate with the brain than the blood supply, so it is no surprise that it stands out as #1. The importance of CAC testing, mentioned earlier, also applies to reducing dementia risk. If there is ischemia in the heart arteries, there is likely ischemia developing in the brain.

Tick, Tick, Tick

The kids were doing well in college, Logan's career had developed into leading projects and being valued for ideas, and the family's financial future was secure. Walking out to the car after a morning workout, Logan was excited about the day but feeling weakened. Physical activities seemed to require more effort lately, and feelings of mild lightheadedness were disorienting. Jamie called over from the next car, "Everything okay?" Jamie was a cardiologist who worked at the same hospital as Logan. "Indigestion, that's all."

An hour later, Logan was at Jamie's office door. "I'm feeling a bit off. Mind taking a look?" By the end of the week, Jamie had taken Logan through a suite of tests that led to a diagnosis: advanced coronary artery disease (CAD). There are perks of working in a hospital, but it doesn't come with health immunity.

The CAD diagnosis was a shock. Logan had always seemed to be in good health, never smoked, and was not the person anyone would point to as a likely heart disease candidate. Now, suddenly, every thought revolved around an impending heart attack. "Why me? What should I do? How will I know if it's a heart attack? I'm afraid to go back to the gym. I'm afraid to climb up the stairs. What about the kids?"

Tick, tick, tick. It felt like a grenade was about to go off at any moment. One wrong move and kaboom!

Ask any CAD patient, and they'll share the feeling of an impending explosion, a walking timebomb. No warning, and then sudden panic. The experience is unique to heart attacks and strokes. We can be feeling fine one moment and laid out on the ground just moments later, fighting for air. For many, there are no warning signs. Just an acute myocardial infarction (MI) and death.

Where do MIs occur? Seventy-three percent of out-of-hospital cardiac arrests happen at home and 16% in public settings. Automated external defibrillators (AEDs) are found in many public buildings but are a long way from being commonplace in homes. There are many affordable models readily available for consumer purchase online.

There is a clear relationship between MIs and lifestyle and age. This is most clearly evidenced by MIs under the age of 50, where at-risk habits are most pronounced. Factors like smoking and sedentary are well known, but it quickly gets confusing to know what other things matter most. The consensus among heart and stroke professionals is that about 80% of MIs and strokes are preventable. For now, the other 20% we can tag with remaining uncertainties that contribute to ischemia and genetic factors.

UNDER THE HOOD

Let's back up and look at basic heart function. It's one of the most fascinating organs in the body for a host of reasons, and its power is impressive. When we're at rest, it pumps about one gallon (3.8L) of blood every minute. Not bad for a little pump that fits in the palm of our hand (Figure 18). The heart of a fit athlete can put out ten times that flow rate, or the power to fill two five-gallon pails in just a minute. Try doing that with a garden hose!

Figure 18: Human Heart Model

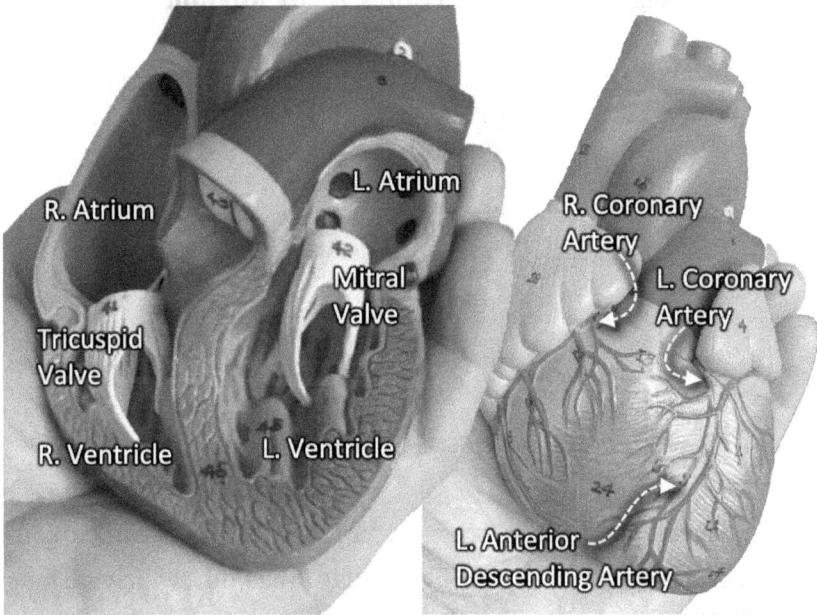

A model of the heart, illustrating the four chambers, two of the four valves (left), and the arteries feeding the muscles of the heart (right).

There are four chambers of the heart, two upper atria dedicated to delivering and receiving blood from the lungs, and two lower ventricles that deliver and receive blood from the rest of the body.

The chambers are formed by fibrous muscles that contract and relax through a beautifully timed sequence known as a Sinus Rhythm. This is what's shown by an electrocardiogram (ECG) via the sensors applied to the chest area. The sensors pick up the electrical activity generated by heart muscle depolarizations, which propagate as pulsating electrical waves, (Figure 19). The doctor or nurse listens to the timing of the four heart valves (mitral, tricuspid, aortic, and pulmonary valves) with a stethoscope to hear them crisply snap shut with every heart cycle. This ECG chart shows five beats of a healthy heart.

Figure 19: Normal Sinus Heart Rhythm

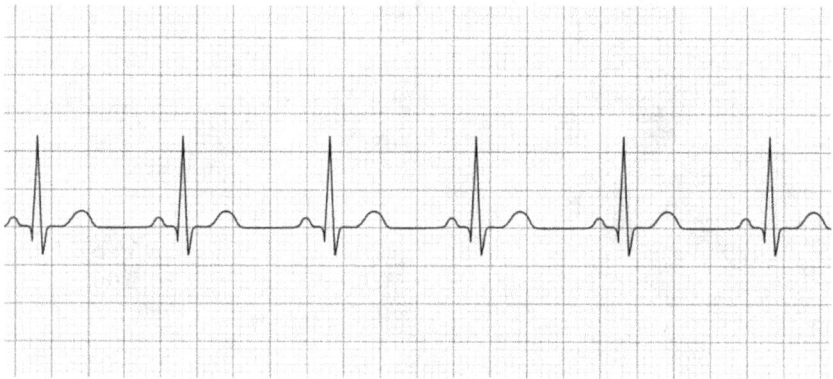

Electrocardiogram (ECG) signal of a normal heartbeat.

Cardiac muscle fiber is primarily comprised of myocardial contractile cells. Unlike the other muscle cells of the body, which are long and narrow, myocardial contractile cells are more uniform in shape, as their job is to contract in multiple directions, not unidirectional like skeletal muscle fibers. Their contraction is a twisting motion that quickly shrinks the volume of the chamber, "contractility," squeezing about 60% of the blood out of the left ventricle, and about 50% in the case of the right ventricle of a normal heart. This cycle repeats over three billion times by age ninety. No other muscles in our body come remotely close to matching that work output.

Heart muscles respond to exercise, in the same way skeletal muscles strengthen with increased physical loading. We may not be able to flex them in front of a mirror or at the beach, but they respond in a way that is far more beneficial to extended health. Strengthening the heart muscles improves the ability to squeeze blood out of the chamber the way we can squeeze juice out of a lemon. The difference is that it only takes a fraction of a second once it is triggered. Increasing the ejection fraction (the percentage of blood ejected vs starting volume) from 50% to 75% increases the available blood supply to the body by 50%. That means the body is supplied with 50% more oxygen and nutrients, thus able to deliver more power to move faster with more strength. The peak performance metric for this is cardiovascular fitness, or more commonly, VO_2max. This assessment utilizes a specialized test that is usually performed in an exercise physiology laboratory. The Cardiopulmonary Exercise Test (CPET) is performed on a treadmill or a stationary bicycle, with increasing power loading until the subject/patient is unable to continue. A CPET measures respiratory oxygen/carbon dioxide exchange and tracks heart activity with an ECG while a technician monitors blood pressure at regular intervals. Elite cyclists and cross-country skiers routinely top the charts with VO2max capacities of over 80 ml/kg/min for men and 60 ml/kg/min for women. By comparison, average fifty-year-old men and women have less than half that capacity. Cardiovascular fitness is trainable.

There are plenty of regularly active men and women over age sixty with VO_2max capacities higher than average twenty-year-olds. There is still plenty of untapped power available under the hood if we choose to invest in it. One of the benefits of a fit heart is that it doesn't have to work nearly as hard at rest, where we spend more than 95% of our time. VO_2max is also one of the strongest predictors of longevity.

A strong heart has numerous physiological benefits that pay dividends in later years, as well as social and emotional benefits that come with an active lifestyle. With all that power comes an impressive network of blood vessels that supply oxygen and nutrients to 60,000 miles of blood vessels and capillaries in the body every minute of every day.

The heart muscles rely on four main coronary arteries on the outside of the heart: the Left Main (LM), which feeds the Left Anterior Descending (LAD), the Left Circumflex Artery (LCA), and the Right Coronary Artery (RCA). These arteries feed several smaller branch arteries, which in turn feed thousands of small capillaries embedded in the heart muscles. These arteries all play a key role in preserving heart function.

At their largest diameter, before they start branching, they are only about a third the diameter of a drinking straw, and get progressively smaller with each branch, just like the branches of a tree. As small as they appear, they are amply designed for normal body function and losses associated with aging. It's not until they are about 60% blocked that they are of clinical significance. Cardiologists normally don't consider intervening until a blockage exceeds 70%. At these levels, it's not uncommon for patients to be asymptomatic. This excess design capacity is terrific, as it provides a significant safety margin for the wear and tear of aging over several decades; however, that also makes it hard to discern any noticeable deterioration until the disease has progressed to an advanced stage.

ISCHEMIA, THE ROTTEN APPLE

Imagine our blood vessels as a set of tires on a car but we don't have the option of replacing them every fifty thousand miles. We're allotted only one set of tires for its lifetime.

Just as our skin cells age, so do the endothelial cells that line the inside of our arteries. Endothelial cells are highly metabolically active and play a key role in several physiological functions. They are permeable by design, allowing chemicals produced by the body to be exchanged with muscles and organs, as well as chemicals produced within the artery walls themselves. The primary source of nitric oxide (NO) is within the artery walls. NO plays a central role in aiding in blood pressure regulation, through a process called vasodilation — the relaxation of arterial smooth muscles that enables them to stretch in diameter when the artery senses a rise in blood pressure. Under high physical effort, Olympic athletes have been measured to have systolic blood pressures of over 200 mm/Hg. These pressure levels are very high and short in duration, but they would be much higher were it not for NO and vasodilation. NO is important for all of us at every age. It's also one of several chemicals whose levels can be restored with exercise.

Over time, arterial endothelial cells slowly become more vulnerable. Damage is accelerated by causal things like diabetes, metabolic syndrome, hypertension, smoking, and physical inactivity. Some low-density lipoprotein (LDL) cholesterol particles enter into the endothelial cell lining, where the immune system recognizes them as a threat. It would be ideal if the immune system destroyed them and discharged them from the body, but unfortunately, that's not how it works. Instead, the body initiates an inflammatory response, not entirely dissimilar to a pimple or a sliver that might embed itself under the skin. The immune system releases a chemical called leukocyte, which acts to form a foam cell trapped beneath the endothelial lining, within the wall of the vessel, known as the intima. Just as one bad apple can destroy a bushel of apples, the dysfunctional endothelium becomes vulnerable to more LDL particles, eventually forming lesions in the vessel lining, allowing even more LDL particles to penetrate and become entrapped inside the wall of the artery.

Again, we see another time factor at play. Young LDL particles are soft and sticky, and if they remain in this soft, semi-solid state, eventually, they can swell and erupt through the vessel lining and be released back into the bloodstream. Flashback to the original Raiders of the Lost Ark movie, as the massive boulder is rolling down inside the cave, threatening to crush Indiana Jones, and imagine that is a clump of LDL fragments flowing inside an artery. The clump is carried down the artery until it hits a dividing branch too small to pass through, creating an immediate blockage, termed an occlusion. Blood suddenly stops flowing to the area, oxygen and nutrient supply to the affected area is quickly expended, and an acute medical event occurs. If it is within, or feeding the brain, an ischemic stroke occurs. If it is in one of the heart arteries, an acute MI event occurs. In both cases, minutes matter. Calling local emergency professional medical care is the priority, and efforts to restore blood flow by cardiopulmonary resuscitation (CPR) and/or Automated External Defibrillation (AED) are normally recommended. Permanent, irreversible damage begins occurring within minutes, followed by death, unless flow can be restored quickly. Minutes matter, which is why medical experts advise calling 911. Paramedics can initiate treatment faster than trying to transport a patient to the hospital and navigate hospital emergency admission protocol.

Most of our cell tissues are epithelial cells. Our skin cells, for example, are stratified squamous epithelial cells. It's easy to spot a pimple or a lesion in our skin cells, just as it's easy to observe changes in our skin as we age. Our arteries are built with simple squamous epithelial cells. The main difference is accessibility. We can look at our hands or in a mirror and observe that our skin cells are showing signs of stress. We don't have that opportunity with our arteries, even though they are aging as well. And, unfortunately, no amount of skin cream is going to help our arteries.

Some of us inherited arteries that age more quickly than others. There's no test to determine this. We'll only find out when issues start appearing, and that's a dangerous strategy because, often, the first indication is a heart attack or stroke. The odds of surviving either of those unscathed aren't good!

We can adjust our lifestyle habits to extend our health or slow the progression of arterial disease. It's not just the brain and heart that would benefit; all our arteries benefit, meaning that all our organs benefit, too. It is one of the most leveraged strategies we can apply. Lifestyle habits, such as managing stress, adopting a quality diet, and engaging in regular exercise, lower the immune system's inflammatory response and buy more time for the body to heal itself.

One of the body's defense mechanisms is to convert soft plaque into stable calcium. This can avoid the volcanic plaque eruption and blockage that leads to a catastrophic event. Instead, the process is slowed, delaying and potentially avoiding a medical event. The build-up of calcium in the artery wall certainly isn't ideal, but it poses a lower acute risk than plaque, which is inherently more unstable. Calcium is less mobile and consumes less volume than plaque, creating a scaffolding effect. The artery stiffens, losing some of its flexibility, but offers improved protection against acute MIs discussed earlier. Over time, however, as LDL particles continue to penetrate the endothelium, the vessel wall thickens, reducing the diameter (a smaller straw) of the vessel to restrict blood flow. This reduction in diameter is termed stenosis, which results in ischemia – reduced blood flow.

Calcium isn't a cure. It is the body's band-aid, and a lesser evil in the short term. It's just a way of buying time by finding places to carefully store the calcium versus a dump truck backing up to the door and unloading everything on the front stoop. Slowing down the process also presents more opportunities for early detection, treatment, and lifestyle interventions.

CHOLESTEROL

Cholesterol is one of the biggest victims of efforts to oversimplify health. One of the worst ideas, in my view, was to start labeling High-Density Lipoproteins (HDL) as "good" and Low-Density Proteins (LDL) as "bad." Both proteins are produced by the body, and both serve very important functions. The body is a hugely complex chemical plant with equally impressive self-regulatory capabilities. Everything it produces is for a specific purpose, all while balancing millions of chemical signals every second.

LDL occupies the spotlight, and so it should, so long as high uncertainty remains. All viewpoints agree that it plays a central role in atherosclerosis, but precisely how remains elusive and the source of polarizing debate. Population data unquestionably associates LDL with heart disease, but the confounding reality is that many people live very long, healthy lives with high cholesterol, and, more specifically, high non-HDL cholesterol. Non-HDL cholesterol includes all the atherogenic artery-clogging lipoprotein particles, including LDL, very-low-density lipoprotein, and intermediate-density lipoprotein. As individuals, getting consumed in the technical aspects of the scientific debate serves little value. In contrast, continuous lifestyle improvements and paying attention to the wear and tear of our arteries are well within our ability to manage.

DIGGING DEEPER

LDL is a general classification of many sizes and types of LDL particles, some much more atherogenic than others. Subclasses of particles like sdLDL, VLDL, and LP(a) tend to be the ones that bind and penetrate the artery lining. We don't learn anything about these from a routine cholesterol panel.

Determining LDL particle information requires an Advanced Lipids test. LabCorp uses a nuclear magnetic resonance (NMR) lipoprotein particle number test that directly quantifies the athero-genic particle values. Quest's Cardio IQ® uses ion mobility lipoprotein fractionation, a technology that uses gas-phase (laminar flow) electro-phoresis to separate unmodified lipoproteins on the basis of size. Both methods provide much more information that may avail the patient and physician better understanding. These are common tests, but not routine. Patients can request their doctor to order the test if there are cardiac concerns.

LDLs aren't single particles. They are composite clusters (Figure 20), serving as vehicles of other, much smaller particles, including ApoB. While the cause remains uncertain, scientists generally agree that cardiovascular risk is more closely associated with ApoB than the classic cholesterol metrics, which is why ApoB is another important number to know.

A popular clinical approach has been to recommend statin drug therapy to all patients with elevated LDL levels, based on popula-tion data that point to lower cardiovascular risk at lower LDL values. While there is abundant research data, patient outcomes remain less impressive for patients with no prior heart conditions. It assumes that lowering LDL slows atherogenesis by reducing the total LDL in the blood. It sounds reasonable and logical, but there are two issues with this oversimplistic approach.

The first is that it assumes that all LDL particle types are reduced equally. That is only determined by lipoprotein particle testing before and after, which many PCPs still do not order, for reasons I won't get into. Blindly assuming that all particle types are reduced equally or that atherogenic particles have been reduced without confirmatory testing is lazy medicine. The second issue is that it assumes individ-ual patient risk is dependent upon population risk. It would be nice and tidy if that were true, but there have been many studies that have sought to understand why it's not uncommon for centenarians to have high cholesterol. For reasons science still can't explain, some people live normal, long, healthy, long lives with high cholesterol. Understanding our individual (n=1) risk is paramount.

A useful analogy is the decision to swim in a lagoon. Let's say there are 200 fish, including two sharks. The rest are harmless and help balance the ecosystem. If the recommendation is to remove half of the fish, there's still a good chance of one, or even both sharks still being in the lagoon. The total fish count is much lower, but there is still significant risk. Statins struggle with the same issue. They lower cholesterol very well, but the risk doesn't change nearly as much as we'd like. Current statins only prevent about one in 39 heart attacks for patients with heart disease, and one in sixty without known heart disease.

Figure 20: LDL Cholesterol, Bad Actors

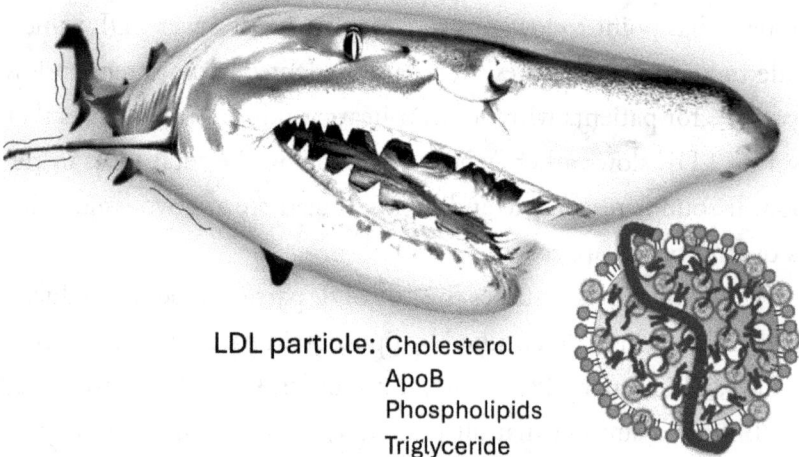

LDL particle: Cholesterol
ApoB
Phospholipids
Triglyceride

Low-density lipoprotein (LDL) causes serious heart and brain health issues when it forms on or in the walls of arteries. LDL is found in a range of sizes and densities, in various compositions of cholesterol, ApoB, Phospholipids, and triglycerides.

Let's use the fish and lagoon example to make another important point. We know there is a basis for concern, so we ask to have a particle size test done to better understand the fish population. The test reports that 50% of the fish are over 200 lbs/90 kg), 30% are medium-sized, and 20% are small. The doctor advises that the odds are that with that many big fish, some of them are bound to be bull sharks. That would surely get our attention. The particle test gives cause to do another test that can categorize the fish species and learn that 100% of the big fish are harmless dolphins. Better yet, sharks don't like hanging out with all those dolphins. Sweet! We're delighted by the news and grateful for the detailed testing. But the doctor isn't sharing our delight. "Turns out the small fish are piranha." In the world of cholesterol, that could be sdLDL, VLDL, and LP(a). Dr. Joel Kahn's book "Lipoprotein(a), The Heart's Quiet Killer: A Diet & Lifestyle Guide" is an excellent resource for anyone looking for ways to manage LP(a).

Many times, doctors and patients are too quick to decide there's a problem, when there isn't, and others are too quick to discount early signs of something brewing. The answer to both is the same: we need more data. Next-level testing puts anxieties to rest or brings focus and understanding of what we're dealing with while it's still early.

Finally, statins also bring side effects for many patients, so one must always consider the risk/benefit ratio in considering statin use, just like any medication. This is especially the case for medicines under consideration for lifetime use.

If this sounds like a recommendation against statins, it isn't. I take a statin every day. I have the particle data to demonstrate its effectiveness, no side effects, and reams of clinical data on its long-term use. But you're not me, and neither of us is the population. We are individuals with unique traits. We need simply to be reasonably well-informed before signing up for any medication and be able to answer four simple questions that any physician should be very pleased to answer:

- Do I really need it?
- What should I expect from taking it?
- How will I know how well it's working?
- What are the alternatives?

Several individual factors weigh into the risk reduction around statins. Risk assessment is a science unto itself and involves many factors, not the least of which are duration (denominator in years) and age. Most studies report modest hazard reduction. One of the benefits of statins is that they accelerate the stabilization of soft plaques that might otherwise rupture and lead to an MI or stroke. In doing so, statins will elevate a CAC score, but it is unstable plaque that is the acute threat that it helps to quench. The biggest levers to address long-term risk are not statins and not supplements; they are a lifestyle.

Our focus is best centered on the root cause, i.e., reducing plaque burden at the source with lifestyle modifications. Most cardiologists now recommend lifestyle modifications as the primary method. They still prescribe statins, but they recognize that the patient holds the trump cards. The bigger disparity appears to sit more with primary care physicians. They tend to be less informed about lifestyle best practices. I encourage my students to involve a cardiologist regarding any concerns relating to cholesterol, the heart, and dementia.

For many people, cardiovascular disease is going to be a long-drawn-out gunfight. Lifestyle modifications are table stakes and totally within our control. Beyond that, being well-informed about our personal data and working with a cardiologist to access all tools available is a good strategy. I'd want every weapon at my disposal.

One of the unexpected therapeutic discoveries to become evident over the last two decades has come from treatment for erectile dysfunction in men. Drugs like Viagra and Cialis increase nitric oxide produced in the artery walls to help dilate the vessel and enable increased blood flow. Preserving blood flow is core to preserving heart and brain function, and several studies subsequently identified a significantly lower incidence of mortality in patients taking these drugs. It proved too late for the manufacturers to cash in on the windfall, or perhaps it was a marketing decision from the outset. Either way, it's a win. Cialis (tadalafil) is preferred, due to its longer acting: 17.5 hrs half-life vs 4 hrs for Viagra (Sildenafil).

We'll look more into heart-related testing later in the book.

PREVENTING AND REVERSING HEART DISEASE

Why does heart disease remain the number one cause of early death? The honest answer is that the root cause(s) still eludes scientists. It points toward parallel interactions between physiology, biology, genetics, and lifestyle that are not yet clear. Hopefully, AI will finally bring us to a much better understanding.

A common biomarker is inflammation. We know that lifestyle risk factors drive high inflammation and compound as the issues pull in other vascular functions (functions reliant on blood circulation and regulation). Figure 21 illustrates study data looking at the relationship between lifestyle risk factors, inflammation, and affected vascular systems.

Figure 21: Lifestyle Impact on Inflammation and Vascular Systems

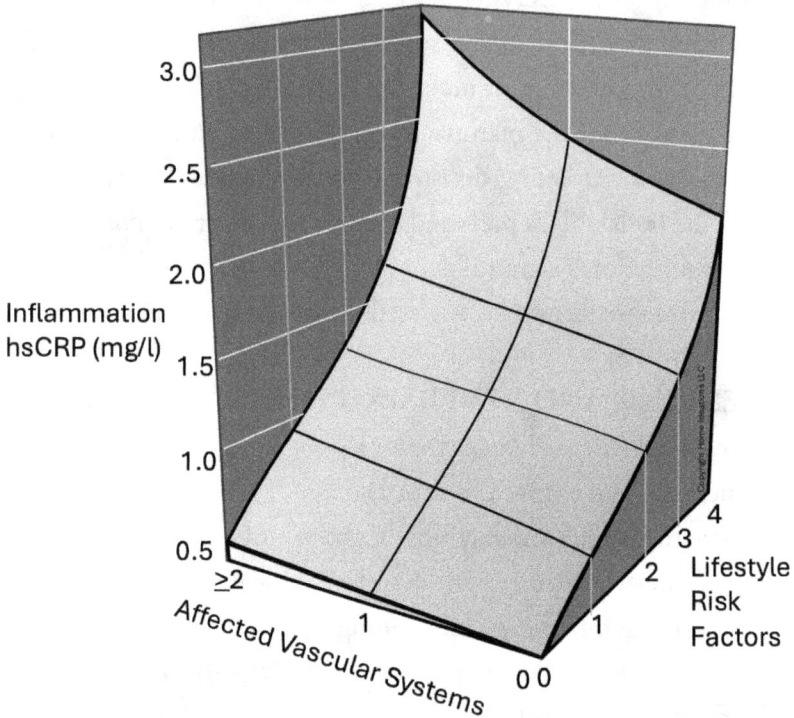

Data source: Bay B, et. all, Inflammatory burden, lifestyle and atherosclerotic cardiovascular disease: insights from a population-based cohort study. Sci Rep. 2023 Dec 8

Lifestyle influences C-Reactive Protein (CRP), associated with inflammation across multiple vascular systems.

A recent study looked back over fifteen years of coronary artery disease (CAD) studies and found that between 40-60% of people are susceptible to CAD due to genetic factors. Add in about four additional years of life expectancy for every generation leading up to 2010, along with a general decline in food quality and physical activity, and it's not hard to appreciate how just these four factors; genetics, rising life expectancy, falling food quality, and physical activity, compound to result in rates of heart disease we are currently experiencing.

The popular saying that genetics loads the gun, but lifestyle pulls the trigger is a way of saying that habits drive outcomes more than genetics. This concept is illustrated in Figure 22. The difference between average and healthy lifestyles has a major influence on our cardiovascular disease risk.

Figure 22: Lifestyle and Cardiovascular Disease Risk

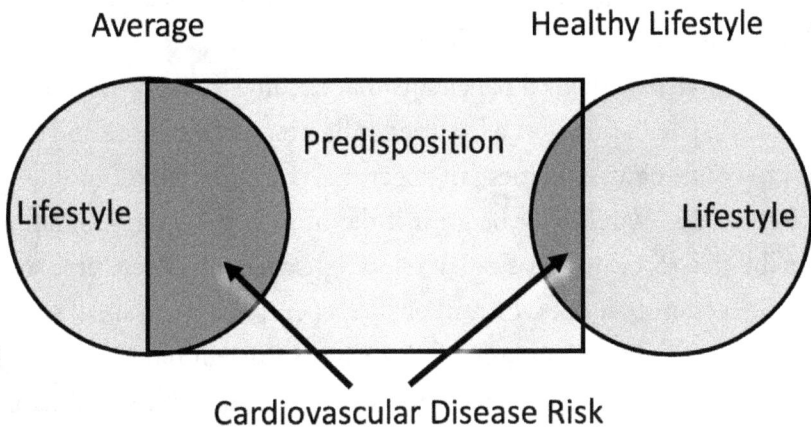

Healthy lifestyle habits reduce the chance of genetic predispositions advancing to disease.

SUPERHERO: COLLATERAL CIRCULATION

We imagine our circulatory system to be fixed, or fully established once we have reached our adult body size. Thankfully, that isn't the case. It's worth taking a moment to review some basics of the circulatory system.

Every living tissue of the body is comprised of cells that need blood to survive. Arteries deliver oxygen-rich blood to our cells, and veins return oxygen-depleted blood to the heart so that it may get pumped back to the lungs to become oxygen-rich once again. We need to focus only on the delivery side for this discussion. Our proximal arteries serve as superhighways, and main surface routes, transporting large quantities of blood from the heart out to all major zip codes of the body with each heartbeat. Distal arteries serve as branch roads between major routes and local regions. Capillaries serve neighborhood streets lined with homes, that we can think of as human cells. In blood terms, that last step is termed perfusion – the flooding of capillaries with oxygen-rich blood for the cells (houses) to soak in the oxygen and nutrients. When everything is working well, every tissue in our body is supplied with blood with every heartbeat. But often, things don't quite go to plan. What then?

We've all experienced paper cuts that become indistinguishable in just days. The cut triggers a localized inflammatory response and rapid growth of new capillaries (angiogenesis) to restore blood supply to affected cells. Wouldn't it be great if the heart had similar rebuilding capabilities to deal with slow-developing ischemia? Given time and the right stimuli, it does. Instead of a paper cut, imagine a small artery becoming constricted and unable to deliver sufficient blood to a small region of a heart muscle. Just as with the paper cut, the affected tissue senses a functional loss of blood flow and triggers capillary growth from adjacent tissue to try and meet oxygen and nutrient demands to the cells. As with a cut, capillary angiogenesis takes time and favorable conditions but can occur in as little as a few weeks.

Figure 23: Collateral Circulation via Capillary Angiogenesis

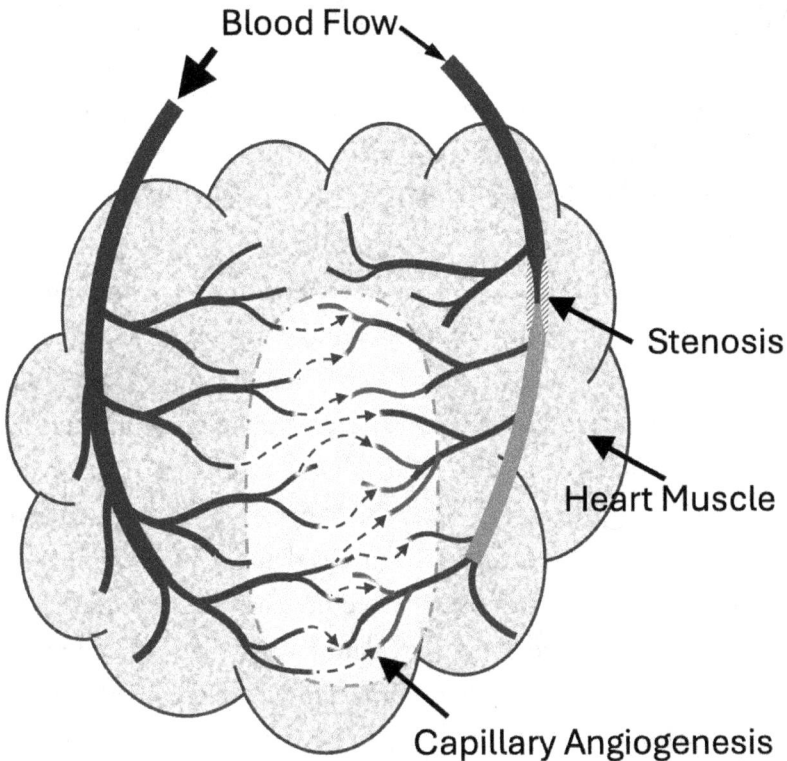

Heart muscle cells starved for blood (right) during exercise, stimulate capillary growth from healthy arteries (left) to resupply starved muscle cells. Frequent exercise over years helps build reserve protection for the heart.

EXERCISE STIMULUS

We can think of capillary angiogenesis as the body's innate bypass capabilities. Instead of grafting an artery from another body location to replace a stenosis restriction, the body grows a new pathway on its own, fed from a completely different source. The muscle doesn't care which artery delivers the blood; it just wants to be fed. There are limits to this, but it's one of the reasons exercise plays such an important role in longevity.

Activities that raise the heart rate strengthen the cardiovascular system, and exercise is the only known means of intentionally promoting collateral circulation. Frequency is the key, which is one reason why daily exercise is so much more effective than just a couple of times per week. Each muscle cell craving for more blood triggers a demand. This is the foundation of fitness and muscle development anywhere in the body, and it holds true for the heart. It is adaptation in action.

This also gets at the underlying benefits of intensity and high-intensity interval training (HIIT). Short-duration stresses are enough to trigger angiogenesis without placing the muscle tissues at prolonged risk. We'll talk more about effective exercise in an upcoming chapter.

Myth: Athletes don't have heart attacks. Unfortunately, exercise isn't a get-out-of-jail card. Athletes can suffer from all the same issues as less active individuals. The difference is that when they do have an ischemic MI, it tends to be less severe because they are more likely to have developed some reserve circulation, thanks to years of regular activity. It effectively buys them more time, and time is the biggest factor in MI outcomes.

"While exercise is one of the best things you can do for health and longevity, it does not make you immune to cardiovascular disease. Athletes with cardiovascular risk factors should be managed (with lifestyle/dietary modification coupled with medications when appropriate) using the same cutoffs/ recommendations as nonathletes. We have a lot of work to do with athlete education as I routinely see athletes with heart disease who believed that they could eat and drink whatever they wanted because they were lean and exercised daily."
Ankit Shah, Sports Cardiologist

BULLETS IN THE CHAMBER

There are still no silver bullets to address ischemic heart disease, but there are several supplements worth mentioning.

Some of these include:

- Vitamin K2, particularly MK-7, may have potential benefits. MK-7 (menaquinone-7) is often found in fermented foods and certain supplements. It is viewed as more efficacious when paired with vitamin D due to synergistic effects. Vitamin K2 is believed to aid in improved calcium balance.
- Vitamin D3
- Coenzyme Q10 (CoQ10) is a naturally occurring antioxidant in cells and plays a role in the production of energy (ATP) within the mitochondria. Statins can reduce CoQ10 levels, and supplementation can help to restore healthy levels.
- Fish oil is commonly used as a heart health supplement due to its high content of omega-3 fatty acids, specifically eicosa-tetraenoic acid (EPA) and docosahexaenoic acid (DHA).
- Berberine
- Curcumin
- Garlic
- Magnesium
- Zinc

Supplements are widely debated, and there are many more options than listed here, but the above list reflects popular options of those interested in filling the chamber. Dose matters, and each should be investigated and reviewed with a physician, as they may counter the effects of some heart medications, particularly anticoagulants. Diet influences choices as well. The healthy approach with any supplement is to get lab tests to confirm and address levels or deficiencies or on the advice of one's doctor. Blindly taking pills because of something posted on the internet is not a mindful strategy. There's no substitute for due diligence.

Chapter 9

DEATH BY DIET

JUST WHEN I THOUGHT there wasn't much more to learn about food, things got exciting. We've learned a lot about food science and new ways to prepare healthier dishes over the last decade. Real food is seeing a revival, at least for some. Habits are hard to change, and perhaps none more than those around food. In this chapter, we'll focus on unlearning several things we continue to hear about food that holds us back from allowing our food choices to promote our health. And we'll do it without spending any more money.

Mick and Marty walk into a diner for breakfast:

Server: Eggs, bacon, toast, and orange juice?

Mick: No thanks. Eggs cause heart attacks.

Server: How about just the egg whites fried with a little butter?

Mick: Fats are bad, so forget the butter and the bacon. Unless it's whole-grain, you might as well hold the toast. And that orange juice should come with a diabetes warning label on it! I think I'll just have a coffee, no cream, no sugar.

Marty, dazed and confused: I'll have a stack of pancakes with whipped cream and sausage; hold the fruit.

After decades of confusing and contradicting guidance, many people appear to have given up trying to do the *right* thing, whatever "*right*" is. Social media has amplified the food confusion even more and made what should be a comforting topic incredibly divisive. Raise the topic of food, and it's an invitation for dramatically different and passionate opinions from self-proclaimed experts who are remiss of any responsibility for public health. The distrust and anxiety around something as basic to health as food is profoundly disturbing. Too hot to handle, politicians kick the nutrition issues down the road for the next administration, and we continue to get sicker. Let's deconstruct some of the confusion, myths, and contradictions, and shed light on consensus and clarity around food and health science.

No one knows what makes a *perfect* diet. We'd need the capability to map an individual's complete phenome and epigenome, match it with a prescribed diet and lifestyle, support it with a closed-loop measurement capability, the knowledge to adjust it by age, and verify it across millions of individual lifespans. That puts it on a best-case timeline more than a century away, and it still wouldn't be perfect because foods themselves are constantly changing.

At the heart of it, people respond differently to certain foods, just as they respond differently to medications. Food is genuinely medicine, but more nuanced, and complex. An optimal diet for the vast majority is going to be well-supported by historical data and paired with knowing our individual health and biomarkers. That said, some may need a reset to help get them back on the road.

Diet is just one of five levers we know with certainty impacts health and longevity. While diet might very well be the number one opportunity for the general population, individually, we should be constantly working to bring the diet into balance with the other 4 MEDAC levers. In 2019, U.S. deaths of people aged 90 and older totaled 494,846. That's a lot of real-life data. Conservatively, 95% of them never attended a nutrition class or ascribed to any particular diet. Few, if any, reached the age of 90 and beyond on a regular diet of hot dogs, fries, sodas, and processed foods. They weren't fanatical about diets. They were just fortunate to grow up in an era where whole foods were the norm and processed foods were the exception.

Few of today's adults and children will have received that head start and are unaware of how far behind they are.

Some of us need a major intervention to address a metabolic disorder, but most of us simply need a series of small course corrections that will steadily and persistently trend us to a better place over several months and years. Drastic changes are sometimes medically necessary, but without the support of a coach, too often behave like boomerangs and come back to inflict more suffering later.

A hyperfocus on diet also tends to place relationships at risk, as it inevitably places unreasonable expectations on others. We've all found ourselves in situations where we felt uncomfortable around the foods being served or the insistence of others that their needs and values weren't being acknowledged. It takes time to build our Diet-IQ, and we need to be mindful that others are at a different place in their journey.

Life Lessons Tend to be Hard

The middle-school lunch recess bell rang, and I hopped on my bike on a mission to do what working people do: spend my first paycheck on lunch. Not quite knowing where working people go, I rode to the convenience store a mile from school, strode in the door, cash in my pocket, and surfed the aisles. A brick of sponge toffee and a two-liter bottle of root beer seemed like the ideal celebratory lunch. I fancied myself a bit of a root beer aficionado, and Hires was the best. Perched on a curb, I opened the root beer to that beautiful gas sizzle of sweet flavor that was soon to hit my lips, but not until a bite of sugary goodness. I'd arrived!

Sugar hangovers don't wait until morning to let us know we've made a bad choice. By halfway through the root beer, my gut threw in the towel. I'd downed it so fast that I'd skipped right on past the sugar high and hit the wall. Defeated, the unfinished soda and toffee got tossed in the trash can, and I sheepishly rode back to school. My dream lunch full of sugar taught me one of life's hard lessons– there really can be too much of a good thing.

That 12-year-old learned a hard lesson. We think we know what we want and what's going to make us happy, but often, it's that voice in our head that is only concerned with immediate gratification. I was lucky. It was such an acute response to an overdose that it was easy to make the connection. Low-dose dietary misuse is far stealthier and operates undetected below the radar, and it brings a host of confounding factors that can take time to sort out.

4-LETTER WORDS

By now, anyone interested in optimizing life outcomes has a good sense of what's wrong with the Western diet. We've effectively crowded out fiber and whole foods with too many processed and ultra-processed foods, wheat, refined and added sugars, calorie-dense foods, industrial red meat and poultry, seed oils, toxic residues from pesticides to preservatives, excess salt, and more.

Before diving into the diet minefield, let's get clear on three important 4-letter words:

- **DIET**, in the medical and nutrition context, is every food that passes over the lips on its way to the gut.
- **FOOD** is everything that contains calories and is a combination of carbohydrates, proteins, and fat. Carbohydrates convert to glucose, protein to amino acids, and fat to fatty acids. Some of these also release fat-soluble or water-soluble vitamins (organic) and minerals (inorganic.). Food does NOT include synthetic additives like emulsifiers, dyes, pesticides, and preservatives. These are passengers that come with industrialized foods, bringing unintended consequences.

- **WFPB** refers to whole and minimally processed plant-centric foods. It may include limited quantities of fish, animal, and dairy products.
- **KETO** is a dietary method intended to promote ketosis, the body's natural mechanism for burning fat. It has historical applications in medicine for the treatment of epilepsy and, more recently, for cognitive impairment diseases like Alzheimer's disease, autism, and brain cancers. It's earned the title of fad diet and popularized low-fiber versions carry serious long-term risks.

DROWNING IN FAT

As with so many foods, attempts to oversimplify "fat" lead to more confusion and debate. Oils are a fat macronutrient. The "oil" distinction comes from them being liquid at room temperature. Let's look at one of many confusing examples: olives. Olives are fruit. Olives are solid at room temperature. Squeeze the olive, and it releases olive oil, a liquid fat. The remaining flesh left behind is a carbohydrate. But wait, the flesh also contains protein, which means the innocent little olive is a fat, an oil, a carbohydrate, and a protein. Several foods contain all three, and many more contain a combination of at least two, which is why oversimplifying food can be problematic because combinations can dramatically change the way our body responds to them.

Let's try to sort out some of the confusion around oils. Oils are either natural, mineral, or synthetic. Edible oils are abundant in foods, commonly found in fruit, vegetables, seeds, nuts, and fish. Their fat classification is based on the number of double bonds in their carbon chain. The more double bonds it has, the more energy that is needed to break it down into molecules the body can digest, which is a good thing.

Fats exist naturally, and some are manufactured.

- **Polyunsaturated Fat:** (multiple double-bonds): Found in fatty fish, nuts, sunflower seeds, flax seeds, vegetable oils, soy products... PUFAs are foundational to a healthy diet.
- **Monounsaturated Fat:** (one double-bond) Found in olives, avocados, olive and avocado oils, nuts, canola oil, pumpkin seeds, sesame seeds, sunflower oil, peanut butter... The key distinction between mono and polyunsaturated fats is the omega-3 fats found in polyunsaturated fats. The body is unable to produce these omega-3 fatty acids, which is why polyunsaturated fats are important to a balanced diet.
- **Saturated Fat:** (no double-bonds): Common in meat, dairy, coconut, palm oil, avocado, cheese, dark chocolate, whole eggs, fatty fish, nuts, chia seeds, olives.... Saturated fats were misunderstood and demonized for several years. Extra-virgin olive oil (EVOO) and avocado oil are back on the healthy list.
- **Trans fats:** These are highly processed fats, engineered for stability and high-temperature frying. They are well-known to be bad news for health. Full stop!

Many foods carry multiple forms of fat, which can quickly get confusing and explains why their health benefits can sometimes be in question.

As a rule of thumb, the less a food is disturbed from its original state, the higher its quality and beneficial nutrients.

- Cold-pressed olive oil, for example, is a healthy food, partly because it requires far less pressure than squeezing the oil from, say, a nut, seed, or leafy vegetable
- Whole seeds are much healthier than seed oils for the same reason

It's easy to see how quickly foods get confusing. The closer we can stick to the whole food in its original state, the more we can rely on its health and nutritional benefits.

Not all foods are created equally. Climate, soil, and farming practices all influence the final food quality. Olives, for example, are not all the same quality. Astute olive growers in regions with the best soil and climate leverage their premium product and publish certified polyphenol (antioxidant) levels in their oils via the ARISTOIL Interreg MED Program. Fresh extra-virgin olive oil has the highest polyphenols. Cool storage and lower cooking temperature help to preserve polyphenol content. A public database on polyphenols for a vast array of foods can be found at Phenol-Explorer (http://phenol-explorer.eu/cite_us). As for polyphenol content, olive oil varies by season, just like wine. The European standard requires a polyphenol concentration of at least 25 mg/kg to be sold as high polyphenol content. Several EVOOs are available in the 400-500 mg/kg range, with some specialties over 1,000 mg/kg, sold for a considerable premium. Are they healthier? It is debated within the EVOO community, but for most of us, sourcing organic EVOO with 250-500 mg/kg polyphenols is a major step up from the typical grocer options.

The Mediterranean region is well known for its olive oil production and consumption, while Latin American cultures rely more on vegetable and avocado oils. Notably, 2020 life expectancies in olive oil-producing countries of Italy, Spain, and Greece (LE: 81.6 - 83.8) were all higher than those in Costa Rica, Chile, and Cuba (LE: 77.6 - 80.3), which consume mostly vegetable and avocado oils. Meanwhile, Japan and Hong Kong (LE: 84.4 - 85.0), world leaders in life expectancy, primarily consume palm, soybean, and canola oils. The oils in Japan and Hong Kong are not the same oils that appear on North American grocery stores' shelves, despite what the label may infer.

Our polarizing habit of demonizing and canonizing certain foods notoriously overlooks the food industry practices behind so many of our food issues. Soybean is a great example. About 94% of U.S. soybeans are GMOs (genetically modified for pesticide application), while GMOs are not allowed to be grown in Japan. Over 90% of U.S. canola is GMO, while Japan grows no GMO canola. We'll take a closer look at this when we get into the environmental aspects of managing health risk exposures.

The experts have flipped on palm oil, as they've come to better understand the role of saturated fats in the diet. Once demonized, palm oil is back in favor as a health food. The deforestation and habitat destruction for orangutans, elephants, and rhinos resulting from palm harvesting, however, are of serious concern. There are better choices for humans and the planet.

Oil choice is only one piece of the puzzle. The other key is how we use it. While many of the oils might appear quite similar in raw form, how they perform under heat varies significantly. Apart from changes in flavor, sufficient heat causes a loss of nutrients and the formation of harmful compounds that result in oxidative stress when consumed. Avocado and olive oil remain frequent oils of choice for cooking, but we should recognize that heating will degrade the quality of any oil. When cooking with EVOO, I try to limit the heat to 325-250 °F. An alternative cooking method such as air-frying is usually more constructive, reserving oils for room temperature use as much as possible.

DEAR DAIRY

Dear diary, why is dairy so difficult? Few things were more special as a child than piling seven of us into the Ford and driving to the dairy for ice cream. I was always on the front bench seat, tucked in between Mom and Dad, and the other four older siblings lined up across the back. There weren't seatbelts back then, so the limit was based on how many bums we could squeeze in.

The dairy was a real dairy, with Holstein cows in the farmyard and a processing plant out back. The storefront was where the action was. Sundaes were made with real ingredients and served in glass boats. We'd choose from ten flavors of ice cream while Milkshakes whirred on avocado-green Hamilton Beach blenders on the back wall.

The dairy process back then was hands-on. The milking was done with pumps but looked nothing like the big, automated operations that dominate the dairy industry today. The cows grazed happily in the fields. Today, most cows spend their time in a barn. It allows for more controlled feeding, less labor, and lower-cost consumer products, but unfortunately, it also means there is a greater disease risk and more antibiotics required. Today's feed is typically a total mixed ration (TMR) of forages, hays, grains, byproducts, and minerals & vitamins, not like the whole foods they once enjoyed. Unfortunately, many of the feed crops carry pesticide residues that are routinely found in dairy products. Organochlorine, organophosphate, synthetic pyrethroid, and/or triazine are typically found in today's milk, yogurts, cheese, butter, and sour cream.

Not so many years ago, scientists thought that getting rid of the fat in milk was better for weight management. In stripping out the fat, they also removed most of the healthy nutrients. Now that fats are better understood, whole milk is back, as the preferred choice over low-fat dairy.

Different dairy sources, like so many foods, tend to get too lumped together. What about goat and sheep milk? These don't just come from different animals; they are chemically different products. This is why some people who are allergic to cow's milk can consume goat or sheep milk. These alternate sources come from outside the major industrial processors and tend to be higher in nutrients, lower in casein, easier to digest, and less likely to have pesticide contaminants in their feed.

Yogurt consumption grew 7x per capita between 1975 and 2013. Americans got the news that the bacteria in yogurt was a good thing for our gut, but unfortunately, what they've been enjoying are yogurts laced with processed fruit and high-calorie syrups with added sugars. As with so many of our foods, we get told that something is healthy, and the food industry rushes in to make it into a dessert food, negating the potential health benefits. There are several varieties of plant-based yogurts available now, but again, the big food producers have loaded most of them with added sugar. Reading labels and looking for smaller brands is often where the gems are waiting. The sheep and goat milk yogurts may not be as prominently displayed, but they are worth investigating. Adding fresh or frozen organic fruit to plain yogurt bumps up the flavor and nutritional benefit, without the added sugar and other industrial processing chemistries.

PROTEIN PANDERING

"Most of us should be eating more protein." It's a statement common to hear from people focused on building muscle mass, but I was caught off guard to hear it coming from Casey, a college graduate student focused on health. "Why?" I asked. "Protein helps mitigate the blood glucose spike from consuming carbohydrates," was Casey's response. That's true, but eating a balanced meal that includes complex carbohydrates addresses a blood glucose spike. Extra protein doesn't improve health and is not the antidote for eating simple carbohydrates.

Dietary protein is a small player in the protein story. The body makes over 20,000 different types of protein, all on its own, from the nutrients in the foods we eat. Why so many variations? Proteins are our workforce, taking on many diverse roles. They act as hormones and enzymes, manage fluid and acidity, nutrient transport, make antibodies, rebuild tissue, and burn as fuel on rare occasions when carbohydrates and fat levels are depleted — a situation most often associated with endurance athletics and extreme diets. The body makes these multiple types of protein using a DNA recipe book filled with instructions for making all the proteins we need. The recipes are based on 20 amino acids, of which only nine are based on dietary protein.

Eleven of our required amino acids are derived from glucose in our bodies. The nine amino acids that we can only source from food are histidine, isoleucine, leucine, lysine, methionine, phenylalanine, threonine, valine, and tryptophan. As such, they are referred to as essential amino acids. The body doesn't care whether these come from plants or animals, just that they are part of our diet. The body doesn't take sides in the protein debate.

One of the most fascinating things about proteins is how they fold. Four-finger origami paper fortune tellers, popular with children, can help to explain how proteins fold. The 4-finger origami reveals a message unique to each finger. Similarly, the way a protein folds influences the message it conveys. Proteins often misfold, causing messaging errors and dysfunction, but thankfully, the body has mechanisms to identify, repair, or discard them. When protein misfolding becomes rampant, the body is unable to keep up, causing disease and aging to accelerate.

Proteins are important but not the star of the show. Animal-based proteins and plant-based proteins contain all nine essential amino acids (EAA.) The differences lay in the levels that they contain. Animal-based sources are relatively few, while plant-based are thousands, so it isn't surprising that there are a range of levels across plant sources.

Vitamin B12 is an important supplement that needs to be part of the protein conversation. It is key to physiological processes and aids the release of bound protein during digestion and transport into the bloodstream, improving protein uptake. Ultimately, it is important for the maintenance of the nervous system and the formation of red blood cells. While the belief was that B12 was important for plant-based eaters, it turns out that almost 20% of the population over age 60 is vitamin B12 deficient.

PROTEIN DOSE

Dose matters with food, just as it does with medicine. As appealing as a big steak or rack of ribs might be, the quantities consumed by most Americans today far exceed a healthy nutritional dose. According to the Dietary Guidelines for Americans 2020-2025, Americans consume more than triple the recommended amount of animal protein (meat, poultry, eggs). We've seen a steady rise in animal protein intake since 1960, mainly coming from a dramatic rise in poultry consumption.

Health experts agree that adults need 0.8 grams of protein per kilogram of body weight or about 0.36 grams for every pound of body weight. Beyond age 70, guidance now suggests that more protein is helpful to make up for lost uptake efficiency and the importance of maintaining muscle mass. Current thinking is that 1 gram protein/kg, or 0.45 gram/lb, is recommended.

Is more better? There's a common misconception that consuming extra protein helps build muscle. Activity promotes muscle; inactivity causes muscle to atrophy. Excess protein not consumed by the body doesn't conveniently convert to muscle; it converts to fat. The 2019 article Perspective: The Public Health Case for Modernizing the Definition of Protein Quality by David Katz et al. offers a healthy perspective on protein for populations living in economically advantaged countries. The National Chicken Council reports a tripling of poultry consumption between 1960 and 2020 (Figure 24), while red meat intake has been in decline.

Figure 24: U.S. Animal Consumption per Capita

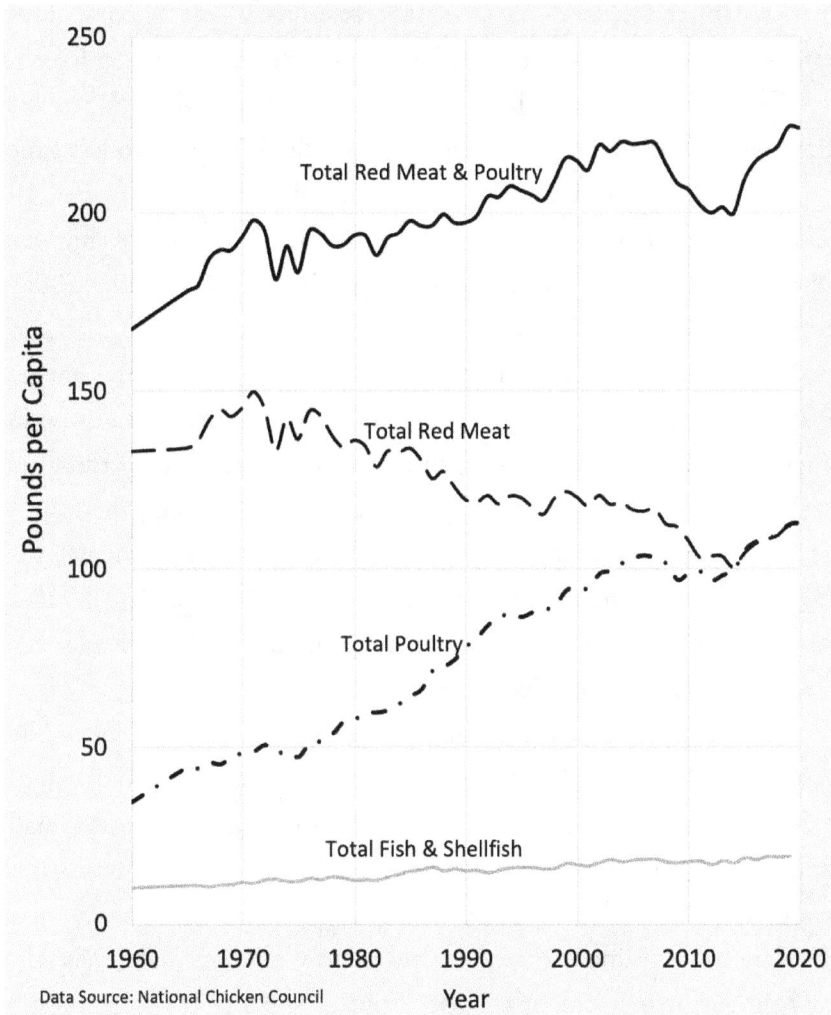

Total red meat and poultry consumption grew 36% between 1960 and 2020, most of it due to a dramatic increase in poultry intake.

When considering our protein source, it's important to consider what comes along for the ride. Mechanistically, animal proteins cause the gut to release various metabolites, including trimethylamine (TMA), into the blood. The liver then converts TMA into TMAO, the oxidized version of TMA, which regulates physiological processes involved in the development of atherosclerosis in the arteries. Both excess intake and low-quality (industrial) sources drive atherosclerosis.

Chickens now weigh in at nearly double the weight in 25% less time on 29% less feed per pound. Yes, double the weight in less time on less feed. The poultry industry has gone almost exclusively to concentrated animal farming operations (CAFOs), which place chickens in ultra-high-density spaces for the duration of their short, 47-day life. Industry lingo like free-range, cage-free, all-natural, farm-raised has become the rage, but in practice, it rarely aligns with the images it evokes in our minds. Antibiotic use and animal feeds continue to align with accelerating weight gain vs the nutrient value of the food or health of the animal. Again, the source of the protein, the source of the protein's food, and treatment with antibiotics all influence the quality of the protein we ultimately consume. Companies like Pasture Bird are changing the game, scaling pasture raising without the need for intense antibiotics or drugs.

Too little protein absorption can result in anemia, evidenced by common blood biomarkers. It tends to be more common among vegetarians, which is why vitamin B12 with folate is important. Small amounts of animal protein may be medically necessary in some cases to achieve healthy blood levels.

The bottom line is that dose and quality matter. Given that animal protein is the highest cost per calorie on many plates, spending smarter helps to keep food costs within budget.

PROCESS THIS

Processed foods have contributed to more deaths than all the lives lost to cigarettes and conflict in the last hundred years combined, yet they persist unchallenged.

My research into leading longevity countries suggests that the health risks associated with a processed food lifestyle have surpassed smoking as the number one risk in some countries. Japan, for example, enjoys about seven more years of life expectancy than the U.S., despite a 50% higher rate of smoking. Japan tends to eat far more fresh food than America. By comparison, U.S. consumers eat four times more beef, four times more chicken, 2.4 times more sweeteners, two times more potatoes, 60% less fish, 50% less soybeans, 70% less onions, 85% less cabbage, and 90% less spinach than Japan. These are not subtle differences in universally consumed foods. Japan also bans GMO pesticide-based crops, so they also consume fewer agricultural chemicals in their food. It's unclear which of these variables contributes most to Japan's seven extra years, but they all make sense based on data from other countries, (without the smoking).

Many studies like to compare the findings of popular leading diets, and not surprisingly, they don't always agree, zeroing in on minor differences. Sanity is finally emerging, acknowledging that even small amounts of processed, particularly ultra-processed foods, have a more deleterious impact than the subtle differences between leading diets. In other words, the foods we avoid matter more than splitting hairs between well-established, medically supported diets. It should be obvious to anyone curious about extending healthspan that foods like sweetened breakfast cereals, soda, potato chips, fried chicken, white bread, candy bars, coffee syrup drinks, energy drinks, bologna, sausages, hot dogs, etc., are health liabilities. These industrialized foods are no doubt playing a role in the rising death rates in the under-age 70 category, which we'll discuss a bit later.

Processed foods aren't new. It's just that the U.S. consumer appetite has exploded. Candy bars like Crispy Crunch, Oh Henry, Kit-Kat, and Reese's Peanut Butter Cups have been around since the early 1900s. Ultra-processed foods skyrocketed in the late 20th century as food scientists continued to formulate more foods that plug into our primal cravings.

The use of sodium as a preservative expired in the 1920s when the refrigerator was introduced to our homes, yet many processed foods are laced with absurdly high quantities of salt. It's there to make low-quality food palatable and contributes to the average American intake of almost 50% more than the recommended daily amount. Add in an abundance of low-quality fats, added sugar, and a long list of chemical processing aids and dyes, like titanium dioxide, that aren't required on labels, and we've paved the way to metabolic syndrome—dramatically increasing our risk of heart disease, stroke, type 2 diabetes, and liver disease, to name just a few.

Dr. Robert Lustig is one of the doctors leading the charge on the processed food that has hijacked child and adult eating habits. Our generation owns the ultra-processed industry, but our children and grandchildren will be the real victims of our food crimes.

FRINGE DIETING

Desperation is a huge motivator. Frustrated enough, we'll try almost anything.

Blinding Success

For three decades, Jack fought a losing battle with his weight. Diagnosed with prediabetes five years earlier, he was well on his way to Type II Diabetes Mellitus (T2DM) when he joined an online Keto diet group overflowing with compelling, heart-touching stories of how Keto changed their lives. Jack shed weight, and his T2DM improved. He was all in, soon professing to all that would listen, that Keto was the only way!

I asked Jack what he knew about the long-term risks of a Keto diet. His head cocked sideways, like I'd asked if he'd ever been to

Mars. In his mind, it was simple. His health had been reduced to 3 numbers: his weight, blood sugar, and A1C. Those were the only numbers he cared about because, in his mind, that had become the definition of health.

Jack's story has become more common in recent years. More and more, we've become slaves to our food, unable to see the bigger picture. Several physicians I know have experimented with a Keto diet, and every one of them has abandoned it. Any short-term health "profit" is accompanied by a long-term liability. It can feel empowering to think we're on the leading edge of changing world health, and like we're the one in the know. Keto proponents justify the rationale by pointing back to when food was scarce, and we'd sometimes fast for days, never knowing if this might be our last meal. Starvation is far from a first-world issue and hasn't been for thousands of years.

Some diabetics respond favorably to a keto diet, at least in the beginning, so it can be helpful in the same way as fasting. The basic principle is to limit the availability of carbohydrate fuel in the bloodstream, which triggers the body to enter a state of ketosis, whereby it switches to burning fat. Eliminating carbohydrates cuts off the supply of fast-digesting energy and helps reduce the insulin hormone spike, most associated with simple carbohydrates. Over time, it can retrain the pancreas' insulin production. Some people respond to Keto for weight loss, but ultimately, healthy outcomes demand a balanced diet. Short-term fasting, increasing fiber intake, and getting simple carbohydrates out of the diet work for most in the short term; it's a sustainable approach and will work for the long-term goal of healthspan.

There is solid data on Keto diets. Its history dates back over 100 years, to medically managing epilepsy patients. More recently, Dale Bredesen, MD, has demonstrated success with Alzheimer's patients' treatment. These are two acute examples where a keto intervention may make perfect sense. However, no population in human history has demonstrated health and longevity on a Keto diet, or anything remotely close to it… ever. There are safer and more appealing ways to leverage ketosis naturally, and reach a healthy old age.

FINAL THOUGHTS

It's easy to get caught up in the diet game, and even easier to give up trying. It's a minefield of potential hazards and rabbit holes that distract us from seeing the big picture. Common sense takes minimal effort and pays big returns over the long run.

It's easy to point a finger at processed foods and believe that we've addressed the core issues with food. There's still a lot of opportunity between processed foods and optimal foods. It isn't nearly as difficult as I once thought. The common theme across Western foods is over-industrialization. The logic of what's good for automating car manufacturing is good for food has proven to be fatally flawed. Having worked on many large industrial processes, it's easy to understand the drivers, but what's missing from the food industry is consumer healthspan. Nowhere does it show up on the industry's list of top priorities. Consumer health in the food industry means not poisoning the consumer. That's a long way from promoting their healthspan.

There are 15 major car companies in the U.S. That's in sharp contrast to the over 41,000 food and beverage companies, according to the USDA. Car companies care deeply about the consumer experience and sense of lasting value. The big-food industry's primary drivers are cost, convenience, and consumer addiction. We know that even if we buy a lemon vehicle, we can replace it. Fifty years of hidden food issues aren't as easily corrected.

Consumers share culpability with the food industry. We refuse to pay a penny more for what is often a higher quality product, but the health-conscious consumer segment is also driving the growth in organic and regenerative-sourced foods. While these don't address all the issues, directionally, they place us on a longer healthspan path and lead the food industry to higher-quality offerings. The type of consumer we are reflects our choices in optimizing health in meaningful ways.

Chapter 10

CHANGE THE GAME

THE BALANCING ACT BETWEEN leading-edge health science and quackery is not always obvious. It demands vigilance. Real science tends to be slow-moving compared to how we measure many other things. I often come upon research papers written 20 years ago that are only now gaining serious attention. The genuine scientific community isn't out promoting products and making big health claims. Real scientists tend to be pessimists, skeptical of others' work and even their own. The slow pace is a real problem, but it's also a safety check.

Figure 25: Balancing Health and Science

Making smart choices can feel like rule-breaking at times, but it can be tempting to take it too far and fall into the contrarian trap. One's identity can easily soon become about opposition and virtue signaling versus intelligent health. Contrarians are quick to point to studies that support their particular brand of dogma, and expend tremendous energy in the hope of being recognized as brave truth-speakers. Internet doctors and self-proclaimed experts promoting pseudoscience prey on those looking for quick fixes to chronic health issues as these consumers jump from product to product, lured by the latest hollow promise.

THE ROAD LESS TRAVELED

One of the moments that continues to resonate in my discussion with Margaret Moore, "Coach Meg," was about comfort zones. We tend to play it safe. It avoids the discomfort of failure, but in doing so, we miss important opportunities to learn. It's outside our comfort zone that we discover things important to our growth. It's unsettling for a short period but soon draws us in to learn more.

Learning happens outside our comfort zone.

I've come to appreciate firsthand the challenge faced by about 170 million Americans aged 40 and above, who are trying to come to grips with how little they know about health. Most days, I feel like I'm one of them, trying to make up for lost time.

The Conforming Crowd

Every day, a million commuters flow out onto New York's Manhattan sidewalks like lava flowing out of a volcano. They just keep coming and coming, pressed tightly together, walking shoulder-to-shoulder. It's the daily routine. Keep moving forward or be trampled by the herd. A red stop light presses the crowd in even tighter, anxious for the light to turn green. The pressure to conform is intense. Cars circle constantly, like border collies working to keep the herd in check. Engines growl, and horns bark over the chatter of the herd. Don't even think about breaking ranks. Conform, and we'll all get to where we need to be today, and tomorrow, we'll do it all over again, and again, and again.

Humans are natural pack animals. We learned early in our evolution that our odds of survival favor us moving together. The New York sidewalk behavior isn't unexpected; it's just an example of extreme behavior. Pressures to conform to societal norms are everywhere. Anyone who's tried to order a meal without a protein feature is bound to be asked, *"Would you like a protein with that?"* The server likely hasn't a clue if there is sufficient protein; they are just trained to ask because people can often be pressured to conform, and that's good for business.

As responsible adults, we know that following is usually the path of least resistance… at least in the short term. There are times, however, that we need to seriously consider taking the road less traveled, especially given the direction of public health these last several decades.

PLAN TO BREAK SOME RULES!

If there's a place to break some rules, it has got to be in our health patterns. Whether it is fear of embarrassment or perception among peers, the evidence is painfully clear that most of us haven't figured it out. Most of the rules aren't rules at all; they are just common behaviors built around conformance. We shouldn't be under any misconception that breaking conformance rules is easy because it isn't. People are easily threatened by health habits that differ from their own; as many have found, it can place relationships in unhealthy tension.

One great rule breaker is redefining convenience. Long-term values rarely include taking twice as long to complete simple tasks, and there's a common assumption that healthy habits take longer, which is why people claim not to have the time. There's a short "Make Health Last" video on the Whealthspan, YouTube channel done by the Canadian Heart & Stroke Foundation that beautifully captures a split-screen look at active convenience.

- Walk-and-talk meetings take no more time than sit-down meetings and get both parties moving.
- After dinner, walks with a partner are a powerful way to reconnect while being active and away from electronics and other distractions.
- Prepare healthy meals that generate quick and easy leftovers.
- Examples like my oatmeal, granola, and chili recipes in the appendix are perfect examples of great food in less time.

Lunch Rebel

For years, Kerri took her own lunch into the office and always avoided the food brought in for meetings. Her colleagues teased her about it for years. Time passed, and one by one, her colleagues ran into health complications, and the nervous teasing transitioned to asking her for health advice. She seemed to be defying aging and sickness. "It's not just the lunch," she'd say. "I keep active, but not as much as you might think. After all, I don't have to work off that crappy food that you guys insist on eating! I've never understood why the company chooses to feed us unhealthy foods or why everyone puts up with it. It makes no sense. It doesn't promote morale or company profits. The only winner in this is the company selling us the crappy food."

There are many healthier food delivery services out there now. They range from semi-prepared, frozen dishes that just require heating to companies like GrubHub that bring local restaurant food to our door. These are more costly than homemade, but for people dealing with long hours of work, commuting, and shuttling kids around town, it's a better option than many fast food options.

INFLECTION POINT

Surrounding ourselves with genuinely smart, curious people is one of the best things we can do to get up the learning curve quickly. They are practiced at spotting fact from fiction. Genuinely smart people keep current with science and continuously adjust their thinking as awareness grows, and the evidence becomes clearer. Many reside in the space between the health professional who is still reciting outdated, decades-old dietary advice and the edgy, self-proclaimed expert who challenges everything coming from mainstream science. Smart health professionals know that change in the field of medicine is slow. It's typically about a 30-year timeline from concept to broad acceptance and adoption. Gathering quality data on humans is slow, difficult, and expensive work that needs to be done safely. The trick for us is to get in early, once efficacy and safety questions have been addressed.

Part of changing the game is knowing where we are in a behavioral cycle. The U.S. Surgeon General's report in Figure 26 illustrates the change in smoking rates between 1900 and 1960. Its rise and fall in prevalence are only evident now that we have the luxury of history to look back on. It followed a classic normal data distribution curve that is often observed in large population studies. This analysis ended in 1998, but the trend continued to fall, last noted as 12% of the population still smoking in 2023, down from 42% in 1960.

Figure 26: Annual per Capita Cigarette Consumption, U.S., 1920-2020

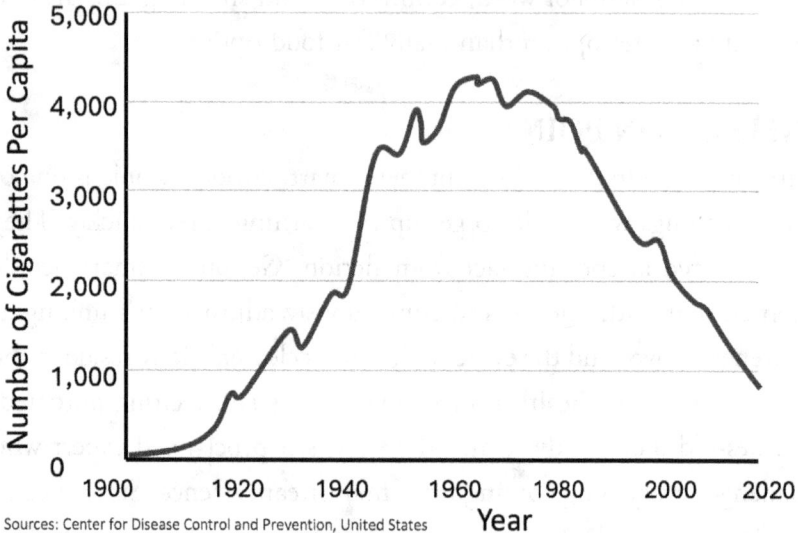

Sources: Center for Disease Control and Prevention, United States
Department of Agriculture and Center for Tobacco Control and Research

It took decades, but eventually, the public responded to the health warnings pertaining to smoking.

Where are we today on health behaviors? I estimate that we are where smoking was at around 1950. It's at an inflection point where change is stalled. A meaningful number of people have started to make positive changes, but many are still falling prey to the systems and common practices that undermine public health. The government eventually took decisive action that placed barriers to smoking. We're not seeing that yet, but times have changed. The consumer market is more dynamic, and governments have become more handcuffed. It may only be after governments see a convincing shift in public sentiment and habits that it feels politically safe to take legislative action to restore public health.

Once the trend changes, the reformed health community will help pull the others along more than legislation could ever hope to achieve. There will be pressure to conform to a new code of norms, making it easier for the rest of society to reclaim health. At our core, the human desire to help one another is strong.

The pattern is well understood in the innovation and adoption cycle, as seen in Figure 27. In innovation language, I think we're at the early adopters stage, and over the next two decades, we'll see significant growth in adoption. Even if we were all to decide to change tomorrow, the support systems will require time to adopt as well.

Figure 27: Innovation Adoption Cycle

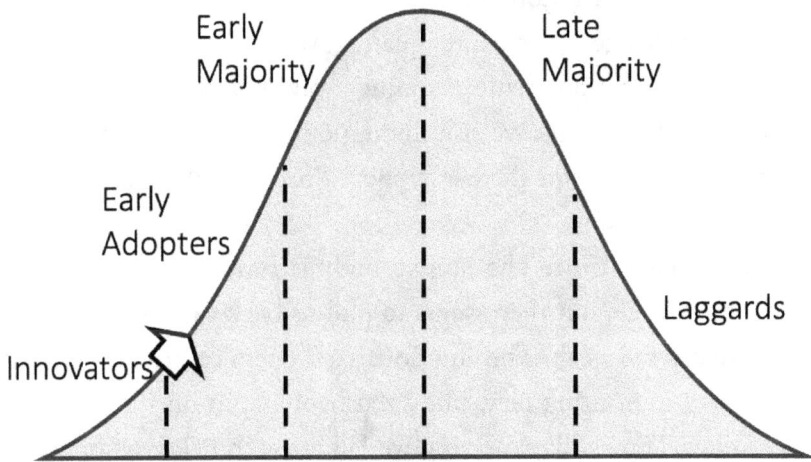

Healthy habit adoption is on the rise, likely somewhere in the early adopter stage.

PREPARING FOR CHANGE

One of the hardest things about changing lifestyle habits is building the foundation necessary to make quality choices stick. As we come to understand our individual "Why," and how that fits into our overall balance and priorities, thoughts of change shift from daunting to appealing.

Change requires more than an aspiration, often a lot more. The pressures to conform and revert to where we started are immense when our dreams of sustained health and happiness are not compelling enough. And the pressures aren't all external. Often, the greatest pressure to conform comes from within, so we really need to spend time seriously thinking about our WHY before jumping into action. Where are those around us headed? How does that fit with our vision? Change typically involves changing our environment and with whom we spend our time. Hopefully, that is just adding new communities to surround and support us. For some stuck at a dead-end, an unhealthy situation can demand wholesale changes. Change inevitably creates disruption, and that can be stressful for a while. No matter what changes we're contemplating, we'll want a community to support us for the long haul. Running away *from* something can be part of the solution, but we risk finding ourselves alone. Running *to* something usually infers there is support already in place and waiting for us to arrive.

Change takes time. The human body is elastic and can tolerate change for a while but then wants to pull us back to where we were. It's not that we're weak. The emotional and chemical reasons for this are real. Try imprinting new, bite-sized habits built on things we already know. Things like knowing we fall asleep quicker without the late-night snack, knowing we're more productive when we get outside for short breaks in the day, knowing we're happier to be around if we have a good workout, knowing we're more relaxed on days we've taken 10 minutes to meditate are a few of thousands of possibilities. Imprinting new habits that stick means we are internalizing the experience and valuing them more than old habits.

None of us is perfect in all 5 MEDAC foundations, and that will always be just fine. We're all in a different place, and figuring out where we need to focus is key to our success. It demands honest objectivity, and that's often aided by gaining external input from others who are well-informed. That might include colleagues, friends, experts, and coaches. Is there a root cause issue we're practiced at avoiding? For those prone to self-sabotage, modest, realistic goals that are baby steps toward success are likely better than trying to rush and leap to the top, only to fall short yet again. If quieting our mind feels forced and frustrating, reflect on activities that bring us to a relaxed state, activities that rely on movement, not substances.

We all have hundreds of opportunities, so there is no need to swing for the fence and try to hit a home run. Getting into the game and getting on base leads to greater success. To take the baseball analogy a step further, we can think of MEDAC as our team lineup. Getting a couple of players into the game helps take the pressure off any one player. Life is going to throw us some curve balls, but by investing in our Community, adding a few more whole foods into our Diet routine, incorporating some physical Activity, and putting ourselves in an Environment that promotes well-being, Mind exercises will be less intimidating because just as in baseball, it's easier to score with runners on base.

Figure 28: MEDAC on Base

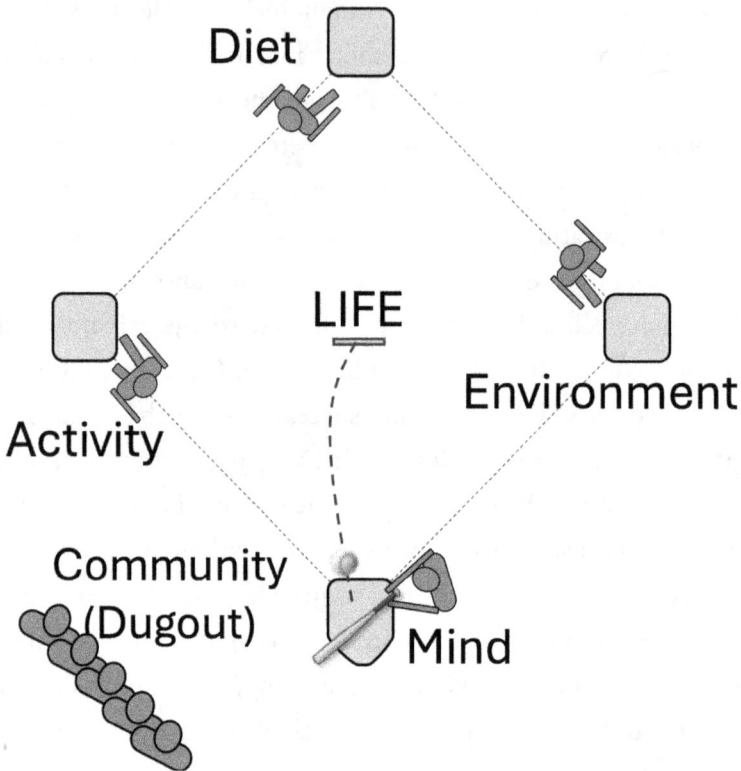

Getting habits on base gets easier with one that is adopted.
It requires a team —teamwork is key.

Unsure where to start? Polls frequently report weight loss, physical and mental health, fitness, finances, personal development, and social goals as common examples. I discourage the familiar trap of a weight loss goal. It's where our shoes can take us that matters. Weight loss can be an important outcome, but it pales against physical, metabolic, and mental health outcomes that are much more meaningful, more empowering, and more sustainable. Think of a bigger meaning that incites a bigger commitment.

I learned long ago that most people are smart and already know most of the answers. It's more about asking the right questions in a way that changes the conversation in our head.

What is the largest imbalance(s) we need to address? There are usually many things, and we need to distill them down to a short-list focused on 1 or 2 MEDAC foundations that can set us up for an easier win.

Why is it important for us to address the imbalance? Is anyone else going to do it for us? Will it resolve on its own?

How can we build a framework that guides and supports us in our journey to get there? How will we know if we're on track? How can we stack the odds of success in our favor?

When will we have the necessary information and support to start? What milestones can we look for along the way? When will we know when we've mastered it?

Answering these questions with depth is unlikely to be easy. Our best efforts may not seem as clear as we'd like, but it's going through the thought exercise that matters most. Often, the answers will only become clear upon reflection, well down the road. A balanced approach is best, with enough thought to provide direction but not so much thought that we become paralyzed and unable to move forward.

As we begin layering in new opportunities, that's often when personal development and self-esteem make demonstrable changes. There are several books on changing habits that share many different approaches. I've found *attachment* to be one of the easiest ways to start. Instead of denial or some new stand-alone habit, try attaching a new habit to an existing habit. Here are a few ideas to help get the creative juices flowing:

- Reduce added sugar to coffee by 10% per week, and consider adding a dash of spice, such as cinnamon, nutmeg, or dark chocolate powder, to help gently redirect the focus of the tastebuds from sweetness to flavor and aroma.

- Add a hill to a daily walk to build some strength and intensity.
- Take a 2-minute break during a walk to close your eyes and focus attention on the sounds and smells as a simple mindfulness exercise.
- Leave 5 minutes earlier for a regular commute and give more space to other drivers to discover how much more relaxing the travel can be.
- Identify three simple things that don't cost much money but would make daily living safer and easier for an older person living in the home.
- Pick up some wild organic blueberries during a grocery trip. Even better, do a side-by-side comparison with conventional blueberries.
- Reach out to some old friends to let them know we're thinking of *them*, not to tell them how fantastic or dismal *our* life is.
- Sign up to try a group activity, a community group, or a new faith and fellowship group just to learn something new and why others choose to attend.
- Order healthy side dishes instead of a main entre when dining out.
- Choose to bake a favorite dish instead of frying.

One of the strategies is to get into the habit of exploration and discovery, or, as in the illustration, just get on base with something new. Not every hit leads to a run. Where it leads is part of the joy and magic of discovering a richer world and a healthier life. We know we've got a healthy habit dialed in when we can't imagine life without it, and we feel the urge to bring others into our discovery.

Chapter 11

BALANCING MEDAC

THE IDEA OF PILOTING a plane always seemed daunting, but at the age of 13, my son wanted to learn to fly. After weeks of study and some training flights, I was invited to join them on his final lesson flight. It was a Cessna 172, circa 1975. Business travel had me in the air frequently in those days, but this experience immediately had a raw intimacy about it that removed any emotional comforts offered by plush flight cabins filled with distracted passengers, flight attendants pushing food carts up and down the aisle, pilots separated by armored doors, and tiny windows that enhanced the sense of being indoors. No, this was the opposite of all that. The six hours of flying time lessons were feeling more than a bit light.

The seatbelt buckles were barely latched when the engine revved up. I waited for the sound of another engine. Nope, that was it, no backup engine either. My eyes darted back and forth between the airfield that was quickly passing us by and the young hands on the controls. This was definitely not a drill and certainly not a dream. Seconds later we were cruising up over the coastline and found myself looking for familiar landmarks and loving the bird's-eye view that this little plane afforded. Calm at the controls; my son appeared twice his age as he nudged the ailerons and rudder, guiding us smoothly on course. The 30-minute tour ended much too soon, as the wheels softly touched down. Takeoff anxieties had been quickly pushed aside by the joy of the flight and the honor of witnessing the event.

In the same way that pilots make hundreds of small adjustments to the throttle, landing gear, ailerons, rudder, and elevators to reach cruising altitude, so too will we find ourselves needing to nudge multiple lifestyle habits simultaneously. In time, as we get into the rhythm of stronger choices and conscious decisions sliding seamlessly into habits of choice, we discover that we're largely operating on autopilot. Stressors transform into foundations of strength and knowledge. Each person's journey is unique and typically encounters challenges along the way, but that's always a part of growth.

Balance looks easy. We see a bird in flight as perfectly natural, yet we know that each of the 7,000 feathers on an eagle serves an important function, whether soaring at 10,000 feet or diving in to capture prey. As a boater, I tend to think of ballast in the keel, but ballast plays just as important a role in flight, as it's ballast that enables level flight, takeoff, and landing. Both balance and ballast are invisible but powerful forces that are easily discounted. We associate the thunder of commercial jet engines with flight but without balance and ballast, they are just very expensive missiles with no control.

INTERDEPENDENT HALLMARKS OF AGING

As we try to promote balance, it's helpful to recognize the different attributes of aging and longevity. A decade ago, scientists arrived at a list of 9 unique factors that could be measured and characterized and named them the Hallmarks of Aging. The original nine included:

1. Genomic instability: DNA damage
2. Telomere attrition: Shortening of the caps that protect chromosomes
3. Epigenetic alterations: Gene expression/methylation errors
4. Loss of proteostasis: Protein folding errors and degradation
5. Deregulated nutrient-sensing: Impaired energy production and cell growth

6. Mitochondrial dysfunction: Energy source dysfunction
7. Cellular senescence: Accumulation of zombie cells
8. Stem-cell exhaustion: Loss in cell/organ regenerative capacity
9. Altered intercellular communication: Functional errors and inflammaging

In 2022, scientists got together again to review the progress and decided that there were more areas of research to add to the list.

10. Compromised Autophagy: Destroying of damaged, old, or redundant cells
11. Microbiome Disturbances: Loss of microbial species diversity
12. Altered Mechanical Properties: Losses in cell structural integrity
13. Splicing Dysregulation: Gene errors in synthesizing proteins
14. Inflammation: Cellular response to the immune system

While it's an extensive list, a significant finding is that there is strong interdependence among the various hallmarks because they all interact with multiple biological systems working in parallel. They tend to track together, which is good because that means it doesn't involve 14 disparate approaches.

The hallmarks of aging are helpful to scientists but have limited applicability for us. Of more value to us are the behaviors that tend *not* to provoke the hallmarks of aging. We can think of these behaviors as the hallmarks of longevity.

HALLMARKS OF LONGEVITY

In studying long-lived people, some traits stand out that provide insights into their success:

1. Humility: Aging is a humbling experience, not due to frailty but by discovering how big our world is, how little our opinions matter, and how fast time slips away.

2. Curiosity: The more we learn, the more we discover how much more there is to learn. Curious minds pay attention to the habits of those who lived well and long.

3. Emotional Resilience: Don't sweat the small stuff is more than a maxim; it's a superpower. They live it.

4. Physical Resilience: Their above-average health promotes extended health and a lower incidence of chronic disease.

5. Positivity: Even when life deals them lemons, they make lemonade and choose to focus on all the good things life brings them.

The ability to build and sustain health in today's reality goes beyond just diet and exercise. Those are essential, but there's much more to discovering the magic.

MEDAC – WHERE AM I?

I've mentioned the MEDAC acronym several times, and it is finally time to put a shovel into the ground. In the same way we think about a home, the framework is only as reliable as the foundations. The longevity framework is supported by 5 key foundations:

- Mind
- Environment
- Diet
- Activity
- Community

We tend to take foundations for granted because they aren't as frequently in our line of sight, but we want to always feel their presence. Reject any thoughts of these being binary concepts. They all serve different needs, but are all interdependent, just as in the hallmarks of aging and longevity.

If whealth and longevity were a large building, our perceptions of the building would depend a lot on our point of view. It's too much to see all at once, yet we know it is there. New York's Empire State Building towers over us from the street. The instant we walk through the doors and into the lobby, all the marble captures our gaze. Looking out from the 86th-floor observatory, we see over building-tops and out to the Atlantic Ocean. It looks dramatically different depending on the time of day, and feels different, depending on the weather. We don't *see* the Empire State Building so much as we experience it. Our experiences evoke emotions within us through what's known as phenomenology – how we experience the environment around us. There will be specific items associated with each MEDAC foundation, but the connection we seek is one of experiencing them, versus checking boxing on a list of action items.

Looking over the five foundations, there are likely some that evoke more emotional connection than others, and chances are the emotions are different. This is our beginning point, our emotional connection with each foundation. Continue sifting round and round, allowing the experience to speak to us. We each have a history of experiences with all of them, and likely some questions. There are no right or wrong reactions. Some may be very positive, others very negative. We are beginning to inform our conscious mind of where we are in relation to each of them. Each foundation is of equal importance for an entirely different set of reasons. While one or two might be easier to identify with, intimately connecting with all of them collectively provides balance and ballast, and achieves a state where Whealthspan champions thrive.

Figure 29: MEDAC Foundation

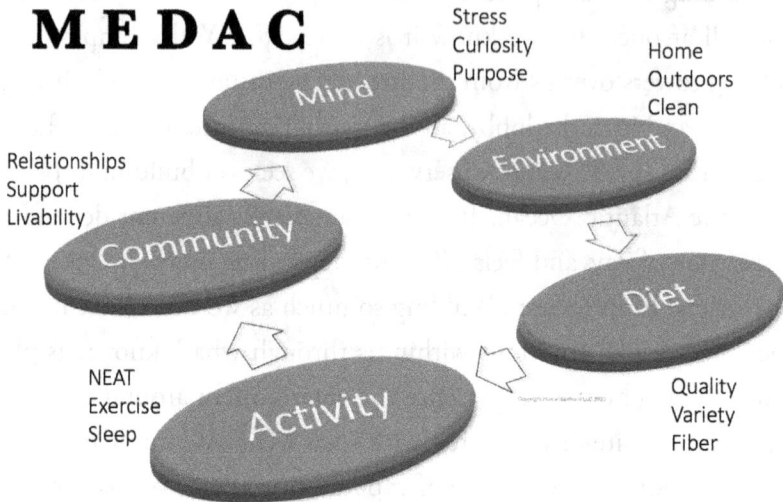

MEDAC

Mind — Stress, Curiosity, Purpose

Environment — Home, Outdoors, Clean

Community — Relationships, Support, Livability

Diet — Quality, Variety, Fiber

Activity — NEAT, Exercise, Sleep

The MEDAC foundations provide a strong base for a personal framework.

MIND: Our mind is constantly in search of a connection with all things amazing, inspiring, and touching, while constantly faced with decisions on where to devote time and energy for the next few seconds. The mind holds our values and priorities, which serve as our guide markers. The composite shapes our attitudes and how we present ourselves to the world around us. It forms patterns of virtual frameworks to help us make decisions in split seconds. How clear are our values? How aligned are our habits with our values? Where are we at ease with them and where are our values and habits at odds? These are the normal tensions that pull us in many directions and influence our choices.

We make split-second quality-related decisions all day long – what we need more of or less of in our lives. These are the decisions we know as habits. We effectively bypass the conscious, rational decision process. This gets at the prompt regarding our connection with the five MEDAC foundations and why our connection is inclined to be different with each one.

Our mind's more than 100 billion cells and neural networks are protected by our skull, our lifestyle habits, and our environment. We can think of the skull as our first line of defense, but there are many threats from which it isn't designed to protect us. Several recent dementia studies have pointed to the role of both lifestyle and environmental toxins. An interesting one, "Dementia in the Ancient Greco-Roman World" by Finch did a historical review of dementia dating back through ancient Greek and Roman eras and compared that with modern U.S. and contemporary Amerindians of Tsimane of Bolivia. The study found that U.S. dementia rates over age 60 are 11 times higher than in ancient and current Tsimane, and the ancient Greeks.

Some mistakenly believe that dementia will increase by promoting longevity behaviors. Unequivocally, that is misguided and false. While age remains a dominant risk factor for dementia, modifiable lifestyle, and environmental factors have a significant influence.

Clint Eastwood's quote, *"Keep the old man out,"* and subsequent hit for the late Toby Keith, resonates because it conveys an attitude people can identify with. It's a conscious choice. Eastwood's tough-guy image aligns with the stubbornness we see in long-lived people. Life isn't always going to be easy. Sometimes we're going to have to fight for our foundations.

Stress can seem hard to put a finger on when life pulls us in many directions. There aren't quick and easy ways to measure it, and it tends to easily take on a life of its own. That's unfortunate because, in the world of chronic disease, stress always ranks as a top contributor. It may seem nebulous, but its teeth are razor sharp.

A large 2020 metanalysis study looked at the association of chronic stress with heart events and the many common disease states associated with cardiovascular risk. Over a 5-year follow-up, standard medical therapies reduced clinical events by 25%. Stress Management training lowered clinical events by another 48%. That's a profound finding and speaks to the impact of corrosive chemistries the body makes in response to chronic stress.

Figure 30: Impact of Stress on Cardiovascular Events

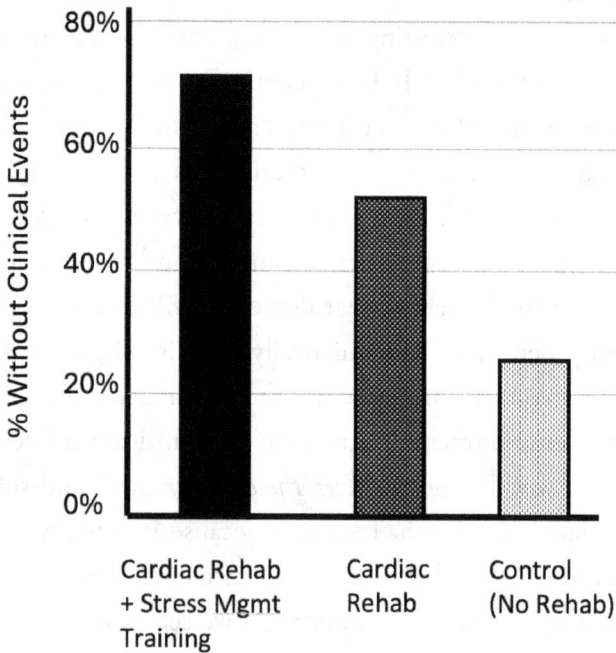

Data Source: Blumenthal et al, Enhancing cardiac rehabilitation with stress management training: a randomized, clinical efficacy trial., 2016

Cardiac rehabilitation programs rely almost exclusively on lifestyle habits because they've proven to be so effective in managing heart health for at-risk patients.

Stress leads us to think of psychological and emotional stress from relationships, financial hardship, career, etc., but there are many sources of stress. Sedentary behaviors, loneliness, and processed foods, for example, are well-documented sources of chronic stress, as are environmental toxins. Anyone who has experienced a hangover can appreciate the effects of acute oxidative stress on the body. Stress impacts both the immune and endocrine systems — primary systems that manage the entire body. We frequently observe people consuming ultra-processed foods in response to psychological and emotional stress, but this only throws fuel on the fire, adding to oxidative stress and cognitive decline. Healthy habits like quality food, friendships, and exercise are far more effective tools to resist and recover from acute stress.

Powerfully Positive Hormones

I found myself in a difficult meeting one summer afternoon. The corporation was under significant financial pressure, and our C-suite boss had made a blind promise they couldn't deliver on. We'd been called in to share the pain. The behavior we witnessed was unbecoming of a leader of people and any question of competency was answered.

I left the office and climbed aboard my "silver bullet" time trial racing bike to vent my stress. The road was a familiar training ground, dead straight out of town for 15 miles, with a slight incline and a modest headwind. I pushed harder than usual. The stress had found an effective outlet — the pedals. I could literally feel my body chemistry changing as the miles slipped by and the wind peeled away the stress. I was "in the zone," as athletes describe it. It's an amazing experience. A wry smile came over my face, connecting with a superpower over negative stress, smiling all the way back. I'd managed to switch on some powerfully positive hormones.

There would be only one more meeting, to inform her I'd arranged for a transfer and that it was a done deal. The silver bullet and I were moving on up.

Discovering we have powerful tools to conquer stress is empowering and fosters resilience. This was a clear example of how different stresses produce very different endocrine responses in a head-to-head contest. Part of our stress-coping toolkit is knowing we have options to turn to. Feeling stressed without positive outlets leaves us feeling cornered and sets us up for chronic stress. We need outlets that aren't substance-related, and we need to know how to access them on demand.

As chemistry in the body, stress is oxidative, like the slow insidious rust on a car body. It triggers an imbalance between the production and accumulation of reactive oxygen species (ROS) in cells and tissues and our ability to quench or calm these reactive products. MEDAC principles help counter stress directly and promote the generation and consumption of antioxidants that give the gift of electrons, which in turn, spares our own proteins, lipids, and DNA, from losing electrons (oxidation). A positive attitude, meditation, activity, healthy food, nature, and gathering with friends are all examples that contribute to better coping with the stresses of daily life. We want to know with certainty what works and have easy options at our disposal. The compounding benefit is that our tolerance for stress increases, knowing we have effective tools to deal with it.

Curiosity constantly grows awareness and results in us being better informed about the dynamic world around us. Curiosity also fosters humility, as it opens our eyes to an expansive world of learning opportunities. It is part of why lifelong learning is a common theme among healthy agers. It keeps our minds challenged and engaged, and on top of changing trends that provide opportunities to leverage and adapt emerging knowledge. Some even go back to college in later years.

Early in my career, it surprised me to see world-class scientists asking seemingly innocent questions. Their curiosity seemed as intact as a young child, constantly curious about the world expanding in front of them. Having worked with hundreds of scientists since those early days, it's clear that lifelong curiosity is a superpower.

Purpose for many is arriving at an answer they hadn't realized they'd been searching for. It's easily recognized by an eagerness to rise from sleep each day with positive objectives that align with a chosen theme or mission. Purpose is often big, much bigger than ourselves, meaning it serves many others and frequently extends beyond the horizon of our lifetime. This gets back to humility, and being very comfortable serving a small role in a much bigger play. It can be like finding love. It finds us when we aren't consciously looking for it, but once it gets its hooks into us, we can't imagine life without it. We'll explore purpose more deeply a bit later.

Faith touches many places in the mind and naturally aligns with purpose. Traditional faith practice brings people together into a community, not just in a formal setting but also in daily life. Values are reinforced through friendships forged through conversations that extend into personal topics that are sometimes more easily broached in faith-based communities. Faith is usually also built around beliefs in what awaits us upon death. It's not uncommon to see older adults strengthen their faith practice as they come to terms with life as finite. Aging in a positive community of others is essential.

ENVIRONMENT

We interact with the environment in our homes, in the outside world, and the external environments that find their way into our homes.

The internal environment is frequently overlooked when considering environmental risks and opportunities. The National Human Activity Pattern Survey (NHAPS) revealed that we spend 85% of our time indoors in summer and even more in winter. Eighty-two percent of our indoor time is spent in our homes. More recent studies indicated that we're spending even more time indoors since the 2020 COVID pandemic. The trend toward more time indoors at home also rises as we age. All that time translates to high indoor exposure. So, while relative risks are usually low, high exposure amplifies their impact. We don't hear much about home environmental risks because they don't make for spicy media headlines, but there are a few deserving of attention.

Mold spores are very common and are reported to be found in about 50% of homes. Some residents experience acute reactions but for most, there are no obvious symptoms. The chronic concern centers on Alzheimer's Disease (AD) risk. Mold has been found to be one of the strong correlations with AD and mold remediation is becoming a common strategy in the treatments for AD patients living at home. It's presumed not to be a dose, but rather an exposure issue. Relocating to a mold-free home can be a solution, but not an easy one. Most obtain the services of environmental remediation specialists.

For adults over 65, we know that about 90% of them plan to remain living in their homes, but fewer than 10% of their homes are equipped to support this objective. This factors into how so many older adults fall off the financial cliff. Those who live well tend to place themselves in supportive environments that make living at home a viable option.

When I founded Home Ideations LLC, a primary objective was to test the receptivity of adults aged 50-70 to functionally enhanced designs over traditional builder/designer options. The response was a resounding "yes." The key is discovering what a functionally enhanced design looks like. These are updated designs and remodels that improve livability across the lifespan, which makes for better living at all ages and contributes to resale value.

I had the opportunity to design and build a home for our family, that I nicknamed the Livability Project. It looks like any other new home but with subtle features that ensure optimal living and maximum options. Things like 1-step entry, push/pull door handles on all doors for when we're carrying things in/out, naturally wide door openings, big windows, and high ceilings that combined create a seamless connection with the outdoors and a big sense of space with a smaller footprint. On the exterior, the grading eliminates the need for steps and provides natural flowing movement. And yes, it includes a main living floor bedroom suite complete with a curbless shower and hands-free toileting. There are several more features, but this provides a sense of what efficient lifetime design provides.

We spend a lot of time in our homes, and it is the one environment that is within our control. It's one of the best places to invest early to extend our healthspan.

The external environment presents many more challenges because so many of the issues are outside of our control. The world continues to grow more toxic every year, changing in ways we can't see, smell, taste, or measure over human lifespans. We've been lulled into a belief that industrial exposures are just a part of modern life. Residents of places like Cancer Alley, the 85-mile (137 km) stretch of land along the Mississippi River between Baton Rouge and New Orleans, LA, which contains over 200 petrochemical plants and refineries, historically have reported 44% higher rates of cancer than the national average. Louisiana ranked 4th in heart-related deaths and 8th in cancer deaths according to the Center for Disease Control in 2021. The impacts of environmental toxins are most closely experienced by the local residents — hotspots well above state averages.

The U.S. has more than doubled agricultural chemical use since 1990, while at the same time introducing new chemicals engineered to pair with genetically modified organisms, commonly known as GMO crops. Engineered GMO crops enable pesticides like Roundup to be sprayed broadly, killing almost everything that comes into contact but the GMO crop. It was a great idea in concept, but as farmers have discovered, ever-increasing amounts were required as the weeds became pesticide-resistant. The problem was compounded as the soils became sterilized, due to the killing of the microorganisms, which play a key role in the crop's nutrient uptake from the soil, and declining organic matter, which results in higher compaction and less water retention (more runoff). The industry's solution? More chemicals, more watering, and more runoff led to yet another problem, more pesticide residue in unintended waterways. In 1991, the USDA had the foresight to implement the Pesticide Data Program to monitor pesticide proliferation, and unsurprisingly, it revealed a 600% increase in pesticide residues in the waterways. The compounding relationship between the start of GMO+presticide crops in the early 1990s, Roundup as a broad-spray desiccant on corn and wheat in the early 2000s, the doubling and introduction of new chemicals (left axis), and pesticide residues (right axis) is shown in Figure 31.

Ironically, it was in the middle of this massive 30-year experiment that I managed the pesticide operations for one of the big global chemical producers, naïve to all that we know now. Looking back over this same period, we've witnessed a coincidental rise in several chronic diseases in the 1990s, followed by over a decade of finger-pointing and denial. Understandably, the chemical and food industry continues to argue for the absence of direct causal evidence. Shareholders of the Roundup brand are feeling the sting of getting caught up in the outfall, with billions in damages awarded by the courts, but I suspect this is the canary in the coal mine. By reasonable measure, it appears that U.S. public health is paying the price for the U.S. food industry's spot as the #1 global food exporter. Farmers are quickly retreating from chemical-based farming and the big food companies are trying to spin it as an environmental win, but the food industry is long overdue for an intervention.

Figure 31: Pesticide Consumption and Residue, 1990-2020

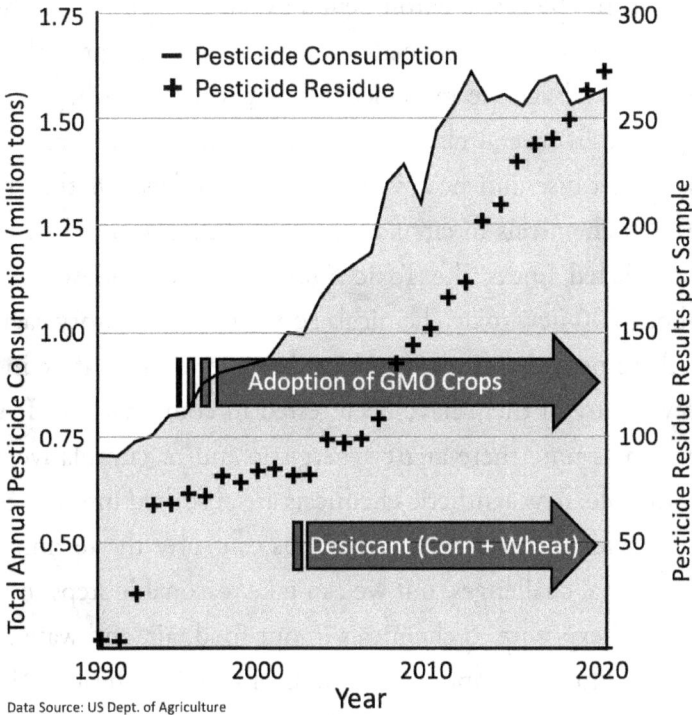

Chemical use has grown broadly, but none as pronounced since the introduction of GMO crops tailored for broad chemical spray. The added use as a desiccant prior to harvesting further exacerbates rising pesticide residues in waterways and pose increasing chronic threat to humans.

Air and water easily transport toxins thousands of miles. The ubiquitous presence of environmental toxins highlights the chronic risks to human and animal health. The environment has been subjected to intense synthetic chemical stress, and our regulatory "safe" levels appear to be inadequate for reasons no one can satisfactorily explain. Historically, this infers that nothing will change until the EPA and USDA agree that there is a problem, and Congress supports a change in the regulatory standards. We can expect decades before regulatory and political processes catch up with the problem and the environment recovers from the impact, through natural bioremediation.

Regardless of which side of the political aisle we line up on, we are all living in the biggest environmental experiment in human history. There is growing confidence that many supposed "safe" chemicals of the industrial age are more accurately toxins, contributing to the dramatic rise in several chronic diseases. The conundrum is which ones are the cause and how vulnerable each of us. Of the estimated 350,000 chemicals in circulation, the EPA has more than 85,000 chemicals listed under the Toxic Substances Control Act (TSCA), with about 700 new toxic chemicals added to its inventory each year. While these new chemicals may have been tested for safety in isolation, few if any of them have been tested in combination. It would be naïve to assume there aren't synergistic and/or cumulative effects when multiple, new synthetic chemicals are absorbed into our bodies.

As individual consumers, none of us can solve the technical, political, or social challenges, but we can take reasonable steps to reduce our personal exposure to chemicals in our food, air, and water. Every reasonable reduction improves our odds of sustained health. Not surprisingly, we tend to find human longevity associated with cleaner environments.

Diet is a gnarly topic for most of us. Earlier we looked at sources of some of the confusion, and coming up we'll take a closer look at approaching diet with a simplified strategy that puts us on a foundation for success. Quality, variety, and fiber are cues that point us to eating well. A healthy approach to eating is surprisingly simple and straightforward, and need not get drawn into the radical diet debates that unnecessarily confuse and frustrate so many relationships.

Activity spans the gamut from a good night's sleep and a daily walk to high-intensity heart rate workouts. As with each foundation, but particularly with activity, understanding where we are now plays a big part in appropriate next steps. Earlier we touched on the role of exercise activity in heart health, and it is key to remember that nothing appears more important to cognitive health than movement.

Like all animals, we evolved to move and to sleep. The more we move, the more likely we are to get better sleep. This is one of the simple laws of nature. Finding how to move in a world that's been steadily moving less is a challenge, but a challenge worthy of us all. We will go into more activity in an upcoming chapter.

COMMUNITY

Community is our 5th foundation, the one that binds us together. It is by working together that we've been able to advance the species and do great things.

Separation of wealth has grown in recent decades, and it can feel like we're growing farther apart. Once excited to answer our phones and doorbells, we approach with caution or avoid them altogether. The digital world has connected us in ways that have separated us as humans.

Looking forward, our community needs to be well-defined and protect human connections. A big part of a community is location. During our careers, work often brings us into a community. What is our community outside work, and after our career ends? We're inclined to think about "what" we'll do in retirement. A more important question might be who we are going to spend that time of life with and how can we support one another. Global data across all cultures makes it clear that we'll thrive in locations of high livability, where aging well is well supported naturally. Looking far ahead, who we are going to spend time with in our late-life years when we're likely to need help from time to time? Everyone's answer to these questions will be unique. Some will plan to move many times, while others will already be in their best location. There are many paths to successful outcomes, we just need to put some thoughtful planning into it.

We might think being alone is easier, but loneliness places us at a much higher risk for dementia. Dementia is no picnic under the best of circumstances. Dementia in isolation isn't something we'd wish on our worst enemy.

COMMUNITIES OF THE FUTURE

My health and housing focus has led to designing communities of the future, both new and upgrades to existing communities. By leveraging the best of what we've learned over the decades in residential and commercial settings, and with the new technologies coming into homes, there are many exciting opportunities on the horizon. Tomorrow's best communities will leverage strong social values and novel ways of bringing people together in ways not possible in many communities today. Through intergenerational mixed housing, naturally active greenspaces, and intentional commercial services, it becomes possible to build more affordably, and bring wider demographics of people together naturally. Look for more to come on this.

ROW YOUR BOAT

A helpful MEDAC balance analogy is a rowboat. Mind directs our path, Environment manages the gear, Diet takes care of fueling and hydration, Activity is responsible for the training program, and Community gets everyone working together. Again, the idea here is that there are many roles to play, and that each one is important to the outcome of the team. The best outcomes are achieved by how well all 5 seats work together.

Figure 32: MEDAC Balance: Working Together as One

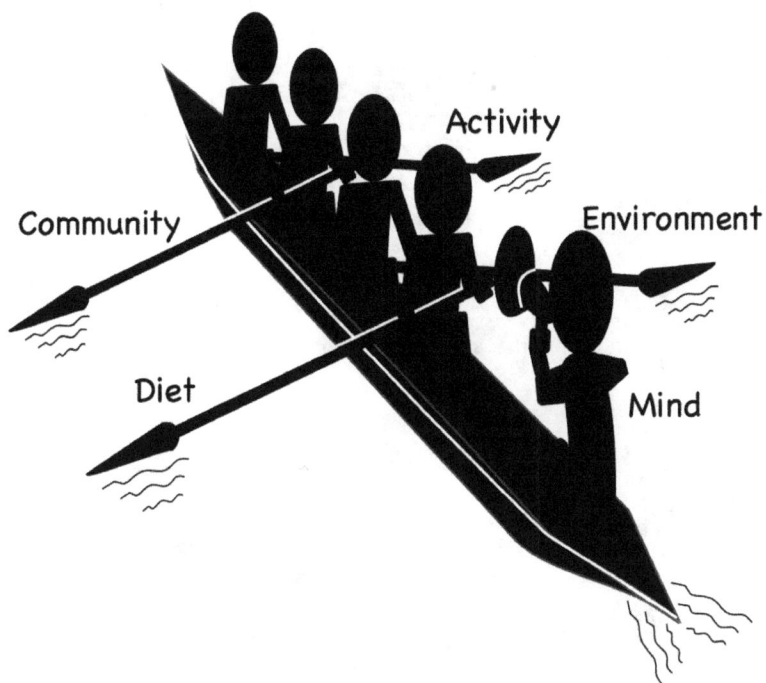

Activity

Community

Environment

Diet

Mind

Chapter 12

HEALTH IN A SICK WORLD

Moments matter

Larry had spent the morning doing what he loved; kicking butt on the tennis court with his mates down in Florida. He wished they could identify with his eight-year up-and-down battle with cancer. He'd try to tell them he likely wouldn't be back, but it was hard for them to make sense of it without visible signs. His cancer had returned again, but this time it wouldn't be letting go. The doctors were out of options. Fit, lean, healthy, active people like Larry aren't supposed to get sick. They aren't supposed to get cancer. And, they sure aren't supposed to die early.

Our last hour together during my visit was nothing short of surreal. I still quiver every time I think about it. It didn't require many words. He'd dropped subtle clues in the days leading up to our goodbye. Even as kids growing up together, we didn't need many words. A look said most of what needed saying, which was how it was playing out that day too. He knew I'd heard what he was trying to tell me. It was our way, quiet and personal, yet this time it had an intensity beyond anything I'd ever experienced. Our eyes both sparkled with a tear as we took one last look at the doorway.

I sat silently in the car, hands gripping the steering wheel, frozen, unable to place the car in drive. The impending loss was profoundly sad, yet the connection we'd experienced was beauty on a whole new level. We'd been allowed to say goodbye on our own terms. Few get such a gift in life. It was as if God handed us each an old soup can joined by a waxed string, like the play telephones we'd made as kids, only this message was crystal clear.

A few short months later he would send his final message. "I'm waving the white flag. Love you, bro." And with that, the physical connection went silent but the inspiration lives on.

Fresh out of college, I was fortunate to be hired into advanced materials research for a multinational corporation. Fate smiled at me early, and I was soon traveling North America, working directly for the company's Chief Engineer. Jan was internationally respected, and as a mentor, I'd struck gold. We'd travel together across the U.S. and Canada, frequently sketching design ideas on the backs of diner placemats. He had access to the latest computational modeling software, but it couldn't match rich, creative discussion, a pencil, and the back of a paper placemat. His blindness never stood in our way, making the experience even more remarkable. We were in the real world, gathering data in real-life situations that the design theory hadn't accounted for. I learned early that real-world data was king.

Years later I found myself back in corporate research and had the good fortune to tag-team with our company's President and CEO at a private investors event to showcase our clean energy technology. David was a leader other leaders tried to mimic, able to articulate a vision that inspired people to work together for a better tomorrow. Twenty years after corporate retirement, he received an honorary doctorate, and he summed up his address to the graduating class in just 5 words:

"Change Everything All The Time"

David followed that up with *"I've met too many talented people who avoid making or dealing with change in their lives."* He was speaking to a corporate culture we'd both lived. These people fall short in life for fear of change, and fear of failure. Worse, they hold others back from living their best life.

"The pressures to conform are unrelenting, but following the crowd assures one thing: that our best will be mediocre."

Thinking differently isn't enough. Positive change requires us to behave differently. These two great leaders put wind under my wings early in my career and helped me see that conformance is a two-sided coin. Knowing when to push the envelope separates excellence from mediocrity.

NORMS ARE NOT NORMAL

We all appreciate the value of conformance with norms on the roadways. Norms help keep us safe, which is why society has laws to promote behavioral conformance and penalties for non-conformance. So why is it that our speeds creep up and we drive a bit more aggressively on Fridays, driving up non-fatal accident rates by as much as 50% compared to other weekdays? It's the day we feel most tired, we're looking forward to time with family and friends, and traffic volumes are increased slightly – all little things that our rational mind would advise us to add more caution, not less. Yet, data from more than one billion trips on U.S. roads daily reminds us that rationalization often trumps rational behavior.

As of 2023, the CDC data informs us that in the U.S., 30.7% of us are overweight, 33.2% are obese, 9.2% are severely obese, and 19.7% of our children are already obese. The overweight epidemic has become one of our new norms. We know from several studies that obesity comes with shorter life expectancy and longer morbidity, the exact opposite of what a rational mind would desire, yet the frenzy persists. It's never been normal to eat 40% excess calories or to stare at screens for 9 hours daily. It's never been normal for children to get 67% of their calories from ultra-processed foods, never been normal to raise children in a chemically toxic environment, and never been normal to live so isolated from one another. We've thrown the responsibility to manage these complex issues onto parents, as though they possess some basic training or unique insights. Our norms have been radically shifted in just two generations, far surpassing the human species' ability to adapt.

Beyond the incredible pace of change, is the vast complexity of the issues in play. Some of the contributions to weight management are listed in Table 1.

Table 1: Factors Affecting Overweight and Obesity

• Inadequate activity	• Sleep hygiene
• Excess caloric intake	• Aggressive marketing
• Low fiber intake	• Medications
• Low water intake	• Leptin resistance
• Calorie dense foods	• Chronic diseases
• Excess dietary salt	• Emotional disorders
• Engineered foods	• Genetics
• Food addictions	• Societal norms
• Food Availability	• Endocrine dysfunction
• Stress	• Insulin dysfunction
• Low food intelligence	• Metabolic Syndrome

Society likes to look at these in isolation as binary problems, continuing to wonder why it can't make headway on changing the trend.

Binary approaches to health are destined to fall well short of expectations.

HAVE AND HAVE-NOT

Data from the Human Mortality Database has much to tell us. Recall that I mentioned life expectancy stalled in 2010 before dropping during the pandemic. There's more to the story.

One of the ways to understand health and mortality trends is to look at death age frequency. Over the last century, the trend saw more people dying at older ages than in the previous decade. Given lifespan isn't infinite, this pushes the distribution closer together, and the most frequent death age gets higher and at a later age. Visually, the mountain gets steep and taller. Looking back at more than 55 million deaths between the years 2000 and 2021, we see the exact opposite occur; a widening gap due mainly to a rise in premature deaths. Figure 33 illustrates the key trends:

- Lifespan frequency above age 90 rose slightly from 2000 to 2019
- Premature deaths frequency increased between 2010-2019 (shaded area)
- Healthy individuals are living longer, unhealthy are living shorter

Figure 33: U.S. Premature Deaths on the Rise

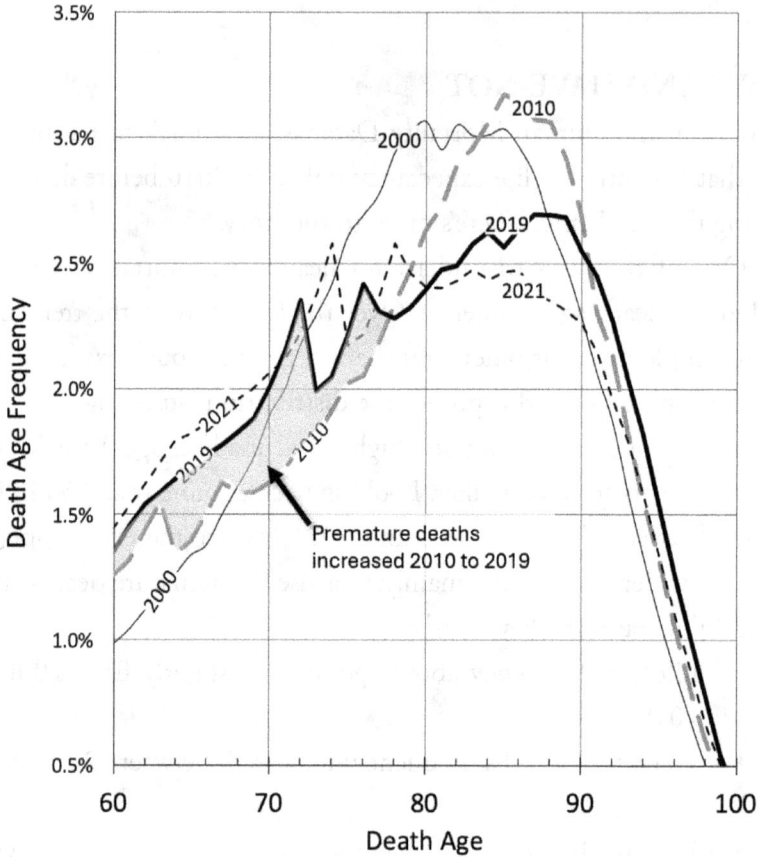

A concerning trend of earlier deaths began appearing in 2010.

The widening distribution exhibited between 2000 and 2019 reflects a pattern of growing disparity in lifespan outcomes among the population that can't be attributed to war, famine, pandemic, or genetics. It points to a growing division between those who have health, and those who do not. For those with lifestyles that align with health, the message is positive. It's worth noting that most of those over age 60 didn't grow up with all the health and overweight issues of today's younger population. Reversing this trend is going to be a decades-long battle. Historical trends suggest the disparity will continue to grow until multiple root cause issues in Table 1 are addressed.

It remains clear that longevity is not the default. The common phrase "people are living longer than ever" would be better stated as "one subset of the population is living longer, while another is dying earlier."

We manage disease or proactively manage health – it's a personal choice.

What does "health" look like? The same as it always did. It's just become less visible, given the shift in norms around us. Health requires more than active management; it requires PRO-ACTIVE management. Let's take a look at a practical approach.

SIMPLIFYING COMPLEX SYSTEMS

Few diseases are more challenging for medical professionals and patients than autoimmune diseases (AutoD), making them an excellent example of an approach to extended health. Odds are good that we're at risk to one or more AutoDs, but completely unaware. They exhibit all the unruly traits of many other chronic diseases:

1. Multifactorial – many contributing variables
2. Significantly influenced by lifestyle
3. Influenced by Hereditable genetics that puts some more at risk than others
4. Operate below the radar for several years
5. Stubborn to manage once they manifest
6. Pervasive in the population, with many undiagnosed
7. Affects multiple systems: immune, endocrine, digestive, renal...
8. Manifest in as many as 100 unique disease states

9. Elevated uncertainties around causes and treatments
10. Tend to be discounted due to the inability to predict and challenge to medically treat

Doctors tend to take a stepwise reductive approach of trial and error to eliminate potential causes, leading to a long frustrating road to diagnosis before treatment can begin. It's easy to understand why people diagnosed with an AutoD can feel overwhelmed and discounted by the medical system.

Allergies offer us some unique insights into AutoD. Nearly one-third of the population has some known allergic condition. For our purposes, let's divide the population into 3 equal groups:

A. Known food or environmental allergy
B. One or more undetected allergies
C. Allergy-free

Keep in mind that the term "allergy" refers to an acute response. However, just like AutoDs, allergies typically take years to develop. In the early stages, our immune system operates as designed and produces antibodies to defend against the attack without identifiable symptoms. This early stage is known as asymptomatic sensitivity. These people are represented by group B. Over time, with repeated exposures, the allergens eventually wear down the immune system's vulnerabilities, triggering an alarm state, elevating us from group B to group A allergy status.

In extreme, acute cases, like allergies to nuts and shellfish allergies, it's easy to know if we're in group A. Answering if we are in group B or C isn't nearly as easy. Slow-creeping allergens are more likely to be associated with fatigue, gastrointestinal discomfort, rashes, sinus issues, mild depression, anxiety, and similar less acute symptoms that could be attributed to many other possible causes that may not even be allergen-related. Awareness is certainly helpful, but testing can be limited. Hypochondria (excessive concern about one's health) certainly isn't the answer, as it feeds negative behaviors and negative health outcomes. Ignorance might feel blissful, but ends the moment we run off the road due to operating in the dark without headlights. Ultimately many have decided that it doesn't matter if they are group B or C. Proactive health management guides one intuitively to take reasonable measures to limit exposure to the many common risks that are within our control. The demand for gluten-free products is an excellent example of evolving consumer behavior and market dynamics. Sales of gluten-free products now far exceed the market size of people with known gluten sensitivities. Consumers are exercising their proactive choice to limit exposure risk. In turn, the increased market demand has helped accelerate the development of many new gluten-free alternative products and has opened peoples' eyes to many naturally gluten-free foods that are just as appetizing and nutritious as their traditional peers. The approach helps to keep inflammation and overall risk low, without sacrificing quality.

ALLERGENS AND INFLAMMAGING

Possibly the most familiar hallmark of aging, widespread inflammation interferes with many functional organs and systems and accelerates the aging process, earning its name; Inflammaging. Low-grade inflammation is normal and slowly rises naturally with age, but the extra burden of negative lifestyle factors increases our levels of overall inflammation and exponentially accelerates the aging process throughout the body. Common triggers of inflammation are allergens. Be they foodborne or environment, they trigger our immune systems to release cytokines into our bloodstream to try and contain the allergen invasion.

Acute food allergies are evidenced by obvious symptoms like nausea, swelling, flushing, itching, and hives. These reactions are a response to a chemical disruption within the body that has dramatically altered homeostasis (balance) evidenced by hormonal upsets and a hyperimmune response. In contrast, asymptomatic sensitivities operate covertly, managed by the innate and adaptive immune systems without our awareness.

As we age, the cellular communication systems naturally weaken and gradually struggle to maintain homeostasis. We can think of our auditory communication decay as a proxy for what goes on between cells. Early hearing difficulties typically involve issues with differentiating sounds. A relaxed dinner conversation between two people at home is clear and efficient. The same conversation becomes strained when located in a busy restaurant. We find ourselves missing certain words and guessing what the other person stated:

"Can you find my hat?" heard as "Can you find my cat?"

"A man is working outside." Heard as "A man is lurking outside."

"I'll pick you up at four." Heard as "I'll pick you up at the door."

These are innocent examples that trigger confusion and incorrect actions.

A natural response is to raise our speaking volume. In doing so, the conversation extends beyond the intended recipient and is broadcast to others seated nearby, akin to an overactive immune response. This causes others to raise the volume of their conversation, further increasing the ambient noise and making the information exchange even more challenging.

Our endocrine system (organs that make and release hormones) is a complex communication system that involves several hormones working in parallel, the way a team works together to perform many complex tasks. It helps cells identify themselves, the same way we identify ourselves in a mirror. This is known as autocrine signaling.

Another form is gap signaling, like handing a business card to someone. Our hormones also possess paracrine signaling, which is like asking the people seated next to us for advice on ordering food. The fourth is endocrine signaling, which broadcasts signals throughout the body via our bloodstream. A proxy for endocrine signaling would be to call out to the waiter across the room for a menu. Everyone hears the message but only the waiter responds, knowing he/she was the intended target. Endocrine system signaling concepts are illustrated in Figure 34.

Figure 34: Chemical (Hormone) Signaling

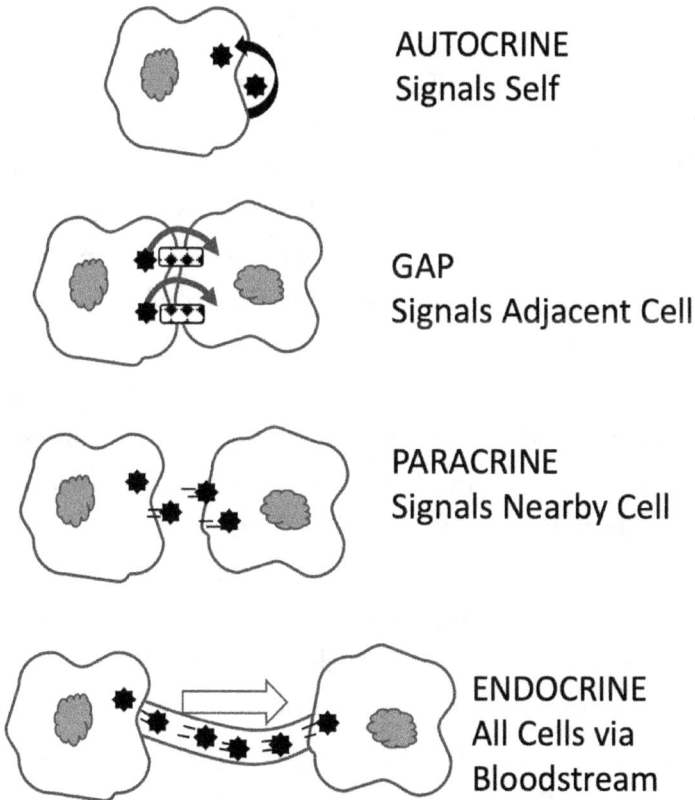

AUTOCRINE
Signals Self

GAP
Signals Adjacent Cell

PARACRINE
Signals Nearby Cell

ENDOCRINE
All Cells via
Bloodstream

Our cells talk with each other in several ways, and even to themselves.

Inflammaging diminishes all of these signaling systems, but it isn't only age that causes inflammation. Allergens also cause inflammation. Earmuffs on a much younger adult are going to result in the same communication challenges. This is analogous to what occurs when we hear the term early-onset age-related disease.

With that analogy in mind, we can go back to the conversation and mistaken words. The same thing occurs within our bodies, except that it is chemical molecules that the body uses to communicate. This can lead to molecular mimicry – a case of mistaken identity, leading to an inability to differentiate between friend and foe. Imagine the challenge banks faced trying to manage security during the COVID pandemic, when innocent customers suddenly donned the traditional face coverings of bank robbers. Not surprisingly, bank robbers seized the opportunity and robberies increased, as banks faced the heightened challenge of differentiating friend from foe.

This is similar to what goes on within our bodies when inflammation impedes our immune system's ability to differentiate friend from foe. Just as we experienced during the pandemic, extra measures were put in place in response to perceived threats, which slowed down multiple functions across the systems of society.

What happens when molecules from gluten or dairy cause asymptomatic sensitivities? Initially, the immune system can manage them, but with constant exposure, eventually, it grows weary of the constant battle and its ability to differentiate between gluten or dairy-associated molecules wanes, and it begins attacking human cells that look surprisingly similar, notably thyroid and joint cells. For people with high sensitivity, this can progress to allergy status in childhood. Those with moderate sensitivity may not experience symptoms until midlife, while those with low sensitivity may present with complex chronic diseases in later years.

Chronic AutoD symptoms cover a wide range, including abdominal pain, anxiety, bloating, brain fog, diarrhea, fatigue, headaches, heartburn, joint pain, nausea, rashes, aches, weight gain, allergies, and fatigue. Lupus, Hashimoto's, Rheumatoid Arthritis, Fibromyalgia, Chronic Fatigue, and Multiple Sclerosis are common examples of advanced AutoDs. Thyroid dysfunction, specifically Hypothyroidism is pervasive, with Levothyroxine being the second most prescribed drug in America. Most physicians view Hypothyroidism and other AutoDs as medically-managed diseases, but for specialists, the first line of treatment is eliminating the food triggers to quiet the hyper-immune response. Tackling it at the source reduces or eliminates the need for medication, and offers the body a chance to heal itself.

For those with mild food allergies, the prudent action is to limit the dose and exposure frequency. Given how common food allergies have become, the same strategy seems prudent for anyone looking to extend their health. Some of the most common food allergens:

- Wheat
- Milk
- Crustacean shellfish (e.g., crab, lobster, shrimp)
- Peanuts

As with all lifestyle choices, it comes down to risk versus reward, and it underscores the importance of quality and variety in our diet. Quality ensures we are eating clean-sourced foods, limiting food-borne toxins (including pesticides) that play havoc with our endocrine and immune systems. Variety naturally reduces exposure to individual allergens and increases our nutrient intake diversity.

We don't need to villainize these foods. Just practicing diligence that aligns with our health goals improves our odds of better outcomes. For the general public, wheat is an important food to address. Between the gluten allergen, high glycemic index, high glycemic load, high carbohydrate values, and pesticide residues, reducing wheat has many health upsides, including easier weight management.

Dose and exposure matter to all things in nature and are deserving of our respect. The bonus is that the same smart, proactive habits that help protect us from AutoDs are the same as the ones that help protect us from heart disease, diabetes, dementia, Parkinson's, and many other diseases.

HOMEOSTASIS

Health is the state of equilibrium. A sailboat floats on water, balancing multiple forces. Buoyant forces keep it from sinking. Wind pushes the sail against the friction of the hull moving in the water. The boat's tilt is balanced by the ballast in the hull and keel while allowing wind to spill off the trailing edge of the sail. A rudder imparts a torque to steer the direction while the keel helps resist the boat from sliding sideways across the water.

When everything is in balance, sailing is a beautiful and amazingly efficient experience, but balance is never static. Small changes in wind speed and direction call for ongoing small adjustments to keep on course. Once distracted and blown off-line, it takes far more effort to bring a boat back on course than it did to hold it there. Airplanes operate on many of these same principles. In living organisms, this balancing act is what's known as homeostasis.

Human homeostasis is infinitely complex, with a network of interdependent autopilot functions designed to persistently track us toward health. Some auto-balancing actions we can detect:

- Sleep to address fatigue
- Perspiration to counteract overheating
- Reduced blood flow to legs and arms to protect our core organs from the cold

- Elevated heart rate to deliver more blood to support physical exertion
- Signals to urinate when the bladder is full
- Signals to eat when the body senses hunger
- Local inflammation to stabilize a cut or sprain
- Elevated body temperature (fever) to kill pathogenic microbes

These are but a few of the thousands of compensatory actions the body simultaneously undertakes to maintain homeostasis every minute of wakefulness and sleep, constantly working to bring us toward optimal health, like making new proteins, enzymes, molecules, and cells while clearing away toxins and debris from accumulating, and maintaining healthy fluid levels in our blood, organs, and cells. Along with each organ, every system of the body is involved in managing homeostasis:

- Cardiovascular system
- Respiratory system
- Integumentary system
- Sympathetic and parasympathetic immune systems
- Nervous system
- Endocrine system
- Renal system
- Lymphatic system
- Digestive system
- Reproductive system
- Skeletal system
- Muscular system
- And more...

When we think of extending healthspan, we tend to think of it in terms of maintaining physical and mental abilities, but it is really by maintaining homeostasis that our bodies can continue to perform the tasks we describe as healthy living. Healthspan then, is the outcome of extending homeostasis, and to do that, we need to preserve optimal signaling communications. Lifestyle choices dramatically impact homeostasis, and as such, dramatically influence healthspan.

Homeostasis infers both upper and lower limits. High blood pressure (hypertension) places too much stress on our vascular system, but low blood pressure carries the risk of not supplying adequate blood to the brain and other organs. Other familiar examples of homeostasis include body temperature, blood pH, osmolality, sodium, and other minerals levels, and many more that fall within the 3 main systems of homeostasis: Thermoregulation, Osmoregulation, and Chemical regulation. These are complex systems unto themselves, and thankfully supporting homeostasis is a lot simpler than understanding it.

LEVERAGING INNATE HEALTH

Our advancing knowledge of the root causes of health and disease has impacted traditional medicine in many ways. The days of sledge-hammer medicine and sterilizing everything in sight are being displaced by precision medicine and methods that support the body's natural drive and innate capacity to heal itself. It has helped spawn an approach to medicine known as Lifestyle Medicine and Functional Medicine. These doctors specialize in getting to the root cause of disease and leverage the body's innate healing strengths. Lifestyle Medicine and Functional Medicine doctors have completed all of the traditional medical schooling. In addition, they have specialized certification from either the American College of Lifestyle Medicine or the Institute of Functional Medicine. As such, they have more treatment options at their disposal, many of them more powerful and more sustainable than pharmaceuticals. It's largely about helping the body get back to a state of homeostasis, where it wants to be anyway.

A lifestyle approach is frequently described as getting out of our own way. At some point, we've all been lost and battled with the choice of continuing our current path, changing direction, or pulling over to seek help. Feeling lost or frustrated should be our cue to take a pause and look for a proactive approach that offers a long-term solution. Part of the experience is growing our health awareness and learning to trust and work with the healing process versus trying to overpower it.

Lifestyle and Functional doctors are more likely to prescribe a prebiotic over a pharmaceutical for a gut issue resulting from a microbiota imbalance. Similarly, they are more likely to prescribe specific exercise activities and methods to manage stress. Some offices have a dietician on staff and some even provide cooking classes for patients. These doctors appeal to anyone who would rather adopt healthier habits than rely heavily on medications for the rest of their lives.

Our desire to intervene and take action is human nature but so is our tendency to take shortcuts. Very few therapeutic (pharmaceutical) treatments are as immediately effective as taking an Aspirin or a Tylenol® for a headache. Our expectations around the power of pharmaceuticals are set early in life, so the default approach to the headache is to take a pill rather than take measures to prevent the next one from happening. Proton pump inhibitors (PPIs) are the 6th most prescribed drugs, used to treat symptoms of gastroesophageal reflux disease (GERD). PPI's are minimally effective and come with the risk of serious side effects over long-term use, such as hip fracture, pneumonia, C. Difficile, and are associated with a 33% higher risk of dementia.

Investing in addressing the root cause versus decades of treating the symptoms can have a tremendous impact on healthspan. GERD was something I struggled with for several years and ultimately ended my endurance athletics. A long investigative search ultimately led to restoring my gut health which finally resolved the GERD and proved pivotal in my health revolution. I've since enjoyed cycling and running more than ever, free of the worry of gut discomfort.

Long thought of as a bacterial cesspool, the gut is now understood to be an intelligent microbially DNA-rich entity unto itself, capable of thought and communication at levels still too vast to comprehend. The gut and brain are intimately connected via the vagus nerve, a superhighway that ensures an intimate bidirectional communication between both organs, also known as the gut-brain axis (GBA). In essence, they are both brains. Besides providing a microbial environment for the trillions of essential bacteria, viruses, fungi, and parasites, the gut also holds the enteric nervous system, comprised of over 100 million nerve cells. These nerve cells control everything from swallowing to enzyme release for food breakdown, blood flow, and elimination. Gut health is evidenced by our stool quality and our emotional balance. If either is off, it's a clear indication that the gut needs tending.

Between 30 to 40% of the U.S. population is estimated to be dealing with functional bowel problems, and scientists now know that anxiety and depression are typically the results of gut imbalance. It's nearly impossible to feel great when our gut is in distress. We know this when we deal with acute gastrointestinal issues, but GI distress is often a signal that there are low-level root-cause chronic imbalances crying out for our attention. These are places where Lifestyle and Functional Medicine excel because they understand that health does not exist in the absence of gut health, and they focus on these root causes.

THE HUMAN FOOD PROCESSOR

The gastrointestinal tract is biology's version of human food processing. There are several steps involved in preparing food nutrients for ingestion. Food ultimately gets processed into:

- Macronutrients (protein, carbohydrates, and fat, all broken down further to amino acids, sugars, fatty acids, and glycerol, respectively)
- Micronutrients (vitamins, minerals, and electrolytes)
- Fiber (consumed by microbes producing short-chain fatty acids)
- Water (absorption into the bloodstream)
- Waste byproducts (stool/feces and urine via the kidneys/bladder)

The time for all of this to occur varies by individual and by their diet. A fiber-rich diet typically results in roughly a 24-hour transit time, while a low-fiber diet can be much longer. Defecation (poop) frequency of fiber-rich diets typically ranges from 1-3 times daily, varying by individual. Low-fiber diets are associated with lower frequencies, sometimes days between bowel movements – not ideal.

The Gastrointestinal Tract diagram (Figure 35) is instructive in illustrating the gut. We might think of our gut as our stomach but in reality, that's only one stop on a long and winding route that starts at our mouth and ends at our anus.

Figure 35: Gastrointestinal Tract

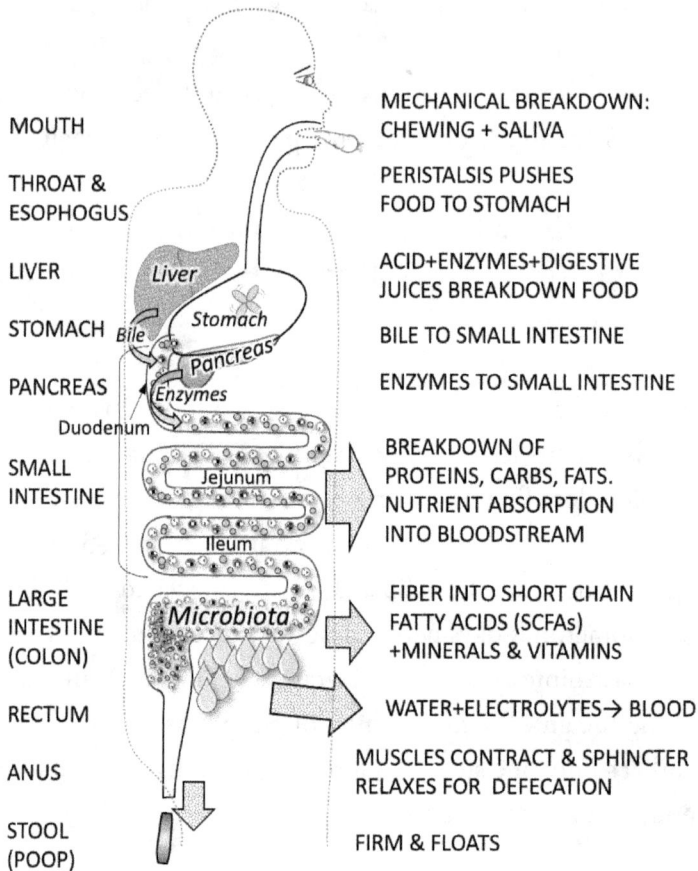

MOUTH	MECHANICAL BREAKDOWN: CHEWING + SALIVA
THROAT & ESOPHOGUS	PERISTALSIS PUSHES FOOD TO STOMACH
LIVER	ACID+ENZYMES+DIGESTIVE JUICES BREAKDOWN FOOD
STOMACH	BILE TO SMALL INTESTINE
PANCREAS	ENZYMES TO SMALL INTESTINE
SMALL INTESTINE	BREAKDOWN OF PROTEINS, CARBS, FATS. NUTRIENT ABSORPTION INTO BLOODSTREAM
LARGE INTESTINE (COLON)	FIBER INTO SHORT CHAIN FATTY ACIDS (SCFAs) +MINERALS & VITAMINS
RECTUM	WATER+ELECTROLYTES → BLOOD
ANUS	MUSCLES CONTRACT & SPHINCTER RELAXES FOR DEFECATION
STOOL (POOP)	FIRM & FLOATS

Liver, Stomach, Bile, Pancreas, Enzymes, Duodenum, Jejunum, Ileum, Microbiota

From food entry to exit, the process of digestion involves several stages that extract nutrients, vitamins, and minerals, while at the same time producing short-chain fatty acids. Its design evolved exclusively on a diet of whole foods.

Our microbiome is now understood to be intimately connected to our health and our diseases. When our operating systems are in balance, our immune system takes care of most threats long before they take hold of us by working in parallel with our microbiota and our endocrine system at the interface of the outside world and our body. In other words, fending off disease occurs routinely, on our skin, eyes, ears, nose, mouth, stomach, intestines, lungs, and sex organs. Each region has a microbiota population comprised of a wellspring of bacteria, viruses, archaea, and fungi ready to protect us against the trillions of common invaders that we share with the environment. Our microbiome possesses hundreds of times more genes than our human cells, which provides a sense of the intelligence of the microorganisms that accompany us through life. They are as important to our survival as oxygen and water.

Our microbiome is analogous to a large workforce operating inside a very large manufacturing facility. We can think of our body as the building and our microbiome as the diverse workforce. An array of over 3,500 microbial species is needed to perform the complex task of processing the wide array of food possibilities. If one group goes out of balance, everything gets impacted.

It's timely here to mention the use of probiotics. Many people are quick to reach for probiotics because they heard it was a good idea to support their microbiome. Even if the probiotic is still living when ingested (many are not), indiscriminately flooding the gut with microbes is reckless health management and likely a waste of money. It would be like a landscaper hiring more workers to cut grass when the reason lawns aren't getting cut is that mowers are in disrepair. It's worse in our bodies because flooding our gut with unneeded microbes crowds out other deficient microbes even more, creating a greater imbalance.

Prebiotics are food for our human microbes, and they are plentiful in fiber-rich, plant-based, whole foods. By ensuring we eat a variety of foods, we are supplying the microbiome with all the diversity it needs. With 100 times more DNA than in our cells, the microbiome is more capable of balancing itself than we could ever hope through some sort of probiotic manipulation. It may take a few weeks to adapt to significant dietary changes, but provided it is fed a variety of quality foods rich in nutrients and fiber, it will reorganize its microbial staff to deliver higher efficiency.

The onection between diet and the microbiome could not be more intimate. Paleo or plant, we evolved to eat a wide range of foods that get to our gut, thanks to several functions carried out by our microbiome. Our small intestine comprises three zones, the duodenum, jejunum, and ileum. It is covered in microvilli that are proficient in absorbing water and digesting nutrients from carbohydrates, fat, and protein. The process slows down significantly in the large intestine where fermentation takes over, and electrolytes, vitamins, and more water are absorbed. Vitamins K and B are produced here as well. Our microbiome drives the fermentation process, consumes undigested complex carbohydrates, lines our intestinal walls with a protective mucosal layer, and helps make enzymes for digestion, along with several other functions. That's why it's helpful to think of fiber, the ultimate prebiotic, as a macronutrient.

ONE CELL BETWEEN US AND THE OUTSIDE WORLD

A one-cell, 5-micrometer-thick membrane is all that separates our blood from everything that enters the mouth. To put that into context, that's about 10 times thinner than human hair. These cells need to be thin to enable vitamins and nutrients to pass through the cell via paracellular and transcellular pathways. In addition to our gut lining being ridiculously thin, it has a massive surface area of about 2,800 square feet. That equals the size of a doubles tennis court! This combination of being microscopically thin and massive in area leaves us far more vulnerable to the outside world through our mouth than through our skin, which is 100 times thicker and 100 times lower surface area.

It gets even more fascinating. Epithelial cells work cooperatively, similar to how the fingers work together when we try and hold water in our hands. We know instinctively to press our fingers together to prevent water from escaping between them and we experience the contact pressure of our fingers communicating with each other to make a seal.

Our gut's epithelial cells behave in the same way, but with more sophistication, (Figure 36). Near the surface, they have Tight Junctions that help them hold onto adjacent cells. They also have Gap Junctions that provide a direct communication link between adjacent cells to ensure they are working as one very large membrane film. Cells stick to each other by very weak adhesion by surrounding forces. It's an incredibly delicate system that can be easily damaged by a poor diet.

Figure 36: Nutrient Transport Across the Intestine

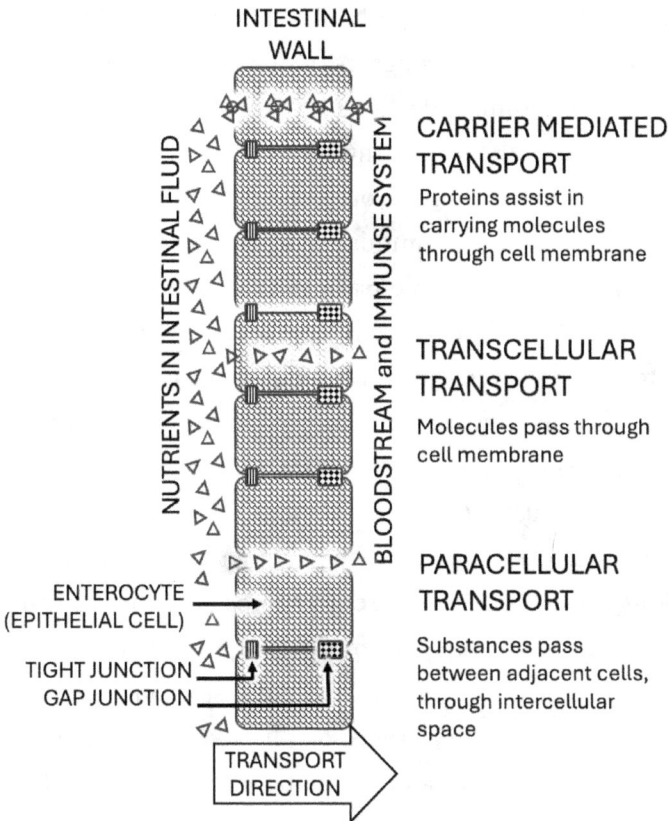

Nutrients normally pass through the cell wall of the intestine either by carrier mediated transport (assisted) or transcellular transport (unassisted). A loss of integrity in the cell wall results in paracellular transport, whereby nutrients pass unobstructed into the blood stream, along with bad actors.

ALL DISEASE BEGINS IN THE GUT

In about 400 BC, Hippocrates stated, "All disease begins in the gut." It is slightly overstated, but certainly, most chronic diseases initiate with the gut. Heart disease, dementia, neuromuscular diseases, and most AutoDs point back to gut dysfunction connections to food. Evidence is never as clean and obvious as we'd all like to see, but the common denominator is the gut.

Earlier we looked at how the epithelial membrane of our gut works when things are in balance. Understanding how delicate this membrane is that separates our bodies from the outside world, it's no surprise that it can go through periods of lost barrier integrity and dysfunction. A common dysfunction is what is often referred to as Leaky Gut, or more correctly, Intestinal Permeability.

Small amounts of Zonulin open the tight junctions between cells just slightly, allowing the immune system to send out frontline soldiers to surround and disable pathogens associated with the food in the intestine. This is a perfectly appropriate response to maintain homeostasis. However, stress, alcohol, sugar, gluten, and common pesticides all trigger *excess* Zonulin production and result in greater porosity in the gut lining. Glyphosate, (active ingredient in Roundup®), is not only used as a herbicide, but it is used as a desiccant on wheat to accelerate harvesting. The glyphosate residue, in combination with gluten, further increases the porosity of the epithelial membrane. Instead of selected nutrients passing normally via transcellular or carrier-mediated transport, partially digested nutrients breach the bloodstream by paracellular transport. It's like the dam breaking and undigested food particles and toxins flood indiscriminately through the cracks in the dam.

This leakage triggers an intense immune response. Instead of sending out small, isolated, tactical squads, the breach results in a full and intense immune response. Daily exposure over months and years eventually leads to immune dysfunction. The immune system loses its ability to differentiate with precision, resulting in downstream functional breakdowns. Many autoimmune diseases discussed earlier trace back to intestinal permeability and the associated immune dysfunction.

We know that diet and lifestyle matter a lot, and making a conscious effort to respect our design operating limits is an obvious first step. Some diseases show quick responses, others take more time to see change, and some need a metabolic reboot to rest the immune system and provide it with an opportunity to relearn normal function.

Recall that the brain has a similar barrier system to the gut. It's no surprise that we see similar barrier permeability across the brain endothelium, causing the brain's immune system to go into overdrive. The consequences for the brain are harder to study but generally contribute to early-onset age-related cognitive decline and are known to be associated with neurogenerative diseases like Alzheimer's.

Gut homeostasis is core to health. The immune and endocrine systems, and the microbiota all work together using complex signaling that makes today's microchips look like something out of a Flintstones cartoon. Thinking about this in terms of the root cause of health, we have an innate defense system capable of automatically putting down millions of threats that come with common whole food sources. It's when we deviate from the design of health and insult it with pesticides, toxins, processed foods, and unbalanced diets that homeostasis is lost, triggering a series of negative consequences. Repeated exposure leads to disease and accelerated aging.

BYPASS PROCESSING

Earlier we looked at normal, healthy, human food processing through the gastrointestinal tract, and we touched on the consequences of environmental toxins in our food. The other big issue we've witnessed is when the normal digestion process gets short-circuited by sugars and processed foods. Unlike other species on the planet, humans evolved with the capability to survive on an amazingly wide-ranging diet. But, surviving and thriving are at opposing ends of the healthspan spectrum.

Aligned with the wide range of foods, are the stages of digestion in our gastrointestinal tract. Short, simple food molecules (sugars) break down first, and the fiber in complex carbohydrates is one of the last to digest. Sweet substitutes jump the line, short-circuiting the normal processing steps developed over millions of years. High and ultra-processed foods cause similar upsets. Stripping out the fiber during processing changes everything. Add chemical food agents into the mix and it becomes mayhem. Flashback to the famous scene of Lucille Ball working at the candy factory when the production line got sped up and it soon became a mayhem.

KAY'S DECADE'S LONG BATTLE WITH FIBROMYALGIA

At age 26, Kay was a rising Ph.D. Organic Chemist making a name for herself in the global chemical industry when Fibromyalgia swept in and stole the healthy active life she had been living. It got so bad that she needed help with the most menial tasks, like brushing her teeth. Determined to get her life back, she researched and learned that exercise helped produce endorphins, which eased the pain, and over the next 20 years was able to use daily running as a means to lead a normal life. Over time, however, her immune function weakened, the fibromyalgia symptoms returned, and she developed hypothyroidism with a TSH of 48, ten times the normal level. At age 50, and fearing a lifetime of medication (Levothyroxine and pain management), Kay threw herself back into the latest research on the microbiome and the role of gut health and found immediate improvement. For someone focused on exercise, it underlined that exercise had its limitations, and that there was a direct connection between food quality and health. It caused her to focus on cleaning up her diet, removing gluten, and shifting to an organic, Whole Food Plant Based (WFPB) diet. Looking back she said, *"I had no idea I was part of the problem, helping put many of these chemicals out into the environment that have contributed so strongly to the sickness we see around us."*

Anecdotal stories like Kay's are common, but unfortunately, re-coveries are rare. While the data underscores that a WFPB approach is best for most of us, how much of it needs to be plants and or-ganic comes down to the individual. Beyond the damage we know that pesticides cause to the soil, water, and wildlife, we know it does nothing beneficial for the human microbiome. For some, it's hard to detect a near-term difference from eliminating inflammatory insults like pesticides, while for others like Kay, it makes an acute difference. Optimally, we want to reduce the uncertainty and choose the best quality, nutrient-dense, high-fiber foods we can reasonably get our hands on every day.

THE ENDOCRINE WIZARD

The master communication system for our body is the endocrine sys-tem. What little attention it gets is usually in reference to our happy, sad, and stress hormones. There are over 100 hormones, several of which scientists don't yet understand. Scientists know that hormones are supremely important, and that many of them seem to work to-gether in transient combinations, but they are a long way from un-derstanding what needs to be known to influence health. It might be described as watching football for the first time, only over 100 teams are playing on one field with 100 balls in play, and it's all happening simultaneously. Many hormones act like wizards and are very challenging to understand. Familiar hormones like cortisol, serotonin, melatonin, progesterone, testosterone, estrogen, insulin, T3/T4 thyroid, HGH, and somatotropin growth hormones are the most studied. Still, there are so many more, and it's clear they communicate in ways beyond current comprehension.

Endocrinology is a latecomer in modern medicine. We know that hormones play a central role in diabetes, thyroid and pituitary function, some cancers, and osteoporosis, but again, these are relatively new fields of study and it's going to take decades to build the scientific knowledge to learn beyond this handful of diseases. Making headway in understanding the far-reaching roles of all our other hormones on human health is still years away. There are currently about 50 persons working in cardiology for every 1 person in endocrinology. We know that the immune system is integral to coronary heart and stroke disease, the number one cause of early death. We also know that the endocrine system is intimately tied to immune function. Yet, none of these fields of medical science are working together in any substantive way. It speaks to our funding barriers and how early we still are in our understanding.

A REASONABLE APPROACH

We could wait until scientists sort it all out, but that's likely lifetimes away in many cases, even with the help of Artificial Intelligence. The most reasonable approach today appears to be one of practical caution.

We know with certainty that many of the toxins we are exposed to in our food, air, and water have some ability to disrupt endocrine function. We don't yet have the scientific understanding to know our individual risk tolerance, but it would be naïve to assume we aren't at risk. We know this because chemicals have regulatory safety thresholds. Testing has shown measurable negative health consequences for known doses, and so regulatory bodies like the EPA and FDA apply factors to limit exposure doses to what are believed to be safe doses for the majority of human and animal life. These thresholds, however, don't consider a cumulative effect of ALL of the endocrine disruptors to which we are exposed. And, each substance is only tested in isolation, not in combination, so we have no knowledge of the reactions and synergies that occur in the environment or within our bodies. The unfortunate reality is that safety tests are incredibly simplistic and conducted in sterile laboratories under ideal control. Evidence is mounting that real-world health is in trouble and regulators can't begin to envision a way to find answers to which of the thousands of toxins are to blame.

The evidence points us to limit exposure, but where and by how much? Populations that breathe higher pollution, drink contaminated water, and work around naturally occurring toxins, predictably experience more disease and live shortened lives. It's hard to say which toxin did most of the damage or why it affected some more than others, and without damning evidence against one, all the approved toxins get a free pass. Frequency data in geographic hotspots informs us with certainty that humans are vulnerable to very low-level environmental exposures, but we only learn the real thresholds after the fact, through experience, i.e. disease and death statistics.

I've zeroed in on food in this chapter because it's easier to see obvious examples of inputs versus outputs, but the same approach applies across the Mind, Environment, Diet, Activity, and Community (MEDAC) playbook. They all impact our health through body chemistry, signaling, and inflammaging.

FINAL THOUGHTS

- Real-world data is king, and by real-world that means "my health data." Trying to make sense of the confusion and public dogma is wasted time and energy.
- Personal health data is our guide to what works best for us, and we must be willing to get the data, consider what it is telling us, and adjust our actions accordingly.
- Focus on feeding our microbiome with a diverse variety of whole, fiber-rich food
- Limit the burden environmental food toxins place on our gut and immune systems by choosing clean foods whenever possible
- Live empowered in the knowledge that we've tipped the odds of extended healthspan in our favor

We live in an era when industrial science has resulted in us being lab rats in thousands of ongoing unintended experiments on humans. Declining participation in the experiment is not feasible, but there are numerous practical and sensible steps we can take to substantially reduce our exposure over our remaining years, thereby enhancing our chances of achieving and maintaining our Whealthspan.

Chapter 13

THE Q.V. FOOD FRAMEWORK

Denise's Surprise
"My father died of heart disease, and now I'm caring for my mother with dementia. It took seeing my mother's decline to finally wake up to life. I recently switched to a plant-based diet, and my LDL-Cholesterol dropped more than 50 points. I'd secretly hoped the plant-based thing was all a hoax, but there was no denying the data. It was empowering and made me realize that I have much more influence over my health trajectory. I've become more curious and enthusiastic about life than I ever was before."

Denise and I met while waiting for a plane. She was intelligent and invested, but confused and uncertain about what to do next. The diet shift and subsequent drop in LDL were powerful evidence of the connection between food choices and health biomarkers, but it also raised many questions. Her curiosity was aroused. She had a renewed sense of empowerment, and could begin to envision a different path than her parents'. Flipping the "diet switch" was her doorway into a range of equally important, life-changing outcomes.

WHERE AM I?
For all the dietary confusion that has persisted for decades, never have we had such easy access to so many great options.
- Abundant access to clean, fresh, and frozen foods
- Healthy options for every budget
- Access to foods from across the world

- Labeling that informs us what's inside packaged foods
- Thousands of delicious healthy recipes for every palate at our fingertips

We can and should leverage that to our benefit. With a little help, most of us can begin making significant shifts in relatively short time frames. However, diet is one of those areas we are quick to make assumptions, so it's important that we place our current vocabulary and habits into context. Take a couple of minutes to write down short answers for future reference. No worries, it's not a test.

1. What does the word "diet" mean?
2. What makes something a whole food?
3. What does "quality food" mean?
4. How often do I find myself making excuses for my food choices?
5. What is the source of my diet knowledge?
6. How vested am I in my current dietary habits?
7. How have my eating habits changed over time?
8. Are my food choices influenced by balancing the desires of others?
9. Are my food choices biased toward flavor, fullness, or health?
10. How do I use food as a reward?

Thousands of books have been written on diets. All but a recent few are outdated, based on what is known today, but we need not be dismayed. With some relatively simple frameworks, food decisions don't have to be as hard as they've been made out to be, and we can easily improve many favorite recipes with some knowledge updates and a little experimenting. There are many ways to eat well, and the more we learn, the better choices we make. There is no finish line in Diet-IQ, just constant curiosity and learning.

Countless studies have debated seemingly endless questions around food, but if I can distill it down to three words, they would be: Quality, Variety, and Fiber. David Katz, MD, coined the phrase, *"Love the food that loves you back,"* and simply targeting quality, variety, and fiber in our food choices sets us up for easy success. It's much easier to understand what those three words mean than what's involved in understanding and trying to follow prescribed diet plans. And, it's easily sustained.

Figure 37: Love The Food That Loves You Back

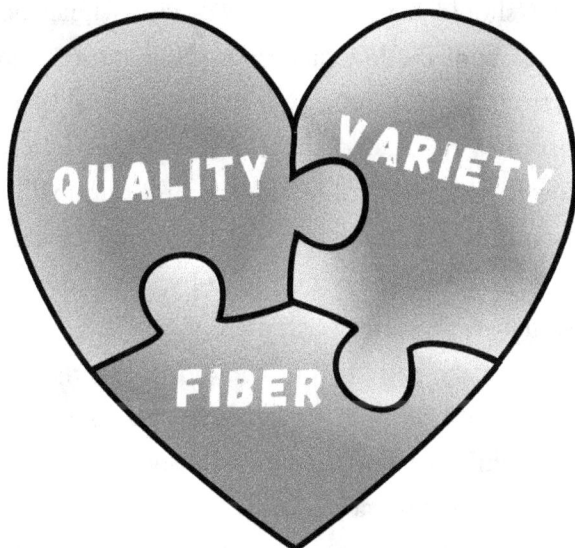

THE Q.V. FOOD FRAMEWORK

Mary cornered me after class one day, looking for help to understand why her cholesterol had risen sharply over the past year. *"I've been eating largely Vegan for several years and haven't made any significant lifestyle changes. I'm quite concerned, and my doctor is recommending I start taking a statin drug. I'd really like to avoid doing that, if possible."* We agreed to defer further conversation until after next week's class on nutrition. Sure enough, she was at the front of the line after class, wearing a big smile, bursting to tell me some news. *"I think I know what's happened. I've been buying those vegan cheeses, ice cream, and beyond burgers, not realizing how high they were in total and saturated fats compared to the other meatless burgers, or how much processing went into making them."* Three months later she reached out, relieved that her lab results had returned to normal and feeling back in control of her health.

More and more we're seeing "Plant-Based" appearing on food labels. This almost always means that they've been processed, a lot or a little, and should never be confused with whole foods. They tend to have many of the low-quality food substitutes and additives for which packaged foods are so well known. As a side note, not all meatless substitutes are created equal. Several of the lesser-advertised brands are low in saturated fat, low in sodium, minimally processed, and quite tasty. It doesn't mean they should be an everyday food, but overall, rank well above the famous, high-hype brands and fit into a high-quality, high-variety, fiber-rich diet.

For all the dietary patterns out there, the experts agree on two simple principles: quality and variety. From plants to beef, sacrificing quality undermines every diet ever published. Admittedly there is confusion on what quality means, and we'll get into that, but simply pausing to consider the quality of any food decision brings a lot of things into alignment, requiring almost no time or effort. Choose any popular diet, and its health opportunity is only as good as the quality and variety of the foods we put into it. What's offered here is NOT another diet. We'd eliminate a lot of confusion by tossing at least half of them away. Instead, think of this as a food framework to draw from when building meals for an infinite number of possibilities.

There are abundant vegan foods that we all know are ultra-processed and unhealthy. Similarly, grocery store-packed meats are typically vastly inferior to regenerative-farmed animals. Vegetables pulled fresh from our garden might not look as pretty, but they are far richer in nutrients and likely free from pesticide residue, compared with the ones picked prematurely and shipped thousands of miles. Given a side-by-side choice, most of us have little difficulty identifying the higher-quality food option. It's usually just a question of whether higher quality is worth the higher price.

Quality can often be described in terms of a food's simplicity. A carrot grown in a home garden started as a seed planted by hand, likely watered every few days, and traveled just a few feet from the garden to the table. The grocer's carrot was likely planted by heavy machinery, sprayed for bugs, weeds, and fungi, and watered with elaborate sprinkler systems. It was then picked with other heavy equipment, washed, sorted, bundled, placed in large containers, and shipped hundreds if not thousands of miles over several days until eventually getting to the grocer, where it sat for another few days until being picked up, carried home and stored in the fridge. Even if it wasn't treated with pesticides, it still can't compare to the nutrient levels in fresh-picked carrots. It's not to say that we all have to grow our own food, but rather, that we can easily understand the benefit of locally grown vs shipped in bulk. The fewer the steps from seed to plate, the higher the quality.

While most big U.S. farms still grow with what's referred to as "conventional" methods, using aggressive chemical herbicides, pesticides, and fungicides, Regenerative Organic farming is taking root across the globe. Grimmway Farms in Bakersfield, California, for example, reports itself to be the largest organic grower in the U.S., growing more than 45,000 acres of organic carrots annually. The quality, production, and pricing of organic foods are constantly improving, making buying decisions easier every day. Given the economic benefits to growers, that trend is expected to continue. Some progressive grocers have stopped offering certain conventional products, which saves them the cost of having to carry both organic and conventional, freeing up more shelf space for a wider variety of food offerings. Committed organic grocers are now rivaling the prices of conventional so-called budget grocers on highly nutritional products like frozen fruit. They are able to offer organic for nearly as low a price as conventional, chemical-based farmed fruit.

Clean diets, consuming whole and minimally processed foods, that are relatively free from synthetic chemicals, tend to promote easier weight management and less stress around calories. It is believed this has to do with not interfering with the endocrine and immune systems as well as overburdening the kidneys and the liver with toxins. Because it isn't ethical to purposefully expose people to toxins, these aren't the types of studies that can be done in random controlled trials (RCTs), but the science grows more convincing every year. It shouldn't really surprise us that our bodies are constantly having to process these low-level food-borne toxins, and that some of us are facing chronic health consequences as a result. Recall that "safe" is a relative term in the food industry. It more closely aligns with acute threats like food poisoning that cause most of us to get sick if ingested one time. The effects of low levels that "might" affect some of us over many years are beyond current abilities to measure, and the regulators have no human monitoring programs in place.

On a positive note, we're continuing to better understand the quality ranges within the many food groups. Just as all proteins are not the same, all meats are not the same. Feedlots, which supply 85% of US beef, retain cattle in confined paddocks with a density of about

100 head per acre where they are fed primarily corn, supplemented with other grains and hormones. Antibiotics are necessary to protect the unnaturally crowded population from disease, up until a withdrawal period just prior to slaughter. It's an industrial approach to growing beef with a priority on low cost.

By comparison, pasture-raised, 100% grass-fed, and finished cattle occupy a nominal density of about 1 head per acre. (Feedlot corn acreage is delivered to the feedlot, so the land-use comparison requires a more detailed explanation than we need to get into.) Antibiotics and hormones aren't typically required, because the conditions are naturally healthier, and the feed is natural grazing grains. The priority is measurable product quality. Many important differences can be measured, as seen in the comparison between Grass-fed and Conventional ground beef, performed by Allen Williams, PhD, Understanding AG, found in Table 2.

Pricing research suggests about a 40-50% premium for 100% grass-fed over conventional beef. Note that there are also mid-range cattle that are feedlot but only grass-finished.

It's long been known that wild and pasture-raised ruminant animals tend to be healthier than industrially grown meat. Regenerative farming practices reflect a composite of the best of science, quality, and managed supply. These reflect the best practices in farming, where the livestock deposit minerals back into the soil, where organic crops can thrive in the next growing season. We can expect to see Regenerative Livestock appear on labels at some point.

Table 2: Grass-fed and Conventional Ground Beef Nutritional Comparison

NUTRIENT	Grass-fed Ground Beef (8oz)	Conventional Ground Beef (8oz)
Calories	432	568
Protein	43 g	38 g
Total Fat	28 g	44 g
Saturated Fat	12 g	16 g
Omega-3 Fat	200 mg	108 mg
Omega 6:3	3:1	35:1
Vitamin E	0.8 mg	0.4 mg
Vitamin K	2.4 mcg	1 mcg
Niacin	18 mg	9.6 mg
Folate	28 mcg	16 mcg
Vitamin B12	4.8 mcg	1.7 mcg
CLA- conjugated linoleic acid	0.72%	0.33%

THE FIXER

Chasing diet perfection ensures constant frustration and disappointment. Though well-intentioned, it is fatally flawed from the outset. There is however a secret weapon in our arsenal with unrivaled power that levels up all diet pursuits… fiber. Fiber has the rare and distinguished ability to fix many common diet flaws in ways that bely its humble reputation. Fiber isn't glitzy. It's cheap, and often the discards of the industrial food processors. It's so cheap that it's nearly impossible for companies to make money selling fiber, so it's no wonder the food industry pays fiber so little attention. Their loss is our win.

As much as our gut needs an array of foods to cover the gamut of nutrients our body craves, fiber is its foundational food. It feeds on a steady diet of soluble fiber, the kind that breaks down during digestion. It helps in regulating blood sugar, naturally lowering LDL cholesterol by binding small cholesterol particles, acts as a prebiotic, and promotes a healthier stool. In the gut, it helps protect the mucosal layer that lines our intestine, protecting the epithelial cells from damage and leaky gut, as we discussed earlier. Its importance to functional health cannot be overstated.

Grains, fruit, and vegetables are the main sources of dietary fiber, but only when it hasn't been stripped away. A great example to look at is in grains, particularly bread. A grain comprises a fiber-dense bran shell, a nutrient-rich germ, and the starchy endosperm. White bread flour processing discards the bran and germ, leaving just the starchy endosperm. This is what gives white bread its bright white appearance and light fluffy texture. It is cake without the icing. As a result, white bread typically only has about one gram of fiber per serving.

At the quality end of the bread spectrum is whole-grain bread. Whole grain means just what it says, all the grain, including the bran, endosperm, and germ. It is darker in color, and less fluffy, but typically packs about five grams of fiber. That's 5 times white bread!

Multigrain bread is the tricky one. It's usually coated in whole grain seeds, leading us to assume it must be loaded with whole grains and fiber. The fiber content of multigrain bread will vary by producer, but frequently contains no more fiber than white bread. It's the whole-grain flour that delivers the fiber, not the decorative topping.

It is a great example of the importance of taking a moment to read the food label.

According to the National Health and Nutrition Examination Survey (NHANES), conducted by the Centers for Disease Control and Prevention (CDC), the average daily fiber intake for American adults is just 15 grams for men and 13.5 grams for women. That's less than half our average fiber intake in 1960. The drop in fiber since 1960 coincides with the rise in meat consumption – meat has no fiber and much higher caloric density than plants. The American College of Lifestyle Medicine's meal plan promotes 55-75 grams per day, given many studies demonstrating fiber's heart benefits. That says the average American would benefit from 2-4 times their current fiber intake.

Fiber is also effective in building and sustaining satiety, the sensation of feeling comfortably full, helping to avoid overeating and excess caloric intake. It's so simple, so powerful, so effective, and so inexpensive, that it's almost deserving of its own superhero status.

Fiber is found broadly across Whole Food Plant-Based (WFPB) options and is one of the key reasons why WFPB eating is, without question, associated with longevity. Chia seeds and ground flax seeds are two of the most effective ways to jumpstart daily fiber intake. Beans, lentils, berries, almonds, apples, quinoa, and several additional inexpensive foods are all packed with fiber. Check out my Oatmeal and Granola recipes at the end of this chapter for help starting a Fiber-Fab day.

There has never been a longevity-promoting diet in recorded human history that didn't include significant quantities of fiber. Several studies have looked at longevity diets that naturally vary by food availability in each region, but typically overlooked the one thing they all have in common, fiber! Interestingly, fiber is also prominent in the Bredesen Protocol, which is used to treat Alzheimer's patients.

FIBER, THE SILVER BULLET

If there's a dietary silver bullet, fiber stands head and shoulders above all contenders. It's partly due to the fiber itself, and the nutritional benefits it drags along with it, because fiber is found in so many high-value foods.

These are some of the biggest studies ever performed on dietary impact on lifespan outcomes. They looked at several million deaths, each one coming to the same findings:

- A 2021 study looked at 3,512,828 subjects in 64 studies and found that increased fiber reduced all-cause deaths by 23% and by 33% for those with an underlying disease.
- A more detailed, follow-up study on this the same found that fiber from nuts and seeds reduced the risk of CVD-related death by 43 %, comparing total fiber intake from a low of 9.2 to a high of 28.2 grams per day. That is still below the American College of Lifestyle Medicine's meal plan recommended of 55-75 grams per day.
- A 2019 metanalysis reviewed almost 135 million person-years of data from 185 prospective studies and 58 clinical trials with 4,635 adult participants and concluded that for every additional 8 grams of dietary fiber consumed, the risk of dying from cardiac disease, stroke, type 2 diabetes, and/or colon cancer fell by another 5-27%.
- A 2015 study looked at nearly one million deaths between 1997 and 2014 and found a 10% reduction in death risk for each 10-g/day increase in fiber intake.

The magnitude and impact of those numbers tower over the studies that hit the headlines. Unfortunately, studies like this don't benefit from industry marketing promotion and don't feed controversy. They're simply too big and too convincing to try and debate.

Thankfully for us, there are plenty of ways to incorporate fiber just by paying attention to fiber content in our food.

GLYCEMIC INDEX – GLYCEMIC LOAD

Both the glycemic index and glycemic load are useful tools for understanding the impact of various foods on blood sugar levels. It is especially important for those with diabetes or insulin resistance but has value for anyone wanting to promote metabolic health.

Sugar is naturally present in many whole foods, but the rate it is absorbed into our blood is dependent on the fiber and carbohydrates present in the food. The Glycemic Index (GI) opened the window to explaining this, but GI has largely been replaced by Glycemic Load (GL). Glycemic Load considers both the speed and the amount of that rise. Glycemic Load provides a more realistic impact of a specific food on blood sugar levels.

Foods with a lower GL yield a lower blood sugar spike, helping to protect insulin sensitivity. Both GI and GL often track together, but there are many exceptions, which is why GL is more informative. Watermelon, pineapple, carrots, beets, and parsnips are just a few examples foods with a high GI but a relatively low GL. Some foods with an unfavorably high GL are brown and white rice, potatoes, and packaged spaghetti. An exhaustive list can be found by searching the Glycemic Index Guide. Low GL foods tend to be high in fiber and lower carbohydrate and align well with proven longevity diets.

SALT

Our relationship with salt is, well… complicated. Salt has long been a hot-button. Just as with sugar, it is naturally present in many whole foods. It is essential for maintaining homeostasis, and that means that there are issues with too much *as well as* too little. The problematic sources tend to come from processed and prepared foods. Restaurant chefs are notorious for overdoing added salt. Hyponatremia occurs if blood serum sodium levels are too low, and hypernatremia occurs if sodium levels are too high. Both imbalances have serious consequences.

Salt is one of the main electrolytes required for chemical signaling, which speaks to its importance. It is crucial for coordinating several physiological processes in the body. Applied levels of blood serum sodium is influenced by salt and water intake and perspiration. Change any one of these three and sodium can get either concentrated (hypernatremia) or diluted (hyponatremia) in the blood, triggering a series of issues. Hyponatremia is the more common imbalance.

Hyponatremia can occur due to various factors such as excessive sweating, vomiting, diarrhea, certain medications, kidney disorders, hormonal imbalances, or drinking too much water without adequate electrolyte intake. It is particularly prevalent among older adults and at endurance race events like half-marathons and longer. An athlete who drinks water to replace water lost due to sweat, without replacing electrolytes, steadily dilutes their blood serum sodium concentration. The athlete appears drunk on their feet, cognitively impaired, and sometimes unable to walk. I've encountered multiple amateurs and pros alike in this state, and it calls for immediate action. In extreme cases, it can lead to seizures, coma, and death.

WHAT TO EAT FOR LONGEVITY

Prescriptive diets are powerful tools for intervention but fail as a long-term solution because we all like freedom in our meal decisions. There's generally little need to be overly prescriptive if our options are grounded in quality, variety, and fiber.

The following are foods we find in the fridge and pantries of cultures with demonstrated longevity.

- Organic fruit & vegetables, many grown within the community

- Abundant variety of clean fresh and frozen whole fruit and vegetables
- Whole grain wheat alternatives like quinoa, amaranth, oats, barley, buckwheat, bulgur, kamut, millet, and corn
- Legumes like lentils, chickpeas, edamame, split peas, soy, fava, pinto, kidney, black, cranberry, and navy beans
- Seeds like chia, ground flaxseed, hemp, sesame, sunflower, pumpkin
- Nuts like raw unsalted almonds, walnuts, pecans, pistachios, cashews, macadamia
- Mushrooms like button, portobello, cremini, shitake, oyster, enoki, beech, maitake
- Goat and sheep milk and cheese (limited cow-sourced)
- Plant-based milk: soy, hemp, oat, almond, macadamia, cashew, coconut
- Fish high in omega-3 fatty acids: salmon, sardine, anchovies, mackerel, cod, herring, trout
- Pasture-raised meat and poultry (3-4 oz serving, up to 2-3 servings per week)
- Eggs that are pasture-raised, free-range
- Fresh and dried herbs and seasonings
- Whole food snacks like apples, pears, peaches, oranges, celery, bananas, pineapple, berries, melons, dates, figs, etc.
- Appetizers like raw unsalted nuts, sourdough rye thins, non-wheat crackers, whole olives, hard cheese, hummus, and vegetables.
- Limited sugary and high-fat sauces
- Minimal added sugars

The meal ingredient options from the above list are expansive. Not all items need to be in our homes, but they reflect the abundance of foods supported by health science and historical evidence of populations totaling in the millions. At least 80% of the protein is obtained from plant sources. Absent from the list are foods that have been over-industrialized or manufactured.

Shifting toward a balance of high-quality established food sources will begin triggering noticeable and positive changes within just a few weeks.

HOW TO EAT FOR LONGEVITY

Routine is helpful to avoid turning to low-quality food options. Again, a framework is more valuable than a prescription:

- Healthy food can and should be unapologetically delicious
- Variety is king – constantly experiment with new foods, flavors, and recipes
- Build an arsenal of substitutes like spaghetti squash, falafels, tempeh, Pumfu, mushrooms, chickpeas, beans, cabbage pancakes (see my recipe)
- Reduce wheat intake, e.g. pasta alternatives like bean, chickpea, and lentil pastas
- Eat raw, steamed, boiled, baked, grilled food, and limit frying (use olive or avocado oil)
- Eat within a 10-hour window, avoid evening snacks
- Prepare batch dishes that are quick and easy to serve and last several days
- Make time to eat with friends and family
- Maintain ≤ 1 serving of alcohol per day (red wine offers the most phytonutrients)
- Shop local markets and the outside aisle of the grocery store
- Avoid extreme diets

None of this is rocket science. It's really just the principles of eating well and crowding out foods that compromise healthspan. Each of us builds our own diet plan based on our upbringing, our cultural norms, and our individual preferences. There's much more to food choices than just taste and satiating our hunger. Texture and smell matter to each of us, as do food sensitivities.

The idea here is to build a framework that works for each of us. No one needs to eat just like me, just like you, or just like some internet doctor who claims to have developed "the ultimate longevity diet". Quality carbohydrates, fat, and protein all have a role to play in supporting our metabolic health. Ensuring they're in balance, that we're getting enough fiber, and that we're not overeating have been the pillars of fueling our bodies throughout human development. The abundance of modern convenient foods, healthy or otherwise, doesn't change what's needed for health.

The options for delicious longevity foods are abundant. If we haven't discovered them yet, it says we haven't explored enough. Discovering new and better alternatives makes it easy and appealing to steadily replace foods that tax our immune and endocrine systems. Just like compound interest, consistency and time do amazing things when we give them a chance to grow and thrive by steadily investing small amounts daily.

COFFEE, TEA, RED WINE, AND DARK CHOCOLATE

What do coffee, tea, red wine, and dark chocolate have in common, besides getting a lot of headlines? Are they the secret to longevity or a quick road to death? All four are healthy choices when consumed responsibly.

Red wine was long promoted for its resveratrol content. Resveratrol is hardly a panacea for anti-aging, and even if it were, the alcohol associated with the quantity of resveratrol needed to make a measured benefit would have us passed out on the floor. Alcohol abuse is the real issue here. Study results are mixed at a dose rate of one serving per day, which effectively tells us that it's near the threshold. Unlike processed foods, alcohol has been in our diet for thousands of years and there is a lot of real-life evidence to lean on. If we're respecting the single serving per day threshold, there are likely 100 other places that will offer higher returns than abstinence. If a glass of wine is part of bringing people together in community conversation, the net benefit of adding the social element is very clear. Most of us know if our bodies don't respond well to alcohol, and that's a reason to reduce or eliminate it from the diet. Opting for a fancy water served up in a fluted glass, garnished with a lemon will address any concerns about not fitting in.

Why red wine over the other options? It's the polyphenols in red wine that make it healthy. Red wine gets its deep color from the skin. In making white wine, the skin is removed immediately, stripping away about 75% of the polyphenols. Mixed drinks introduce excess calories, typically high in added sugars, the worst of all calories to consume. Interestingly, some single malt scotches and bourbons fare almost as well as red wine, due to their simple ingredients and processing. The quantity, of course, is a smaller serving size, and all bets are off when it comes as a mixed drink cocktail.

Dark chocolate, 70% and higher, is a sure win, again due to the polyphenols, anti-inflammatory, and blood pressure-lowering qualities found in dark chocolate. Other chocolates undergo more processing that strips away the polyphenols and tend to have more added sugar that none of us need. Looking for dark chocolate with less than 10 grams of sugar per serving and limiting intake to about 25 grams per day appears very reasonable.

Coffee is the flavonoid choice of Americans, not because it's the highest concentration or quality, but because we drink so much of it. A daily dose of 2-4 cups seems to be the sweet spot, with drip and espresso as the preferred brewing methods, for those for whom caffeine doesn't induce adverse effects. Is decaffeinated better? No. Processing to strip out the caffeine also strips out some of the healthy flavonoids. All bets are off once the coffee is laced with sweet syrups, whipped cream, and sugars. If our idea of coffee is a sweet treat, it's time to re-evaluate priorities. Birthdays come once a year, not every time we walk into a café. Non-sweetened cappuccinos, lattes, and flat whites are examples of healthy coffee variations, as these include just coffee and dairy or non-dairy milk.

Last, but certainly not least, is tea. Tea stands above all of the options in this group. A 2019 study looked at 30 different teas and found green tea possessed the highest antioxidant capacity and total phenolic content, which was also a richer source of polyphenols, especially catechins. Traditional teas all tend to offer significant health value. The best ones are the ones we enjoy.

CALL ME SWEETIE

I'm frequently asked for an opinion on the best artificial sweetener. Recognize that this is playing with fire, and dose makes the poison. Most of them are chemicals created in laboratories and the question is one of safety. It's not a question of health benefits but of safety. The answer should be obvious, but our taste desire for sweetness often trumps logic. The chemicals involved in any of the artificial sweeteners tend to interfere with gut bacteria and are cause for multiple concerns. Research continues to shed light on the metabolic and insulin response our bodies have to these additives, and the answers remain unclear but concerning. Again, low-dose, processed chemical exposures over lifetimes are extremely hard to measure, and there's no consensus in the medical community that these are better or reasonable alternatives to real foods.

Natural, sweeteners like stevia, honey, maple syrup, monk fruit, and old-fashioned sucrose are much better understood and known to humans for thousands of years. Yet again, this is a question of dose. Disciplined use of natural products is the road to freedom when it comes to all sweeteners.

EVERYTHING IN MODERATION

"Tell me about your diet." Is a question I ask frequently. Popular responses are "I eat pretty well" or "I eat everything in moderation." It says nothing about what, how, when, or why they eat. A vague response indicates they aren't fueling for nutrition with a conscious strategy, or they fear judgment. It's understandable, given today's climate around diet.

People are more likely to order unhealthy foods if they see others ordering them. We rationalize that we're not eating any worse than others, and possibly avoiding conflict. It's unfortunate but all too true. We have a nasty habit of putting people on the defensive if they aren't imbibing or feasting along with the rest of us.

Moderation is a convenient way of describing oneself as somewhere in the vast chasm between Froot Loops and organic whole foods, and typically the excuse for weak food habits. A better response would be "Everything healthy in moderation." It infers unapologetic, conscious thought and purposeful choices. Their focus is on quality, variety, and fiber. It doesn't require a high Food-IQ to adopt and follow that simple mindset.

WATER WELL

Water is another question that comes up frequently. It's a responsible question, given the state of broad contamination of surface and groundwater. Municipal water is highly regulated and subject to frequent testing and audits. In addition, the sources are typically well-protected and located far away from common contamination sources.

Chlorine is added to kill and prevent bacteria sources in pipes etc. from being dragged into the water during delivery, but its work is done once it exits the faucet. Chlorine doesn't support a healthy gut microbiome, and although levels are low, it's considered wise to pass drinking water through a charcoal/carbon filter prior to consumption.

Homeowners who rely on well water should respect both the benefits and risks. On the upside, they may be getting minerals that have been stripped out of municipal processed water, depending on their specific source. Well water, however, also comes with the responsibility of routine testing to ensure water quality. Most heavy metals etc. are detected during the initial drilling, but things can change in groundwater sources over time. More common issues are coliform bacteria and viruses that can form in the absence of chlorine. Annual, or semi-annual testing is typically practiced.

Common methods for filtering water are charcoal/carbon, reverse osmosis, or a combination of the two. Both remove a wide range of contaminants from water, including heavy metals, bacteria, viruses, pesticides, and pharmaceuticals. A water test is the best way to decide what level of filtering is required. For most of us, a Brita-style jug or an inline fridge filter is sufficient. Bottled water is a last resort, given the uncertainty of the source and the plastic waste stream associated with disposable bottles.

WHEN TO EAT

We fast every time we go to sleep, just like all the other animals on the planet. Its benefits are hotly debated but unfortunately, most of the data is from animal studies that consistently prove less remarkable in humans. Findings are mixed and not something we need to overcomplicate. We can reduce the fasting options down to three.

1. Intermittent fasting (IF) simply means an intentional break from caloric intake for at least 12 hours, something we should all be doing anyway. A 12-hour IF means either no late-night snacks or breakfast and no trips to the refrigerator during the night. Dropping the evening snack usually offers the biggest return, as it is typically a low-quality food choice and interferes with sleep. There have been a great many studies, but results are mixed, and gains are small. It's hard to find consistent results beyond a 10-hour feeding window (14-hour-fast). A 14-hour IF likely translates to a late breakfast or an early dinner, or skipping one of them. More aggressive approaches restrict the feeding window to as little as 4 hours or consume only water for 24 hours. This can help the body detoxify at a frequency of 1-3 months. IF can help anyone trying to take control of their metabolic health, as it provides additional gastrointestinal rest time, retrains the body to burn fat by enabling ketosis, and helps promote lower total caloric intake. Arguably, the most important benefit of all is that IF helps us to take control of our eating instead of it controlling us.

2. Prolonged fasting (PF) involves multiple days and can be a powerful tool in resetting metabolism, but these require medical supervision. Extended versions last up to 30 days at some fasting clinics. Connecting with medically trained experts is important to understand specific potential health risks and benefits of a PF reset. True North Health Center and Fasting Escape are well-respected in this area.

3. Caloric restriction (CR) is one of the fasting methods, even though not as rigidly designed around a timing pattern. It is simply reducing daily caloric intake, which tends to happen naturally with an IF strategy by skipping evening beverages and snacks. CR caps the daily calorie intake, usually to something at or below 2,000 calories per day. Caloric restriction has the most robust data and is the easiest to adhere to over many years, as it simply comes down to instilling healthy habits. CR and IF studies frequently yield similar results, suggesting that whichever method helps us to manage calories, go with the one we can sustain.

TECHNOLOGY TO THE RESCUE

A few new apps can equip us with amazing speed to assess food quality in our pantry and at our local grocery store. Simply point the smartphone's camera at the UPC package label and the app reports on multiple food quality parameters with an overall food quality score. They are a huge step forward and put quick knowledge into consumers' hands. The one I like best is Yuka.

THE BEST DIET FOR ME

There clearly is no single *best* diet for everyone. Diet fit is influenced by our genetics, age, culture, food availability, activity level, and health. Without question, we need to start doing a lot better job of addressing the dietary needs of children and getting them better informed and on track from an early age. It's criminal that Western culture has enabled the undermining of the health of millions of young, vulnerable children. Every child raised in a low-quality diet environment is disadvantaged for life and will spend decades trying to make up for the health liability imposed on them. Poor diets cross all socioeconomic boundaries, and unsurprisingly, the quality of our diets has been declining with successive generations.

Some people battling disease may require an intervention diet to transition them to a healthy track, but most of us need to just focus on adopting a sustainable longevity diet built on quality, variety, and fiber. The endless debates have got us focused on everything but core dietary needs. Our diet should support getting us into our health lane. That means getting down to basics and focusing on whole foods. We can tweak things once core healthy habits are established but the constant excursions and cyclic weight-loss diets are bad news for our physical and mental health and waste precious time and resources.

The best diet will be unrelenting on quality because quality delivers the best nutrients and crowds out everything else. When quality is coupled with variety, it ensures we're consuming a wide range of foods rich in a vast array of nutrients, and most of us will naturally land on a healthy balance of carbohydrates, protein, fat, and fiber.

The Mediterranean Diet is by far the most studied and associated with people living exceptionally long healthy lives. The Flexitarian Diet is a very practical approach to eating well and is based on the Mediterranean Diet, as are the DASH, MIND, and PEGAN diets. The subtle differences in these diets are overshadowed by how individuals interpret and practice them. Four people, each following one of these four diets, could sit down together and enjoy the same meal with little or no observable differences, as they are all grounded in the same principles:

- Whole foods
- Plant focus (fruits, vegetables, legumes, whole grains, nuts, and seeds)
- Heart-healthy fats (extra-virgin olive oil and avocado oil, fatty fish)
- Limited animal products
- Limited saturated fats
- Responsible caloric intake (typically about 2,000 calories daily)

This approach to eating has been demonstrated to promote healthspan and longevity globally for centuries. The delicious food options within this framework are enormous, and that's often the biggest surprise to people who have been sheltered from whole foods. For those of us who love to eat, it also allows us to enjoy healthy-sized meals that are nutrient-centric, not caloric-centric. Working within this framework addresses most metabolic needs and makes it easy to make subtle optimizations or adaptations as medically needed.

VEGAN DIET

One topic sure to cause excitement in a group setting is a vegan diet discussion. Recognize that veganism is more ethos than diet, which explains why there are many ways to practice a vegan diet. A vegan diet for human health resembles the previous four diets, but absent animal products. The Ornish diet is a strict and clear version of a vegan diet and has been shown to slow, and in some cases, even reverse heart disease. The absence of red meat and the abundance of nutrients and fiber are wins for managing heart disease. Many people do very well with a quality vegan diet, provided they can maintain healthy red blood cell levels and avoid anemia.

Earlier dietary guidance to avoid eggs and cheese helped spur on the vegan diet, as well as issues around industrialized animal welfare and fish contamination. It has been instrumental in bringing those issues to the forefront.

A vegan diet may be medically advised for some, but extensive research in recent years into diet points to quality and dose matter around animal products, be they dairy, meat, or fish. Insist on quality and they can play an important role in maintaining a healthy balance in a support role. Quality and responsible dose management across all of these diets is the key to health success, far more than the label we place on them.

WHO HOLDS THE POWER?

It's easy to find ourselves feeling powerless over food, but no one holds more power than the person who does the shopping. It's virtually impossible to establish healthy dietary habits surrounded by low-quality food options. It's like trying to quit smoking when everyone in the home is a smoker. Convenience is powerful. A bowl of potato chips in our lap is hard to resist. It's in sight and within easy reach. A bag of chips in the pantry is out of sight but comes into view when we're feeling the urge for a snack. The same bag of chips at the grocery store only comes into view when we go into a food store, and we might even prevent that by not shopping the junk-food aisle(s). The idea is to put in place barriers far in advance of the urge. If we're the shopper, we need to take responsibility. If we're not, then we need to have the conversation and work together on bringing better food options into the home. That might also mean we need to shoulder some of the responsibility of the grocery shopping.

Displacing unhealthy foods is only part of the solution. We also need to make quality and variety convenient. Leftovers are fantastic ways to drive convenience. Cook once and eat twice. It's an effective way to leverage the effort required for meal prep by making one effort count multiple times.

If cookies are a weakness, commit to baking them at home with healthy ingredients. This raises the barrier and improves the quality when we do decide to make the effort. On the topic of baking treats, look for opportunities to reduce the sugar and salt ingredients. We can train our tastebuds to appreciate sweetness more by eliminating the exposure to ultra-sweet foods like hard candies and the icing on cakes. It takes a few weeks, but soon ultra-sweet tastes awful. It works the same with salt.

FOOD FOR THOUGHT

1. Take time to self-assess where we are currently within a healthy dietary framework.
2. Make Quality and Variety an unrelenting priority.
3. Set a goal of maintaining over 55 grams of fiber daily.
4. Become a label-reader and look for the fewest number of ingredients, and low added sugar and sodium levels. Consider what's NOT on the label, like herbicides and pesticides.
5. Insist on <u>whole</u> grains and replace wheat with healthy alternatives.
6. Experiment with new fruits and vegetables and consume multiple servings daily.
7. Explore the many forms and sources of protein.
8. Invest in cooking at home and try to make extra for quick and easy leftovers.
9. Take a power position and put barriers in place to low-quality foods.
10. Keep searching and experimenting. Quality food can be unapologetically delicious.

Chapter 14

ACTIVE BOOTY, ACTIVE BRAIN

"Your new goal should be to achieve a level of fitness that allows you to comfortably move as many parts of your body as possible through the greatest range of motion until that day when you are standing over the final putt on the 18th hole of your life."

Dan Zeman, You're Too Old to Die Young

In 1971, the legendary hit TV sitcom put American values on public trial. Norman Lear, its creator and producer, anchored Archie Bunker in his favorite chair watching TV for most of the show. It was a trend Lear had observed well over half a century ago, and a trend showing no signs of change. Lear went on to celebrate 101.4 trips around the sun, evidence that he had indeed figured a few things out along the way.

Losing movement happens so easily – it's the path of no effort.

It is easy to forget that to be human is to move. As breathing is to life, so is movement. Movement takes on many natural forms. Exercise is simply an elevated, typically more structured form of activity, but we need not think of activity in any limiting way. Universally, we are out of touch with our true physical capabilities. Life lulls us into coasting on memories. Never having participated in organized sport as a youth, my immediate attraction to Ironman endurance triathlon made no sense. Nevertheless, I couldn't deny the motivation and intrigue of seeing men and women in their sixties and beyond, finishing amazing feats with a smile. It tugged on me hard and wasn't about to let go. Within months I was feverishly investing time in understanding the training and equipment needed to attempt such an event.

My first race was a half marathon at the age of 45. The start felt like jumping out of a plane, trusting there was a parachute to ease the fall. A maximum security penitentiary marked the final hill. Its stone walls pushed high against the sky. Looking up at the guard towers, I was overcome with a heightened sense of freedom and gratitude. I knew I could finish. My challenge was trivial compared to the challenges men faced within those walls. Crossing the line, came the realization that I was a runner. What a bizarre thought. Then came the discovery that I didn't suck, finishing respectably several younger runners. Twenty years later, that moment seeded many more adventures. We are capable of so much more than we realize.

As a coach, I've seen how people quit on themselves far too early. Elite-level athletes make it look easy! I've had the good fortune on occasions to tag alongside some pro and elite-level athletes in a few sports, and learned that it's one thing to watch them on TV, but quite another to share the same playground.

The Love of the Game

As a longtime shinny hockey player, I was called to stand in as goaltender and was quick to let Fred, the other team's center, know that it was me or a pylon in the net. I hadn't stood between the posts since my elementary school days, and I wasn't an appealing pick then either. In sharp contrast, Fred had played hockey for the Boston Bruins in his younger days, and like many pure athletes, his love for the game kept him involved in the sport many years after retirement from the NHL. Now in his mid-50s, and one of the 'old boys', Fred was still faster and had more moves than anyone on the ice, seeming to glide around other players at will.

It was bound to happen. About halfway into our friendly game, Fred decided it was time to have a little fun with us and turned on the jets. A cloud of snow trailed behind Fred as I heard his skate blades biting the ice. In a handful of seconds, he'd swept past every player, despite their best attempt to dispossess him of the puck. Reaching our blueline, he was on a charge for the net, and the only thing standing between Fred and a certain goal was me, frozen in fear. He looked up, reminded of the neophyte hiding behind all those pads, shot me a grin, and proceeded to lob the puck from 60 feet out, right into my outstretched glove. He'd had his 5 seconds of fun.

People who have invested deeply in team activities and overcome life's toughest challenges have a habit of showing exceptional gratitude and respect to their fellow man. I came to know Fred as one of the most upstanding and respected people in town. His continued love for the game revolved entirely around a love and respect for people. I was never much of a hockey player, but the gift of camaraderie that came with playing with Gilly's misfit crew of doctors, attorneys, and teachers every week for 25 years was nothing short of resplendent. And, without exception, every elite athlete I've occasionally found myself alongside has always shown up prepared to help lift us to the next level.

If we just show up, growth opportunities inevitably seem to find us. We never know how far we can go with activities until we try. Sure, being the best is always fun, but the moment is always fleeting. Breaking a sweat with others is where the magic happens. It's easier to enjoy many activities than just one because it naturally helps keep our expectations in check. Regardless of the activity, they all begin with showing up, and then progressing step by step, up the learning staircase.

Never failing means never trying,
and that's the biggest failure of all.

THE UPSIDE OF DISCIPLINE

Discipline likely evokes negative thoughts. It's viewed as countering creativity and stealing one's identity. While the connection between data and discipline was well understood, it wasn't until I learned to follow prescribed athletic training activities that I internalized discipline in a new way. It was building to something much bigger in the future, much bigger than could be imagined in the moment.

For anyone who's done a 10k race or longer, this plays out in a very predictable way. One study looked at 876,000 marathon results and found that only 13% of finishers did a negative split, that is, they ran the 2nd half faster than the 1st half. That means that about 85% of runners went out faster than they could sustain for the distance.

The body experiences a premature accumulation of lactate during anaerobic glycolysis (transformation of glucose to lactate), leading to muscle fatigue and the burning sensation in our muscles. Our sympathetic nervous system tries to support our eagerness to go fast, but eventually, our parasympathetic nervous system steps in and starts downregulating our pace to a lactate production rate our muscles can tolerate. It's a normal process but when it occurs early in an event, we spend more time going slower than we did early on going fast, resulting in a slower overall pace. In other words, there's no such thing as putting time in the bank so that we can afford to go slower later.

By good fortune, I picked up a book early in my training; Going Long, by Joe Friel and Gordo Byrn, and latched onto the importance of learning one's capacity and this concept of negative splitting. The lactate accumulation is delayed to a point where the sympathetic nervous system, driven by the mind, has a fighting chance against the parasympathetic nervous system that urges us to ease off. I latched onto this early, likely out of fear of falling apart late in a race, but I came to find myself achieving better results than others who were faster and more fit. Planning and discipline often win over fitness, and that's a nice bonus because it also carries over into life and aging well.

TT Time

Calgary, set against the Rocky Mountains and host to the 1988 Winter Olympics, is a triathlete's playground. One quiet August morning, I returned for a third attempt at a 40 km (24.8 mile) bike time trial (TT). Earlier attempts fell short of expectations. With 1,000 miles of flat prairies to the east, an 8-foot shoulder on both sides of the road, and a rumble strip for protection from infrequent traffic, it was about as good as it gets for threshold speed trials.

I started rolling out at 98% functional threshold power for the first 5 miles. It felt ridiculously easy. The next 5 miles were 99%, then 100%, putting more power into it each 5-mile segment. By mile 20 my quads were on fire with lactate buildup and the mind was in full game mode. Why put up with the pain? This wasn't a race situation. No one would care but me. Lactate pain is temporary. It ends within seconds of resting the muscles. The pain of quitting with only 25% to go wasn't going to fade away so conveniently.

With a mile to go, my legs were fighting to hold power. It's the blessing and curse of training with power. It doesn't care about the wind, the temperature, or how the rider feels. Power is power. I call it the Truth Meter. I was on track to break the hour mark. Over the line, I'd bested previous attempts by 5 minutes with a time of 57:18, (26.0 mph / 41.9 kph).

The phone wouldn't be ringing with offers from cycling teams to join their ranks, but it was respectable for a guy who not long ago was overweight and tracking toward serious health issues. Time to get back to work and build on the learning.

Gordo Byrn had kindly offered to coach a small group as part of a pilot program for the new coaching business he was building with Alan Couzens. Leading up to my A-race, Ironman Coeur d'Alene, Gordo posed the question in our weekly call, "What in your life will change if you win your age group?" We'd never discussed such an outcome, nor had it ever entered my mind. It seemed out of the blue, but the question has stayed with me ever since. The obvious answer was an invitation to the Worlds In Kona, Hawaii. But, Gordo prefers deeper waters, as do I, and I decided that it was a question we need- ed to answer for ourselves. Closing in on the age of 40, Gordo was coming off the peak of life at the top of the athletic world and was passing along a life lesson to his athletes. The obvious answer was that nothing would change because like everyone else in my age group, I'd be going back to work next week. Yet the question lingered.

The last lonely 20 minutes of that delightfully pain-filled 57:18 time trial would eventually lead to my answer to Gordo's provocation. The absence of crowds and awards at my private little TT was an unexpectedly important gift. It cleared the way for bigger learnings, and it's proven to be more valuable than all the medals stashed away in a cardboard box. Strong finishes are always fun, but it's what we do when no one is looking that holds the real significance.

I went on to participate in four races the following year and wouldn't return to a start line for over a decade. Life had gotten even busier and the disruption of career changes and multiple home reloca- tions left little time or passion for racing. I should have boomeranged back to my fat, sedentary ways, but I didn't. I'd discovered a passion for human self-propulsion that didn't rely on any outside reinforce- ment. I'd come to love movement with a passion that defies explana- tion. Still passionate about the sport and the people, I had long made a point of encouraging others and checking in on their race days.

On a whim, I signed up for a half-ironman in 2022, motivated by the return of life norms coming out of the COVID pandemic and having come through a cardiovascular event. It would be my first triathlon in 13 years. With a surprisingly small but much more targeted training volume than in earlier days, I was able to execute a cautious, but steady effort, with enough in reserve to launch an uncharacteristic sprint to the finish. Finishing just out of the top 10 of my age group at one of the biggest events on the East Coast, was yet another reminder that I was capable of more than I realized. Little habits add up to big returns over time, but only if we continue to make daily investments.

The more we learn about exercise and aging, the role of proper recovery stands out as paramount. Unsurprisingly, its importance goes up as we age. This stood out in my conversation with Cal Zaryski, 9-time World XTERRA Champion. At the age of 53, Cal won both the World XTERRA title and Ironman 70.3 Age Group Championship; a feat never before achieved. He continues to perform at an exceptionally high level.

The pursuit of awards and recognition is fraught with disappointment. Many rely on variables beyond our control and often come with a dark side. They come with a very real risk of slipping back into unhealthy habits versus staying on a path of personal growth. Big Hairy Audacious Goals (BHAGs) help us work toward things far beyond today, but success or failure won't define us. It's the small things we do day after day that define us. This, I decided, was my answer to Gordo's question. Had I qualified for Kona, I might have gone, but maybe not. I'd already passed on an opportunity to race the Worlds in Europe, without regret.

Very few of my athletic memories are of races. They are about the people I've had the privilege to spend time with and special moments 1-V-1 with nature's terrain:

- Doubling Sonoma-Napa-Sonoma via Trinity-Oakville Grade Rds, with over 15% grades
- Time trialing up Mt. Figueroa, west ascent, from Jackson's Neverland Ranch
- Epic descent down Tepusquet Peak on Chuckie V's wheel and then being dragged home by Trevor Wurtele after absolutely blowing out my legs on the final training day
- An unrelenting 50-mile southern ascent to Highwood Pass, AB Rockies, undertrained, undernourished, and underhydrated.
- Multiple >12% grades up from the Shenandoah Valley to the Blue Ridge Parkway more than 15 years later and still loving the challenge

Scott with his son Stephen at Ironman, Canada finish

Scott with his son Michael at Bragg Creek, AB

Learn to Love Hard Things

So many hard things come down to just putting one foot in front of the other. It becomes a moving meditation. Ideas come pouring in, troubles get resolved, and stress gets left behind, as it can't match the hormones that flood the body in response to physical exertion. Great climbs are opportunities to pit oneself against a new physical challenge. Steep grades quickly separate the climbers from the sprinters, but we all delight in regrouping at the top. Success gets measured by how well we managed the day, not by whether we were first or last. Hard things bring out the best in good people, and the worst in others. They are excellent tests of character and guide us to whom to keep close. These are people who will help us to reach above the crowd and appreciate the real values in life.

So much of what matters happens when no one is looking. It's the good habits we continue to do that align with our long-range ideas of the person we're trying to become. All of us are capable of far more than we realize. We must resist our fears of failing. Fear steals dreams before they get a chance to start and more moments than we can count.

FOGETABOUTIT!

The sport and exercise community is frequently guilty of applying an overabundance of technical jargon, implied expertise, and expensive equipment to join their select clubs. Training zones language and expensive gear do not make anyone an athlete. A recent group ride of about 20 cyclists was a fresh reminder. One by one, cyclists fell off the pace until there were just us two "old" guys riding what many would describe as vintage bikes.

There aren't shortcuts to doing hard things. Invest time in doing. Don't let finishing last prevent us from joining group activities. It's healthy conditioning for our humility, a helpful trait for longevity. Before long we're bound to get a little more proficient and soon someone new is going to show up to take our place at the back of the pack.

ACTIVE DEFENSE AGAINST DEMENTIA

The link between activity and dementia is not an obvious one. We associate exercise with strength, aerobic capacity, and balance... but the brain? Seemingly along for the ride, while the heart, lungs, and muscles appear to be getting all the benefits, the brain enjoys a collateral boost in blood, oxygen, glucose, and hormones that lasts for hours. I can't count the number of times I've been on a run or a bike ride that ideas came flowing in, like an external life force channeling messages into my brain. It's become a running joke (pun intended), coming up with acronyms to try and remember all the ideas once back home.

Eleven prospective studies followed adults over decades, well into their later years. The findings were significant: Regular exercise reduces the risk of developing all dementias by about 30%, and Alzheimer's disease specifically by 45%. No other single lifestyle factor matches this level of positive cognitive impact because none of them have as many compounding benefits. Exercise challenges the mind, relieves stress, gets us outdoors, inspires positive eating habits, and pulls us into supportive communities. It checks a lot of important boxes. A 2023 study of 356,052 participants between 2006 and 2021 looked at 39 potential risk factors and arrived at the same conclusion; nothing protects cognitive health more than a physically active lifestyle, including grip strength.

Another large study released in September 2023 found that seniors who sat for 9.3 hours per day were 39% and 55% less likely to develop dementia within seven years, than those who sat for 12 and 15 hours respectively. There's no getting around it, movement matters a lot!

As a defensive strategy against dementia, physical activity towers over every other mitigating strategy we might find easier or more convenient. As a proactive strategy, no others offer the emotional and pleasure rewards of increased dopamine, serotonin, testosterone, and estrogen provided by exercise. Few addictions can be described as healthy, but dopamine and serotonin are responsible for the natural high sensations that explain why active people tend to remain active with little need for encouragement, and why they tend to be happier people. Coincidentally, these same hormones help multiple body functions and help to auto-regulate body weight.

EXTENDING THE RUNWAY

More and more we're seeing records set in older age group athletics. Occasionally it is attributed to equipment, but more often we're seeing older adults shatter beliefs about being too old for a long list of things thought meant for younger people. I recall turning on the TV and the immediate excitement of following Jack Nicklaus as he captured his 18th major championship at Augusta at age 46. It foretold what was about to unfold across the world in masters athletics.

- Lester Wright set the 100-meter world record of 26.34 sec at age 100
- Don Pellmann set 5 world records at the long jump, high jump, shot put, discus, and 100-meter dash at age 100
- Julia Hawkins set women's 100-meter world records at ages 100 and 105
- Mike Fremont set world record marathons at ages 80 and 90
- Sister Madonna Buder became the oldest female Ironman finisher at age 82
- Diana Nyad made a record 110-mile swim from Cuba to Florida at age 64
- Yuichiro Miura became the oldest person to summit Mt Everest at age 80

It's tempting to think these records are attributed to there being more seniors now than ever before, but it's happening just as frequently in athletes' 40s and 50s. Active lifestyles result in a series of behaviors that extend the runway of vibrance and resilience. Many of them didn't get into athletics until their second half of life. We understand health better now, and we understand that it requires a holistic approach to live our best lives.

As children, our amazing signaling network sets us on a controlled and predictable growth path. It decides how fast we should grow, when our voice should change, when puberty should start, and when to ignore everything our parents tell us. It's like our health is on autopilot, and by age 18 or so we've come to trust this autopilot implicitly.

Unfortunately, it sets many of us up for failure, assuming our bodies will just continue taking care of things independently of our lifestyle habits. Why would we think any different?

Age 40 comes along, and many of us discover little health problems aren't going to be solved by a sportscar or a facelift. We begin to notice simple cuts take longer to heal, but far less apparent is what's happening inside our bodies. Cell division starts to falter and DNA fragments during cell division. Our late-model body starts to require more maintenance.

At the same time, our body's innate repair rate begins to decline due to a drop in several body chemistries. We'll discuss some of these chemistries momentarily, but the important news is that age is only one factor. Activity levels play a big role in the levels the body chooses to maintain. Active bodies also do a better job of taking out the trash by removing senescent cells and clearing the signaling pathways. In contrast, lazy sedentary habits result in higher rates of senescent "zombie" cells that interfere with cell-cell communications and create dysfunction.

MASTER REGULATORS OF HEALTH AND AGING

For as long as I can recall, we've been taught that exercise is good for us. For a long time, scientists didn't really understand why, but the correlations were irrefutable. Fast forward to today, and science is getting to the root cause of health and disease and confirming a lot of our suspicions about the benefits of exercise. It turns out that active humans look remarkably different in many measurable ways *on the inside*. What's most impactful are the compounding benefits that address the uncertainty many have regarding the potential return on the investment. If it takes an hour of activity to earn an extra hour of healthspan or lifespan, is it really worth it? It's a fair question. Let's pop the hood and take a look.

Health is a team sport. Sending one player down the field while the others sit back and watch never works. The opposing forces are too strong and too sophisticated to conquer with just one player. When we talk about sustained health and longevity, there are what I like to call the 5 Master Regulators of Health and Aging (5MRHA). They all serve multiple roles, and together they are a formidable force. We don't need to overcomplicate things by going into depth, but it is helpful to recognize the 5MRHA's comprise a team of chemistries working together for our best health outcomes. Each plays a critical role in concert with the others. They all decline with age but every one of them responds positively to active movement. Earlier in the genetics discussion, we touched on principles of extending healthspan by slowing DNA damage rate and preserving DNA repair rate in Figure 14. Some of the chemistry behind how this occurs is tied to preserving 5MRHA levels. Collectively, they form the team we know as health and longevity promoters.

- Nuclear factor erythroid 2-related factor 2 (NRF2) regulates gene expression in our antioxidant defense system and initiates enzymes that neutralize reactive oxygen species (ROS) and detoxify harmful substances. It also helps to reduce chronic inflammation.

- Nicotinamide adenine dinucleotide (NAD+) acts as a coenzyme, facilitating electron transfer, essential in reduction-oxidation (REDOX) signaling and reactions, and signaling to redox oxidative stress. It's also involved in glycolysis and cellular respiration, which are central to energy metabolism.

- Nitric Oxide (NO) regulates arterial dilation which in turn regulates blood pressure. It's also a neurotransmitter. By age 60, the average person will have lost about 80% of their NO levels. Regular exercise and a healthy diet can restore it to 40-year-old levels. Restoring healthy NO levels is causal in cardiac health, exercise performance, healing, erectile function, reduced blood pressure, and improved respiratory response.

- Glutathione (GSH) is commonly referred to as the master antioxidant because it plays such a major role. It aids in protecting cells from oxidation, participates in detoxification, is central to immune system function, regulates normal cell death (apoptosis), is neuroprotective, and acts as an anti-inflammatory.

- Mitochondria (MT) are the engines (organelles) within all our cells, converting nutrients into energy (ATP), heat generation, central to metabolism, regulating programmed cell death, and playing a role in the immune system.

They all do more than what is listed above, but what is likely evident is the amount of overlap. They work in collaboration, not in isolation. Similarly, they all respond positively to exercise stimuli.

The endocrine system also suffers from wear and tear associated with aging, but thankfully it too responds positively to an active lifestyle. Recall that our endocrine system plays a central communication role in partnership with our immune system. It is one of the few systems that releases chemicals we can associate with emotion. Dopamine increase, for example, is responsible for our positive feelings associated with accomplishing a task and the high we feel after a strenuous activity. Elevated serotonin is associated with the same activities, as well as healthy eating, receiving acts of kindness, and getting quality sleep. Epinephrine, more commonly known as adrenaline, is what triggers our fight or flight stress response.

- Dopamine, Serotonin, Epinephrine, and Norepinephrine hormones are neurotransmitters that naturally decay with age. Exercise stimulates their production and clears their pathways, restoring higher function. They also appear to be neuroprotective against cognitive decline, particularly effective against dementia and Parkinson's Disease.

- Neurotransmitters like dopamine, serotonin, epinephrine, and norepinephrine are crucial for brain function. While levels may fluctuate with age, exercise can boost their production and optimize neural pathways. This not only enhances cognitive performance but also offers neuroprotection against conditions like dementia and Parkinson's disease. Exercise promotes synaptic plasticity, facilitating efficient neurotransmission and cognitive flexibility.

- Brain-derived neurotrophic factor (BDNF) is a protein that protects and promotes the growth of brain neurons and helps them communicate with each other. BDNF levels are increased 2 to 3 times higher after intense exercise and correlate positively with improvements in cognitive functions. Vascular endothelial growth factor (VEGF) is also stimulated by exercise. VEGF is a protein that promotes healthy blood vessels and has been shown to improve cognition In dementia patients.

That's a short list of 10 key signaling players (NRF2, NAD+, NO, GSH, MT, dopamine, serotonin, norepinephrine, epinephrine, and BDNF) that are all causal in promoting health that all respond positively to exercise. Additionally, they all appear to help protect the brain from dementia and neuromuscular diseases. Leveraging their power simply requires activities that raise the heart rate and muscle tissue stimulation.

We are constantly baited by supplements that promise to restore levels of many of these molecules, but it's a slippery slope once we begin looking to chemicals to artificially support homeostasis over a lifetime. Even if these supplements did as they promised, they come at a financial cost and uncertain physical cost to our kidneys, especially those in capsule or pill form, which bear the burden of clearing the excess excipients and fillers used to deliver these supplements. More than 1/3 of Americans over age 65 suffer from kidney disease. We need to be mindful that our choices may carry unintended consequences.

VO2 MAX

At the cellular level, we can think of fitness as our efficiency in delivering oxygen and extracting spent oxygen as CO_2. At the systems level, with circulating blood, we refer to this aspect of fitness as cardiovascular efficiency, specifically VO2max.

The oxygen powers a metabolic reaction within our muscle cells that provides energy (adenosine triphosphate, aka ATP) to do work. People who participate in aerobic exercise over several years maintain VO2max levels up to 50% higher than the average person of the same age and sex. This is a big part of why cyclists and runners maintain such high levels of performance into their 60s and even 70s. They have a Ferrari engine while the average person operates with a vintage 4-cylinder engine.

This might not seem important until we appreciate that VO2max is one of the best predictors of lifespan. It follows that individuals with high VO2max are living day-to-day with cardiovascular systems that are less prone to failure. That also means that they are delivering blood to the brain and body with relative ease versus the average person. They aren't immune to failure but are inherently better protected from the leading cause of early death.

I subject myself to VO2max testing annually, not because it's fun or easy, but because it is a strong test for fit individuals of all ages. It can detect things not evident in standard stress tests, because standard tests are designed around average or diseased patients, not fit, healthy humans. In his book, Outlive, Dr. Peter Attia recommends that his patients maintain a VO2max at the elite level for peers 10 years younger. This likely sounds like an outrageous expectation, but it's not. I surpass Dr. Attia's criteria by more than a decade and I'm no-where near an elite athlete. How? Through 30 to 60-minute targeted exercise sessions 4 or 5 days per week, and one longer activity with friends, I can easily keep my weight in check. It enables me to still have fun playing with younger athletes and is another example of how fitness yields compounding returns.

VO2max has genetic, exercise, and body mass components. Parts of it are largely fixed, but overall, our cardiovascular system is highly responsive to training. Exercise develops skeletal muscles we can see, and heart muscles buried in our chest. Hybrid aerobic and anaero-bic training also improves lung capacity and more efficient O_2/CO_2 exchange. Optimal VO2max relies on high-intensity interval train-ing (HIIT) in combination with aerobic and strength-based training. Once a week I'll typically push the heart rate well up into the anaero-bic regions, between 85 to 90% of my maximum heart rate for short (~1-3 minutes) intense efforts. Hills leverage gravity to increase the workload. Run intervals with increasing speed for each interval are effective as well. Plyometric exercises also provide terrific options for intensity, as does stair-climbing.

SAFETY NOTE: VO2max training should only be attempted by experienced, fit athletes, only after medical clearance from their health professional, and only after a complete warmup. Bypassing any of these steps poses serious, potentially fatal health risks and is never a shortcut to fitness. Age and cooler temperatures call for a longer warm-up. I require at least 25 minutes on a warm summer day, and longer on cool days.

AN EXTRA GEAR

One summer morning ride out in the country found a young German Shepherd in hot pursuit of a pound of flesh, mine. Dog encounters are part of the great outdoors, but this was like no other. As he closed in, the sound of his nails striking the asphalt grew louder and his panting grew more intense. Tucked down into an aerodynamic position, my legs thrust into the pedals until I had no more to give. He clocked in at 33 mph before finally giving up the chase. The adrenaline dump was intense. Stopping on the shoulder, a mile down the road, my heart rate refused to come down. The sympathetic nervous system was still in flight mode, still responding to the adrenaline. It was a clear reminder that body chemistry is very real and highly dynamic.

An unexpected lesson emerged from the encounter; life inevitably throws curves at us. None of us get through life unscathed or without some close calls. The difference comes in our ability to react and adapt on our feet. There are always going to be moments when we need an extra gear. It's the extra gear that helps us navigate serious health threats with less risk and disruption, and it's the extra gear that enables us to get back to doing what we love. The extra gear is only going to be there for us if we proactively make a daily investment.

Everything you want is on the other side of hard.
Monty Williams, NBA coach

LIFE IS MULTISPORT

With fall came a visit to the amazing freshwater lakes of Ontario, Canada — the playground I'd spent many a childhood summer. The rented cottage was beyond amazing, and the view out over the lake was more than I'd hoped for, so calm and inviting. A stack of books

I'd brought for the week waited patiently on the side table. This was a week to unplug, recharge, and refocus.

Colorful leaves of autumn were beginning to blanket the ground. The first snow was due any day. The owner's canoe lay resting near the shoreline, beckoning me to give it one last trip over the liquid paradise. The paddle pierced the water and the canoe sliced forward out into the open lake, aided by a steady wind at my back. Not a human for miles. How rare and so very special.

The wind picked up as more open water lay behind me. It was time to turn back before it grew any stronger. It was at this same moment that Mother Nature flexed her muscles. Making it back would mean going the old-fashioned way, earning it. Holding course into the shifting headwind became a growing challenge. Kneeling in the bottom of the hull, I stabbed the paddle deeper with each stroke, progress was slow but steady. The situation was not uncommon, but this canoe and I were on a first date. A rising wave came over the gunwale as I leaned into the paddle. In an instant, I knew the chilly northern lake and I were about to get very intimate. It was followed by another thought; how grateful I was that I'd taken up multisport and embraced the humbling experience of relearning to swim after decades away from the lap pool. My face hit the frigid water, but my confidence was high. Finding the bowline, I tied it to one ankle and began swimming to an island, dragging the water-laden canoe behind. Jack Lalanne would have been proud.

Once reaching the island, I was able to empty the canoe of water and set off back into the headwind toward the cottage, a bit wiser, and eager to do more reading.

Clarity comes in rare moments like these, reminding us that life is a multisport. There is little value in being great at one thing. Life is a long and winding road. We need to be good at many things and prepared to act in an instant if we hope to be resilient in our later years.

ACTIVITY TRIANGLE

Being on our feet is good. Moving on our feet is better. Doing it with others is best. The goal is to build out our foundation in 3 directions for optimal compounding benefits. Think of these as building a stable tripod to support our brain, heart, muscles and stability.

Figure 38: The Activity Triangle

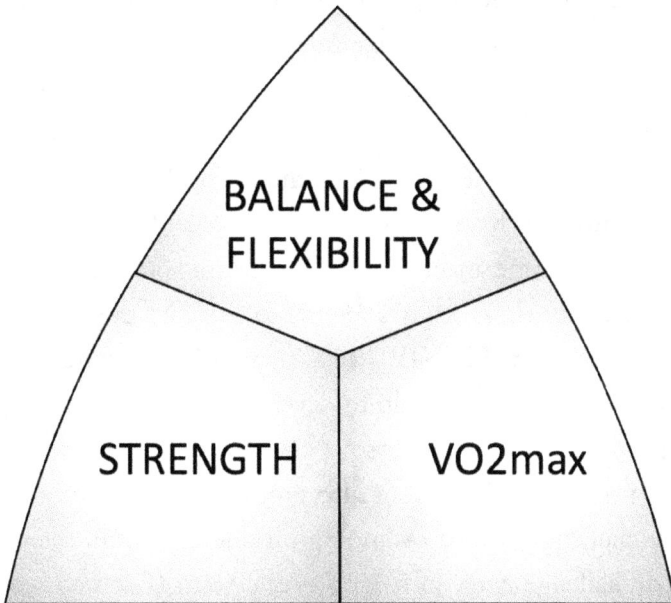

STRENGTH is one corner of the triangle. Our big muscles are where the majority of our mitochondria reside. More muscle leads to more mitochondria, naturally doubling our ROI. Strength also comes with aerobic activity, but in strength, we're talking about resistance-based activities. Some like weight training but resistance bands are a more convenient and economical way to work in resistance training. Bands travel well too. A third option is using body weight to load and unload muscles. Sit-stand-sits, squats, pushups, and calf raises are all good starting places.

VO2max, discussed earlier, is commonly referred to as aerobic or cardiovascular fitness — movements that elevate the heart rate. The body recognizes aerobic activity and gets several body functions involved. Ideally, we spread the aerobic activities across different interests. Walking is popular for those just getting back into an active lifestyle. Over time we can add time, distance, hills, and increased pace. These will naturally influence heart rate response and develop our cardiovascular efficiency. Hiking is popular for those who live in areas with trails and hiking clubs, and of course, running is a next-level activity for those up to the challenge. Dance is one of the best aerobic activities because it engages the brain in a spatial context that trains both the body and the brain simultaneously. In addition, there is cycling, and gyms have a range of ellipticals and stepper machines, etc. Blending in some anaerobic VO2max effort optimizes the return on investment for those ready and able to consider the option.

BALANCE and FLEXIBILITY complete the third corner of the activity triangle. These help to develop and preserve stability and range of motion. One of the reasons I like body-weight strength exercises is that many of the actions also promote balance and flexibility. A simple challenge is to try standing on one leg for 30 seconds. An advanced challenge is to do it with eyes closed. (Far more challenging than it sounds.) One-legged Squats and Calf-raises, for example, require both strength and balance. Starting with Side-Leg-Press outward or Knee-Raises while stabilizing with a chair are easier options to start.

The 4-minute workout is a terrific exercise that can be done anywhere, multiple times daily, requires no equipment, and costs nothing. It involves a series of squats, followed by sets of arm raises, circular arm swings (non-jumping jacks), and shoulder presses. Search YouTube for a video demonstration.

Yoga and Tai Chi have many positions and movements that foster excellent balance and flexibility. These usually have the added bonus of doing it as a group. Flexibility, the ability to move muscles through a full range of motion, is often forgotten, but it improves both function and body awareness, which helps with posture, balance, and movement.

All the above activities help to build and maintain body awareness and prevent falls and injuries in future years. The investment in practicing now will be bonus returns down the road.

These are just a small fraction of the options available to us. There are court sports, golf, swimming, pilates, umba, rowing, kayaking, basketball, and any activity that captures our interest. Just say go! Take it a day at a time, and gradually increase duration and frequency. The more variety, the better! The notion is that we are building toward results with intention. As adults, it usually requires specific intention, because many more distractions and self-identity issues compete with our choices.

Walking, running, swimming, cycling, and weightlifting are good examples to illustrate how to build forward, but the principles apply to every physical activity. There is both a measurable advancement in activity capacity as well as an intentional system to support that growth. As a high schooler, many of us could have probably run a 5k event without any training. Beyond age 40, the likelihood of success is going to be low if we've not made a point to be active most days. The bigger the goal, the more time it will take to prepare ourselves, and the more that we'll benefit from support.

For many, walking is their thing, but if that's not expanding our limits, there are many options. A recent study followed a large cohort of over 450,000 adults and found that climbing 5 flights of stairs daily reduced heart and stroke events by 75%. No gym membership is required and it works in all seasons. The physical adaptation benefits from walking versus stair climbing will be markedly different. No matter the goal, it should place us beyond our comfort zone. Failure must be a real risk, otherwise, we're not pushing our comfort zone and missing out on the whole point of the goal.

BHAG 140.3

I stood looking out at the water, surrounded by over 2,000 strangers, all waiting to attempt an Ironman race. I'd swam the 2.4 miles a handful of times, but never in such a large mass start. Numerous 100-mile rides on the bike were my strength, but I'd never run more than 20 miles in training, and never that far on tired legs.

What had brought me here? It was a big hairy audacious goal (BHAG) that was about to get real in 5 minutes. Consumed in hundreds of hours of training to get to this point, I hadn't ever visualized this moment. I'd seen others compete, and I'd raced shorter events, but this was so far beyond my comfort zone it was impossible to envision the 140.3 miles that lay ahead.

Fifteen minutes at a time. That's all I could envision and so that would be the approach. Hundreds of short steps and hundreds of ways to fail.

It wasn't always pretty, and it wasn't without discomfort, but with a mile to go, I could hear the party going on at the finish line. Twelve hours earlier, an unimaginable BHAG was now in range. Small steps strung together can accomplish big things. It works!

Figure 39: Building Results

BUILD RESULTS

SUPPORT

ACTIVITIES

Be adventurous

Run 5-10k

VO2max test

Cycle 20 miles

Hire coach

10,000 steps/day

Intensity 2/week

Join team/club

Run/Cycle 30 minutes

Biomarkers

Strength 3x/week

5 flights stairs 4x/week

Smart watch

Balance daily

BP Cuff

Exercise bands daily

5,000 steps/day

Wherever we are, there are opportunities to build and improve. Goals, a range of activities, and support systems help move us up the ladder of success and build results.

Having a plan and ways to measure our activities are core to success. Some people benefit from engaging a coach early to get them started along a path, while others benefit from a coach who can take them to the next level. The measure of success is when activity habits are a daily part of life, and we wake up looking forward to them each morning. How fast or far we went, or how much we lifted can serve as short-term motivators, but health success is measured by sustaining many activities over several decades.

THE FREQUENCY-VOLUME PATTERN FACTOR

Multiple studies and millions of coaches will confirm that frequency counts the most. One simple example is a study that compared the number of maximal voluntary eccentric bicep contractions (lowering a heavy dumbbell in a bicep curl.) Group A did 6 contractions once per week. Group B did 30 contractions once per week. Group C did 6 contractions a day for 5 days per week. After four weeks, neither group A nor B showed any changes in muscle strength. Group C, however, (6x5) saw significant increases in muscle strength; 10% in just 4 weeks. Frequency matters.

For most of us who are non-athletes, we should be able to point to a minimum of 2 activities on any given day. Ideally, they will be different activities, and one of them in the morning. Over a week, we should be able to point to at least 5 different types of activities and have completed at least 3 unique activities each of Strength, VO2max, and Balance & Flexibility activities. The more of them we do outdoors in clean air, the better the result.

These align with World Health Organization minimum intensity and volume guidelines (2022):

- 150-300 minutes of moderate intensity, or at least 75–150 minutes of vigorous-intensity aerobic physical activity; or an equivalent combination of moderate- and vigorous-intensity activity throughout the week.
- Additional health benefits are gained by exceeding these minimums.
- Muscle-strengthening activities at moderate or greater intensity that involve all major muscle groups on 2 or more days a week, as these provide additional health benefits.
- Adults aged 65 years and above should do varied multicomponent physical activity that emphasizes functional balance and strength training at moderate or greater intensity, on 3 or

more days a week, to enhance functional capacity and prevent falls.

HEART RATE VARIABILITY

Increased fitness leads to a lowering of resting heart rate (RHR) and an increase in heart rate variability (HRV). RHR is easily checked in the morning before rising or it can be monitored with a smartwatch. An increase in RHR and a decrease in HRV are signs of inadequate recovery or illness.

Heart Rate Variability is counterintuitive to most folks. High is desirable. A high HRV is an indication that at rest, the heart has plenty in reserve, like a muscle car idling at an intersection, so under-challenged that it sounds like it's on the verge of stalling at any moment. The light turns green, and it fires up and launches forward with precision firing. With increasing fitness and overall health, HRV rises and is easily tracked by today's smart devices. More on this is upcoming when we discuss acquiring data.

SLEEP ACTIVITY

Sleep is an activity? You bet it is, and it's one of our most important activities. We spend a lot of time doing it, so doing it well makes a big difference over several decades. Quality sleep protects the brain for future years because that's when some of our most important brain activity occurs. It would be nice if sleep were simply about logging hours. That's a hard enough task for millions, but there's more going on with sleep that's worth understanding.

Rest is part of sleep but sleep is deceivingly complex. It's a bit like the store that opens in the morning, ready for business, and by the end of the day, a lot of the inventory has gone out the door and into customers' homes. Once the doors close for business, the night shift comes in, restocks the shelves, makes repairs, and cleans the surfaces so it's ready for another busy day of business. It might look routine and simple from the street, but inside, it's a whole different story.

Normal sleep follows a loose but predictable, albeit seemingly chaotic cycle, starting with N1 (wakefulness to sleep), dropping quickly to N2 (light), and then N3 (deep, slow wave) sleep. Assuming it makes it that far, it then cycles upward and then downward again, with deep sleep taking priority in the first third of our sleep. The cycle continues to repeat, but shifting upward with increasing time in REM sleep, typically ending with a REM sleep segment before waking.

Rapid Eye Movement (REM) sleep is the easiest to identify because it is the dream state. REM sleep is about memory consolidation, emotional processing, and learning. Most of our muscles are temporarily paralyzed to prevent acting out our dreams. Trying to physically outrun a dragon or fly like Peter Pan while in our sleep would be very problematic! REM sleep helps to process memories and emotions, and plays a role in determining what memories to retain and how to integrate the new learnings into existing knowledge.

Deep Sleep (N3) is focused on physical cellular repair, rebalancing energy into our cells, and restoring immune cell levels. Deep sleep is also when memory gets organized and consolidated, so that important information can be located and recalled in the future, in the same way that a library stores information. This is also a period of detoxifying the brain by clearing waste products and toxins. When we are getting adequate N3 sleep, we feel rested, cognitively alert, and able to solve problems effectively.

The following example is data from across 4 nights. Each night achieved at least 8 hours of sleep, including restful periods. Deep N3 sleep averaged 1:08 per night, while REM was about 1:19 per night. How we get there varies by night, and is a function of many variables, including the prior night's sleep experience.

Figure 40: Sleep Patterns Over Multiple Nights

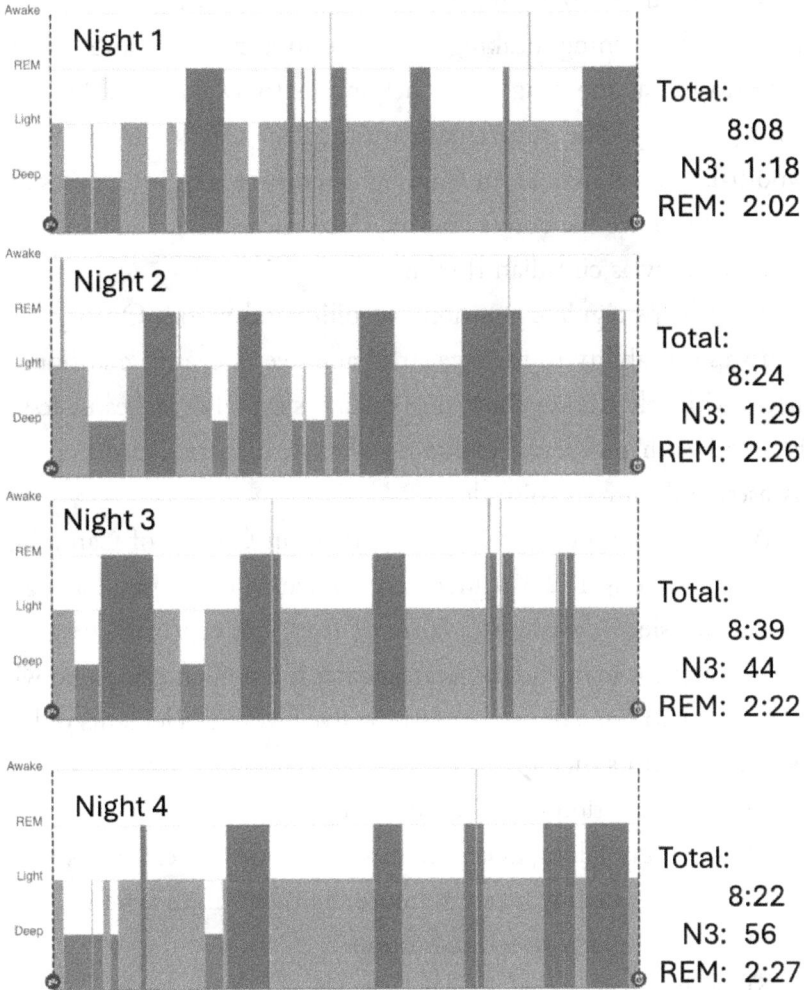

Sleep cycles vary somewhat from night to night, typically dominated by deep N3 sleep during the first third of the night, and REM dream sleep dominating the final third.

All phases of sleep are important, and they all require time to perform their tasks. Several research studies point to between 7 and 8 hours per night as optimal for adults.

The endocrine system is also busy at work while we sleep. The pineal gland in our brain increases the secretion of the hormone melatonin in the evening, peaking 2-4 hours after midnight and naturally decreasing as morning nears, helping us to awaken and feel alert during the day. The suprachiasmatic nucleus (SCN) in the brain's hypothalamus receives input from light-sensitive cells in the eyes and helps synchronize the body's internal clock with sunset and sunrise — what we know as circadian rhythm.

Sleep helps regulate emotional stability and mood. Quality sleep improves our ability to manage stress and keep negative emotions in check. Multiple studies show that quality sleep also makes us less at risk for health problems, including obesity, diabetes, cardiovascular diseases, and immune disorders.

A 2023 study published by the American College of Cardiology found that among 172,321 men and women who reported having all five quality sleep measures (a score of five), life expectancy was 4.7 years greater for men and 2.4 years greater for women compared with those who had none or only one of the five favorable elements of low-risk sleep. Factors included:

1) sleep duration of 7-8 hours nightly
2) difficulty falling asleep no more than two times a week
3) trouble staying asleep no more than two times a week
4) not using any sleep medication
5) feeling well-rested after waking up at least five days a week.

Several over-the-counter dental devices help manage airways and prevent grinding during sleep. Dentists also have some terrific devices. Mouth-taping is also another option worthy of investigating.

SUCCESS IS A CHOICE

We tend to place too much pressure on ourselves, expecting to love an activity instantly or to see unrealistic results in just a few weeks. NOTHING HAPPENS FAST IN LONGEVITY. A Whealthspan mindset chooses to play the long game every day until it becomes second nature, and it's no longer a conscious choice. Home-based activities are usually the most convenient, but social support is important too. There is a group of a dozen or so, older men who meet at the YMCA 3 mornings a week to swim together. It's hard to tell if they like the swimming or the camaraderie more. Exploit all the options, as each has something different to offer. One or two activities might be favorites, while the others fill the gaps. That's okay. It keeps life interesting and keeps one from burning out. It also leaves us prepared to try new things and adapt to changing situations.

We've got to push fear aside and place ourselves beyond our comfort zone to discover what's waiting on the other side. It's not supposed to be easy, so welcome the awakening of muscle and body awareness that will accompany us on the journey. Find whatever and whomever it takes to kick us in the butt to get moving every morning. Make some new friends who are already active. Learn from them and feed off their energy. Be forewarned, it's contagious.

Let's get active together!

Chapter 15

DATA WHEALTH

TWO PATIENTS VISIT THEIR primary care physician (PCP) for a routine annual physical.

Jordan's Annual Visit

Doctor: Good morning. How have you been feeling this week?

Jordan: Sorry I was late. The traffic was bad, and I discovered I needed gas. I probably should have given it more thought. Um, I'm feeling ok, I guess.

Doctor: Anything more I should know about?

Jordan: Not that I can think of. The usual craziness but I guess that's why I'm here –to check things out.

Doctor: We'll schedule the routine bloodwork. Anything special we should discuss?

Jordan: Not that I know of. I can't recall if I did bloodwork last year. Anyway, I'm sure you'll let me know if anything is abnormal.

Jan's Annual Visit

Doctor: Good morning. How have you been feeling this week?

Jan: My resting heart rate's been a bit high, and my blood pressure's been up about 5 points, but still in a good range.

Doctor: Anything more I should know about?

Jan: My parents have needed more help lately and I've needed to travel more for work, so it's been a challenging year. I've felt more tired, but assume it's been the added stress. Otherwise, I've been managing to hold it together.

Doctor: We'll schedule the routine annual tests. Anything special we should discuss?

Jan: I was advised to ask for ApoB and hsCRP labs. I didn't see either on last year's labs. Could we get those tests?

In the 9.5 minutes remaining, how much progress is the doctor likely to make with these 2 patients? How do these patients signal an investment in their health? Do they view their doctor as a health partner or like their auto mechanic? Most importantly, which patient has the best odds of the doctor detecting the early stages of disease within them?

Ideally, patients would want to partner with their PCP in their health journey. Sadly, this has rarely been the case. Doctors are under constant time constraints and genuinely can't afford the time to listen to long-winded stories or laundry lists of normal aches and pains caused by sedentary habits, trying to guess which ones are real or phantom. Other patients skip annual physicals leaving the doctor with very little data with which to work. Then there are the patients who rely on the internet to self-diagnose their issues, expect to be handed another prescription, or are quick to challenge the doctor's diagnosis. To compound things even more, physicians are taught in medical school that patients aren't likely to follow their advice anyway, so don't waste time and get on to the next patient. There are patients waiting, bills to be paid, and an office to manage. And we wonder why early disease diagnoses slip through the cracks!

The system wears down PCPs, overloading them with paperwork, and making it nearly impossible for small offices to survive the administrative and financial overhead. Unlike in private business, PCP's fees are set by the big brokers in healthcare. They are pawns in the world of healthcare spending, accounting for less than 6% of all healthcare dollars. The system is fraught with failings, and nowhere is that more evident than at the primary care doctor-patient interface. Change is inevitable. The trajectory of the current model is not financially sustainable and we're running out of people to resource it.

DATA TALKS B.S. WALKS

Part of what I've always loved about my work has been having one foot in research and the other in the real world to help solve big, complex challenges. Laboratory research might lead us to believe that science is known and predictable. At best, research guides us to reasonable predictions, subject to a long list of assumptions. In my engineering days, occasionally I was hired as an Expert Witness to help resolve legal disputes. We'd replicate the event in question and gather copious data on as many aspects as possible. Often these would be accident reconstructions, supported by multiple sensors and high-speed video. Every case sent the other side packing. Research studies and world-renowned professors' opinions don't stand a chance against real-world data. Studies and opinions are best guesses at the gaps in information. More data fills the guesses with facts, greatly reducing uncertainty.

Today's pervasive, overly simplistic internet health theorists, eager to carve out their niche, may be well-intentioned but most serve to confuse more than clarify many matters of personal health. Real-world health data is both multifactorial and highly individual. This is why clinical data is so important, as it is real-world data, and it pertains directly to one's specific health, i.e. n=1, "my" data. It can seem compelling that 10,000 test subjects had positive, statistically significant outcomes with a certain drug, food, or supplement, but there is no certainty that we'll experience the same outcomes. For many reasons, we might not be a good candidate. Worse, we might even experience adverse reactions due to factors unique to us.

Data is more about information than answers, so we should resist the temptation to draw conclusions too quickly. Often, we need to triangulate a question with multiple data sources to be able to arrive at reasonable answers and take action toward getting on track toward health.

PRECISION PERSONAL MEDICINE

One of the fastest-growing consumer market segments is personal health data. About 1 in 4 people already wear a smartwatch, and it is still early days for that technology. It is projected to triple within a decade, which means more wearables, more data captured by each device, and far more data to interpret and guide us. The healthcare system was designed around doctors and scientists holding all the data, not patients, and that is creating new tensions beyond what the internet brought to the table.

Enter Artificial Intelligence (AI) and physicians are struggling to know how best to proceed. When I speak with Physicians, it is evident that most don't know what to expect, making it hard to know how to prepare. None of this was in their training and the rules of engagement are evolving quickly. AI will play many roles in transforming healthcare, but the one that matters most to this conversation is analyzing personal health data with far more breadth and precision. With personalized medicine that AI is expected to provide, we'll be able to learn about foods and habits our bodies thrive on and which ones create unhealthy stress. For example, learning that our body responds better to a 20-minute intense activity than a 90-minute walk might shift our views on how we spend our time. These types of data are bound to empower us, by feeling more aware and more in control of our health and our future.

Precision medicine will also leverage emerging genetic data and its connection with common chronic diseases. Researchers have already found about 60 genomic variants that are present more frequently in people with coronary artery disease. Most of these variants are dispersed across the genome and do not cluster on one specific chromosome. These data, together with lifestyle and other clinical data, hold tremendous near-term opportunities for patients, but extend far beyond the capabilities of a lone physician to resolve. AI will distill it down into manageable data for physicians and patients to work with in ways not possible today.

What if we could see a disease risk trajectory from within hours of childbirth, and that food allergies, heart disease, certain cancers, and dementia risk could be reduced by 95% instead of waiting to discover it decades later when there's little that can be done? Hospitals are already doing genetics screening on 95% of newborns for up to 50 diseases within 48 hours. It's only a matter of time before early screening will expand much further. I'm willing to bet that's also when we'll see the biggest shift in public health because we'll be working with people at a point in life when they are malleable and healthy lifetime habits can be established early.

Research on dietary habits has also revealed that persons with a Mediterranean-MIND diet score of 7.5 or higher also score better in late-life cognition. Mediterranean-MIND Diet Score is a 15-item dietary assessment tool for assessing obesity, heart disease, diabetes, and dementia risk. The questionnaire covers green leafy vegetables, other vegetables, berries, nuts, olive oil, butter, cheese, whole grains, fish, beans, poultry, red meat, fried foods, sweets, and wine. As more is learned about the nuances of key dietary components, more will be refined into precision health medical practice.

If 3 simple healthy habits would cut our risk of dementia in half, would people try to adopt them? In my audiences, the answer is an overwhelming, yes, because many have experienced the family impact. Just a passing mention of Alzheimer's in one of my talks usually motivates someone to corner me afterward with questions regarding a family situation. They're understandably fearful, but they are also highly motivated. The fear of dementia drives behaviors in people far more than concerns about obesity, heart disease, and cancer, despite them sharing many root causes. Discounting dementia as just another chronic disease says we've almost certainly never had to face it. Listen closely to the families that are dealing with dementia. They have much to teach us.

Our genes get most of us to midlife without issue, but the odds of cracks in our inner armor only increase going forward. The finance folks remind us that past performance is not indicative of future results. In health, we know for certain our second half of life will look a lot different than the first. In the same way we put defined financial guardrails in place, there are several more biomarker guardrails available to us, and more on the way.

Our brains tend to hold on to motivating stories of people who have beat cancer but suppress the statistics of those who weren't so fortunate. It helps our attitudes but hinders our actions. It's a delicate balance that's best managed by knowing we are taking intentional actions to promote all aspects of our health. Assuming we're living up to that promise to ourselves, it is easier to keep a healthy, balanced mindset and be empathic toward those dealing with disease.

Healthy lifestyle habits are good for the brain.

Some empowering news comes out of the CHAP and MAP studies that involved cohorts of over 12,000 participants spanning 10 years, with a recent 18-year follow-up. Compared to participants with poor lifestyles, the risk of Alzheimer's dementia was:
- 37% lower in those with 2 to 3 healthy lifestyle factors
- 60% lower in those with 4 to 5 healthy lifestyle factors.

The healthy lifestyle factors all fall within the MEDAC principles mentioned several times already. All very doable by everyday mortals like you and me! The other great news is that one approach addresses all the common chronic diseases equally.

GENETIC PREDISPOSITIONS

Earlier we discussed our genetics, but what about our genetic predispositions to diseases? The Human Mortality Database is filled with data to help us answer this question, and I'll try to distill all that data down to knowledge we can use.

By looking at mortality data by age, we end up with a frequency distribution that enables us to see the differences across the human lifespan, as well as changes over the decades. About 97.4% of us will live beyond the age of 40. Great! Only 0.027% of us will live beyond the age of 100. For all the hype about the centenarian population growing, it will remain a very select club. For our purposes, it's reasonable to say that all deaths beyond age 100 are attributed to Natural Causes. After accounting for deaths due to accidents and suicide, it says that about 99% of those, aged 40 and above, are predisposed to one or more chronic diseases. In other words, we are all effectively predisposed to one or more chronic diseases. While it shouldn't come as a big surprise, it places our predispositions in a definable context. The questions then are:

- At what point does our immune system lose its ability to address early disease as it sparks?
- How effective will it be in slowing the disease(s) progression?

Science unequivocally tells us that health is <u>not</u> sustained by living in a bubble or playing it safe. I know of no centenarian who lived a sheltered life. It's reasonable, and probably wise, to accept that our protection against chronic disease has limits. At what age chronic disease finally reveals itself, however, is negotiable, and that's where we have some leverage. Making the top decile for a female is currently age 94, and for a male, age 90. In a community of health-minded people, that is a very reasonable target and instructive for planning purposes.

We may be stuck with our genetics, but unlike Las Vegas, we can stack the deck! We get to choose many of our cards and how to play them. Sure, the house is ultimately going to win in the end, but the game of life is the best one in town, and extending it at no added cost, is a great reward.

Figure 41: A Winning Hand

DATA AND THE HAWTHORNE EFFECT

Data changes behavior when managed effectively. Data can also promote what's termed the Hawthorn Effect, or the Observer Bias, and in doing so, influence behaviors and outcomes. A few common examples:

- A clock indicates it's mealtime, triggering us to feel hungry.

- A weekly public weigh-in more effectively promotes weight-loss behaviors because the data is shared within a group.
- Posted workplace safety performance statistics cause employees to be more careful because they don't want to be the ones to spoil the positive streak.
- Roadside radar speed signs flashing "Your Speed ___" to cars exceeding the posted limit cause drivers to slow down.

The introduction of smart personal devices is quickly changing the landscape. Apps are devoted to tracking all sorts of daily metrics, even how far the dog walked last week. Humans love our own data because it compels us to meet or exceed targets that no taskmaster has thrust upon us. Data is usually intimidating at first, but once we get over the initial learning curve it soon becomes empowering.

Smartwatches are 21st-century observers and serve as validation for the wave of smart health devices that are coming. Their success is due in no small part to them being so accessible. It goes about doing its measurements autonomously, with or without our attention. Interact with it or don't, it doesn't care, and it does its thing without us having to be tech wizards. The human interface is drop-dead simple, and that's been the game changer in the world of smart technology.

Data from smart devices feed into massive databases that compare us with millions of other people, informing us how our physiology fits into the world of humans. Whatever level we're at, we're naturally inclined to do the work and maintain habits that support us in advancing toward or preserving optimal levels. It's as anonymous as we choose for it to be, and it's accessible to us 24/7. Need a fix? Check the app and see how we're doing. The result of this is an opportunity to build and maintain a support network that never leaves our side, leveraging the observer effect to our own benefit.

SMART BIOSENSORS COME HOME

Smartwatches are the first generation of wearable smart biosensors to be placed in consumers' hands. Wearable health devices track a range of health-related data, provide real-time health status, and help educate us on issues that affect our bodies.

Wearable biosensor patches are commonly placed on an arm or the abdomen, depending on the function. Continuous glucose monitors (CGM) are the most common in use today. CGMs have revolutionized the management of blood serum glucose for diabetic patients, thanks to their real-time tracking and ease of use. For many diabetics, CGMs have replaced the need for multiple, daily manual finger prick blood tests.

Wearable electrocardiogram (ECG) monitors are simple, provide straightforward heart analytics, and quickly detect irregular and abnormal heart readings, thanks to AI technology. They support remote patient monitoring (RPM), so the doctor's office can be alerted to trends that might be of concern, or just check in on their patients' well-being.

Wearable blood pressure monitors enable those with hypertension issues to keep a constant watch over their blood pressure by biochemical changes in the body associated with hypertension. The traditional BP cuffs can't compete with the convenience and live tracking offered by a wearable device, though these are not quite ready to displace familiar BP cuffs.

Hearables are in-ear wearable devices that are about to hit the market. These will be an upgrade over many wrist wearables, and able to provide a lot more medical information, like blood pressure, ECG, blood oxygen, breathing patterns, as well as biomechanical changes in movement habits that can all help predict events before they occur.

Therapeutic patches that deliver medications and monitor in real-time are in various stages of commercial development. These deliver superior results to the blood concentration swings common to traditional pill distribution. They are also consistent in minimizing dose, which is particularly helpful for medications with a short half-life.

Sleep monitors have also made tremendous leaps forward. Traditionally, doctors send the patient into a sleep lab for an *all-in, one-night* sleep assessment. Expecting a typical night's sleep in a strange environment with multiple wires strapped to the body and a breathing monitor is unlikely to replicate normal sleep, but until recently that was the only option. Home versions can now be used over several night's sleep to generate a more realistic and comprehensive sleep profile for assessment and treatment. Again, more data in a real-world setting is always preferred when possible.

STEALTH MODE

We are quickly heading into a new paradigm in health management, whereby default, many more consumers will be flying below or adjacent to the radar of the healthcare system. The consumer marketplace is fast encroaching on the role traditionally held by PCPs, as consumers gain greater access to more online testing services and therapies. This segment is growing as the introduction of new diagnostic tools is outpacing the healthcare system's traditional slow pace. The move is further fueled by the sharp growth in lifestyle and functional medical practitioners who are trained in lifestyle therapies and understand how to leverage the new holistic health science. Lifestyle and Functional medicine are the care of choice for consumers seeking proactive health and more advanced treatment options. Many physicians are going back to school to get certified, but in the short term, it may take some digging to find a trained physician. Note that many clinicians advertise that they practice functional and integrative health, but are not medical doctors. Due diligence is required to understand the qualifications behind what is being offered.

The list of things we can measure in real-time is growing quickly, and the trend of where we're going with data collection is clear. Consumers are going to bring a lot more intelligence to the personal health discussion. Medical technology companies are staffing up with their own physicians who can prescribe where necessary and make data directly accessible to consumers. It's all going to push the medical establishment well outside its comfort zone and PCPs who resist adapting will be left behind.

Many physicians are nervous about how patients will use and interpret the data. It's a legitimate concern, but it says more about patient education and engagement gaps than patients' ability to receive data. A look around at how much information we all take in today, says that our tolerance for data is higher than ever imagined. Some patients already tend to over-manage their health, creating their own set of issues, but this happens with or without additional data. Humans adapt to change that is positive and empowering. Most of us already walk around with smartphones with 256 MB of data and processing capabilities of trillions of operations per second. Humans crave information! Western society is currently paying an enormous price for its lack of basic health education, and it's clear that we need to start putting a lot better information in consumers' and patients' hands. These diagnostic tools will do just that.

3P APPROACH

The medical system was never intended or designed to proactively promote health or prevent chronic disease. It was developed to cure acute illness, which it does remarkably well. Western medicine has made tremendous advancements in reducing childhood fatalities over the last century through medical hygiene, prenatal, delivery, and neonatal care, imaging, antibiotics, and vaccines. The opportunities for step-change improvements around acute care are growing fewer, evidenced by the shift toward age-related disease treatments. These have proven more challenging to address, due to both the nature of these diseases and the traditional acute-care approach, under which the healthcare system operates. Treating something that's been slowly advancing over 10-40 years is very different than something that developed over just days and weeks. It requires our involvement in ways the medical system is challenged to provide.

Optimists like me get enthused by opportunities to treat chronic health, but it requires a different dance with the healthcare system – one that can test our resolve at times. The dance I'm referring to is learning how and when to lead and when to follow. The Patient-Physician-Partnership (3P) approach is one of healthy tension that recognizes neither partner holds all the answers. The odds of enabling health are exponentially improved by combining both the patient's and physician's knowledge and resources.

The patient visit examples at the start of this chapter speak directly to this poInt. The opportunity to dance starts every time a doctor walks into an exam room. Wanting to work together isn't enough. Both the patient and physician need to be ready to participate the moment the door opens because the clock is ticking down. Play it too casually, and it becomes a social visit, and not much is learned. Play it too intense and the patient gets nervous and forgets to convey key facts.

The 3P approach isn't for everyone, but it is arguably the only one designed for optimal health. A PCP who isn't willing to work with an informed and contributing patient isn't offering the best care. A patient who isn't willing to put in the effort isn't enabling their doctor to deliver their best care. The patient holds the knowledge of lifestyle and symptoms. The doctor holds expertise in interpreting the information the patient provides, along with patient health records and diagnoses, to know where to lead the patient. Sometimes it's a direct line and sometimes it's a process of elimination.

Patients Jordan and Jan, in the earlier example, will both eventually receive a cancer diagnosis. The odds of Jan getting an early diagnosis are significantly better than Jordan's, and Jan will benefit from having far more options, some of which will likely be less invasive and disruptive. Jan has initiated the 3P approach by being prepared for visits and being proactive with specific and informed requests.

Looking forward, the introduction of AI into patient diagnoses is going to offer more benefits to the proactive and informed patient due simply to their ability to provide more accurate and comprehensive health and lifestyle inputs. The more quality patient-specific data in hand, the more reliable any analysis and diagnosis is going to be.

Our physician's responsibility is to try and pull us out of the ditch after we run off the road. It's our job to try and not end up there.

The objective here is to keep our health within the lane markers as we continue on the long journey of life versus waiting until we're off the road in a ditch and forced to call 9-1-1. Today's advanced cars come with lane and object detection that redirects the car's motion in advance of crossing the lane or hitting an object. The same things are happening in patient health data technology. I can romanticize about driving the circa 1950 VW Beetle that my dad and brothers converted to a dune buggy in 1970, but I'm confident the odds of a 2,800-mile cross-country road trip without incident would be much better by leveraging the technology in today's cars.

DECIPHERING LAB REPORTS

Getting in touch with our health means getting intimate with our personal health data. For years, I'd visit the doctor for an annual checkup every year or two, file the lab report, and forget about it. I'd done my part, or so I'd thought. Over the years, I slowly started paying closer attention and came to learn that most PCPs don't get involved until we are well outside the normal range for a given biomarker. I can point to a series of lab reports over 3 consecutive years where physicians missed or chose not to bring a recurring blood marker issue to my attention. It wasn't an acute threat, so no action was deemed necessary. It did, however, present significant chronic risk if not addressed. My own research confirmed the pattern by looking at three other related biomarkers. A minor dietary adjustment brought them all back into range, but it required me to take the lead in sorting it out. I've encountered this with students' and clients' labs as well. It's another reason to spend a bit of time reviewing current lab reports with previous reports, as that's the only way to identify trends early.

Lab reports are transitioning from a list of numbers to more intuitive visual reports. As AI comes more into play, we'll also begin seeing more disease scores that encompass a series of biomarkers. If we take prediabetes as an example, we're more likely to see a Disease Risk Score based on a suite of biomarkers such as 2-hydroxybutyrate, aromatic amino acids, adiponectin, acylcarnitine, branched-chain amino acids, C-reactive protein, ferritin, glycated albumin, glycine, linoleoyl-glycerophosphocholine, triglycerides, isoleucine, glycine, proline, glutamate, lysine, serine, citrulline, 2-aminoadipic acid, and palmitic acid. Labs can measure them all today, but PCPs aren't in a reasonable position to make sense of such a large and complex data matrix. In contrast, that's going to be an easy task for AI to resolve down to a more reliable Type 2 Diabetes (T2DM) risk score than we have today. It's tools like these that will improve primary care in the very near future.

The other point to note is the sliding scale. Most of today's lab reports indicate Low, Normal, and High. There are a couple of shortcomings to consider. Is it better to be on the lower, middle, or high end of normal? For example, if last year's fasting blood glucose value was 99 mg/dL, and a recent one comes back at 100 mg/dL, that crosses the prediabetes threshold and conveys something much more serious. What to do in this case if we're the patient or the physician? Responses will vary widely. From a data measurement perspective, splitting hairs to try to differentiate between 99 and 100 is not the best use of anyone's time, as one mg/dL is likely beyond the laboratory's measurement capability at a 95% confidence interval. A sliding scale, such as the top one in Figure 42, is more intuitive as it places biomarker values into a more meaningful context. A patient who is interested in optimal health naturally feels motivated to strive for optimal value versus just being normal.

The second slider is an example of a disease risk score. These reflect a composite of many biomarkers, each one weighted in context with the others in the mathematical matrix that goes into the score value. As a simple example, we require both height and weight biomarkers to arrive at a Body Mass Index. A more advanced BMI would also consider patient waist-to-height and waist-to-hip ratios, because these are known to be strong health markers. Disease scores are much more complex, but apply the same principle.

Figure 42: Interpreting Lab Reports

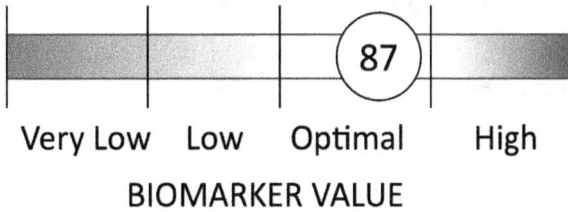

Very Low Low Optimal High

BIOMARKER VALUE

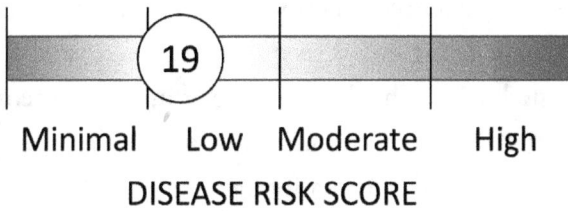

Minimal Low Moderate High

DISEASE RISK SCORE

Taking time to review past lab tests helps prepare us for where we'd like the next labs to be. Some results will be specific biomarkers, but as AI comes more into medicine, expect to see more disease scoring that comprise groups of biomarkers.

This brings us to ask, what is "normal"? In the case of laboratory testing and reporting, most of the time, ranges are based on the test results from large groups of healthy people. Within these population data are a wide range of individual biomarker data. Normal is a statistical representation of many different people who all have their unique composite set of biomarkers, which is why there are ranges of normal. Being in the exact center of normal isn't necessarily ideal for a given individual. It's just a statistical reference point. Our genetics influence many of these values and we might benefit by being on the higher side on one biomarker and the low side on another. Our optimal may not coincide with a population average because of lifestyle factors. Athletes, for example, often fall outside a normal range because their body is responding to stimuli not common in the general population. Recall also that several biomarkers operate collectively, and health is better defined by patterns than by single biomarkers. Ideally, all our biomarkers are normal, but sometimes individual factors make that unrealistic. Doctors are typically well-positioned to explain this to a reasonably informed patient.

BUILDING A HEALTH DATABASE

For better or worse, we own our health. We likely inherited flaws more significant than the outwardly apparent physical traits we see in the mirror, and experienced a period in life when we paid less attention to our health. Some habits seem hard to shake, and some habits seem hard to stick with. Thankfully, none of us need a medical degree to become better caretakers of our minds and bodies. Just like planning a road trip, we need information on where we are now, where we want to go, a course to get us there, and a means to track our progress. Wherever we are today, there are many options available to us to move forward. Data is our empowering friend and offers abundant opportunities to reinforce small successes along our journey.

What labs should I ask for at my annual medical visit? It's always a great question because it says we intend to engage the doctor in an informed discussion and are looking to get the most out of the visit. An overlooked value of baseline routine testing is the historical reference it provides. Without personal data, we've only got population data for comparison, and that pales in value to personal data. Humans are not robots, and there are surprisingly wide ranges of biomarkers among healthy individuals. These data may also reveal some surprises that we'd want to know at the earliest opportunity.

Is a lab result typical for a given patient or has something changed in their health? We only know with certainty by having a thorough historical patient record to look back on. This comes up frequently with very healthy, fit people. Their fitness and dietary habits can mean that some of their labs look different from average population data. I run into this all the time, and it's getting worse as doctors become more desensitized by an increasingly overweight and diabetic patient population. The absence of an acute issue is an invitation for a PCP to dismiss further investigation. It's Unfortunate, but it's common. Recall that the system was designed to treat the sick, not cater to the healthy.

Most lab tests are very inexpensive, so unless cost is a significant barrier, more labs are better. Again, the idea isn't to create problems, but rather, to get a clear and comprehensive baseline. We never want to be in the position of having to trust just one number. It's patterns and trends that tell the real story.

It's common, and preferable, to have our PCP order tests for us, as they are in the best position to interpret the results and can infer more from the data. That said, some doctors continue to be minimalists when it comes to ordering labs. These are historically difficult physician partners. Of all the places to save money in a $4.5 trillion national health spend, labs are one of the last places we should be scrimping. Sometimes physicians require justification to order the lab to ensure it is covered by insurance. Regardless of the barriers, we all have a right to understand our health and sometimes we just need to feed the system information it needs to support the request. There's nothing like shortness of breath, blurry vision, abdominal pain, etc. to help incentivize a doctor to order more tests. It also helps in verifying the need for medication, particularly medications that are likely to stay with us for the rest of our lives. One of the most common examples we see is in addressing heart disease risk based on a basic lipids panel. Two recent examples:

A Tale of Two Patients
Jerry, age 60, has a history of high cholesterol, including high LDL and high non-HDL, and has a family history of heart disease. At

*previous appointments, Jerry's PCP recommended a statin, based sole-
ly on an elevated LDL from a simple lipids panel. An avid runner,
lean, Jerry has always been conscientious about diet and proactively
arranged for a Coronary Artery Calcium scan (CAC). It came back
at zero – the lowest score possible, indicating a low likelihood of arterial plaque. Jerry also requested a comprehensive lipids panel, which
came back with a particle profile that indicated low atherosclerotic
risk. Above-average LDL and excellent cardiovascular health are not
the norm, but taking a drug for no underlying disease shouldn't be
normal either.*

*Kim, age 52, has always had normal cholesterol and triglycerides,
eats well, has never been overweight, and always maintained an active
lifestyle. At the last physical, Kim asked the physician about getting a
CAC, to which the physician responded, "No need, your numbers are
great. Most of my patients would love your numbers!" Dissatisfied,
Kim called the local radiology clinic and was able to book a CAC scan
without a prescription (prescription requirement varies by location.)
The day following the CAC scan Kim received a call from the doctor's
office. It was the doctor. "The lab sent over your results and your heart
calcium is surprisingly high. I'd like to get you in to see a cardiologist."
Kim's CAC score came back at 341 – moderate to severe heart risk.*

Both situations happen all the time with heart disease, and this is
one of several reasons ischemic heart disease remains our number one
cause of early death. The medical system remains far too casual in proactively screening heart disease, relying too much on population data,
and not enough on thorough patient-specific data. It's on us to be
proactive in getting all the reasonable data we can get our hands on.

Kim is heading to the cardiologist with the expectation of getting
additional tests that will more accurately assess the heart's functional

risk. Heart screening tests don't tell us anything about functional risk, and that's what really matters. We'll come back to this shortly.

Competition for our attention is rising, with several health technology and online health companies providing in-house licensed physicians authorized to write prescriptions. These data will come directly to us and are usually copied into our medical records. There are several companies providing these services. They are often storefronts for the same familiar laboratory service companies used by our regular doctors, such as LabCorp and Quest.

While baseline data is invaluable, depending on budget, age, and overall health, not all tests are needed annually. Here is a list for consideration and discussion with a physician. As always, health is individual and that should be factored into our decisions. The goal is for adult patients to understand their care. Known health issues and family history should point to additional tests.

Annual routine lab tests to consider:
- Bloodwork (Complete Blood Count)
- Comprehensive metabolic panel (CMP incl. Hba1C, FBS...)
- Hemoglobin A1C (HbA1C...)
- Standard lipid panel (Cholesterol)
- Inflammation (hsCRP, IL-6)
- Thyroid (TSH) and Insulin Growth Factor (IGF-1)
- Hormones (Cort, P4, TSH, T3, T4, Testosterone, Thyroid Peroxidase Antibodies)
- Prostate screening (PSA) to track progression where there is family history
- Whole Blood Nutrients (Vitamins, Minerals, Metabolites, Amino Acids, Antioxidants)
- Anemia panel

Supplemental:

- Genetic tests (one-time) for CVD, incl. LP(a), diabetes, other familial disease histories
- Advanced Lipid Panel incl. lipids fraction (biannually for elevated cholesterol or familial heart disease)
- Hearing (every 5-10 years, more frequent over age 65)

Heart Disease:

Cardiovascular Disease (CVD) deserves a deeper explanation, because it is so much more prevalent. There are several tests available, and CVD can be much better managed with early intervention.

Cardiovascular Disease starts as plaque formations as early as in our teens, and progresses slowly over decades, eventually calcifying in the walls of the arteries. The Coronary Artery Calcium scan (CAC) is an early first screening test. This is a quick and inexpensive CT scan for heart disease that detects calcium under X-ray and reports it as an Agatston score, as well as a population percentile. It infers the likelihood of soft plaque but does not measure arterial soft plaque. Radiation levels are low, as is the frequency of testing. The key is timing. Those with a family history of heart disease or with diabetes would benefit from testing by age 35-40. Some cities don't require a physician's prescription. A call to a local radiation lab will confirm the requirements. Most labs charge under $150 for the test, which only takes a few minutes. No preparation required, no needles, no dyes – super easy.

The medical guidance for screening age has slowly been coming down from age 50. This is based on high certainty of a positive result for atherosclerosis. A lot of the damage has already progressed by this age. Knowing this information 20 years sooner leverages time in our favor, particularly given we now have several lifestyle tools to address it very effectively.

Plaque is of much bigger concern than calcium, because unlike calcium, plaque is in an unstable state. Calcium contributes to slow progression of stenosis (restriction) but plaque can erupt into an acute myocardial infarction – heart attack. For positive CAC scores, subsequent CAC scans offer little value. Arterial blood flow tests matter from this point forward, because they are direct measurements of heart function. Reversing existing calcium would seem logical, except that the calcium is only part of the volume causing the restriction, and there are no demonstrated methods that don't place the patient at more serious risk and complications. Lifestyle practices are the best tools to slow progression.

Restricted flow is typically evidenced by weak heart contractions and/or slow response rates on an ECG during a treadmill stress test. A treadmill stress test can be replaced by a pharmacological stress test where a patient may be physically unable to perform a treadmill test or if there are concerns of triggering a heart attack.

Another test mentioned several times is the VO2max test, which is performed at a cardiology-equipped lab, capable of measuring and evaluating heart performance with ECG, and results reviewed by a sports cardiologist. Typical sports performance labs do not have cardiology + ECG capability. The VO2max test makes sense for very fit individuals who would not be sufficiently challenged by a standard treadmill stress test.

The simplest of all screening tests is the noninvasive Carotid Intima-Media Thickness (CIMT) ultrasound test. This test focuses on measuring potential stenosis of the carotid arteries leading to the brain. Recall from the heart discussion, that atherosclerosis occurs throughout the body, so the carotid arteries also serve as a proxy for the heart. Apart from this test being noninvasive and inexpensive, it can differentiate between tissue, plaque, and calcium. It is also able to measure vessel intima thickness and can measure stenosis progression over time. Its reliability is limited by the technician's skill, but given the upsides, it gets a thumbs up. The test costs about $250, and like the CAC, it isn't typically covered by insurance. While that might sound like a negative, keeping it outside of insurance helps keep the cost low. For tests like these that might only be required a couple of times, it makes good sense.

Next level testing is a CCT-Angiogram, which is an X-ray scan with a dye that reveals blood flow and perfusion. Several hospitals also use software that can analyze the CCT-A data to produce a 3D color "heartflow" model and add greater certainty to the test.

When a cardiologist suspects flow is significantly restricted, he/she is likely to recommend a Coronary Angiogram (CA). The surgeon inserts a catheter, via the wrist or thigh, that is fed up into the main heart muscle arteries and releases minimal amounts of dye. Flow and perfusion are detected with a short burst of X-rays that generate a video of the coronary arteries in action. If stenosis is limited, the test is complete. If appropriate, the surgeon may opt to insert a stent to re-open the artery. The patient is fully awake during this procedure and able to participate in the decision. If stenosis is significant and a stent(s) is not an option, Coronary Artery Bypass Grafting (CABG) may be a recommended follow-up procedure. Many hospitals are now using robotics for CABG, because it is less invasive, has higher precision, and results in faster patient recovery.

Genetics Testing

An emerging area is genetic health testing. We have 23andMe® to thank for making genetic testing affordable and accessible. While most think of genetics as tracing family roots, the main use is now medical. Availability is limited by current scientific understanding, but we're seeing more coming available to consumers every year. Searching online for a specific functional system or disease will render available options. Genetic testing looks at both genes and gene variants and includes chromosome, DNA, biochemical, and protein truncated studies. These have become common tests for assessing risk to a long list of common diseases like Alzheimer's, numerous heart diseases, diabetes, cancer, and several more. Availability ranges from prescription orders via physicians to consumer-direct services like 23andMe.

The Alzheimer's Association offers a test for the APOE4 gene. About 25% of people with European ancestry have one copy of APOE4, doubling the chances of developing late-onset Alzheimer's. Another 2% to 3% of people have two copies of the variant, which places them at almost 10 times higher risk. Those with a family history of Alzheimer's are usually encouraged to get tested early.

ROUTINE HOME TESTS
Clinical screening tests are important but no substitute for what our body communicates to us on a daily basis. Vital Signs are a good place to start. These include body temperature, heart rate (pulse), respiratory rate, and blood pressure. Most of us know these, but just for grounding, normal vital signs:

Body Temperature:	98.6 °F (37 °C)
Resting Heart Rate (RHR):	50-100 bpm (high fitness tends toward lower RHR)
Respiratory Rate (RR):	12-20 breaths per minute
Blood Pressure (BP):	90-120 (systolic) / 60-90 (diastolic)

All of these metrics are readily measured in a home setting in a relaxed state.

BLOOD PRESSURE
Everyone benefits from having a blood pressure cuff at home and doing weekly checks while seated and restful. Falling outside these ranges isn't necessarily a cause for alarm, but at a minimum, signals

value in understanding why. The value in regular tracking is being able to quickly identify a change from normal. Blood pressure typically follows our circadian rhythm, highest during the day, dropping in the evening, and lowest during sleep.

A home test can be to take 3 readings daily for a week, morning, midday, and evening. Recording each value, and calculating an average Systolic (SBP) and diastolic (DBP) blood pressure will prove very informative. The next level would be hourly during the day starting before rising out of bed and the last being at the end of the day when back in bed for sleep. This yields about 16 data points with a BP profile versus time and a reference for single BP measurements in the future. MEDAC lifestyle practices help reduce blood pressure, and when that isn't enough, medications are very effective. Elevated blood pressure should never go untreated, due to the seriousness of the damage it causes over time.

HEART RATE VARIABILITY

One of the more interesting biomarkers to come along in recent years is Heart Rate Variability (HRV) because it's one of the rare indicators of baseline stress. Also rare is that it is readily available to consumers with several smart wearable devices.

HRV refers to the natural variability of heartbeats. Assume we are sitting at rest and our resting heart rate (RHR) is 60 beats per minute – a convenient single beat per second. Our heart is not a metronome. It constantly adjusts its rate based on a balancing act between the autonomic, sympathetic, and parasympathetic nervous systems. If we looked at every beat on an electrocardiograph, we'd be able to measure slight deviations in times between beats. At rest, our autonomic nervous system, our "autopilot" takes care of maintaining the body's active functions as we coast along. Apply stress and we're likely to experience an increase in heart rate. That's our sympathetic nervous system kicking into action. Once the stress is removed, the body works to bring itself back to a calm, restful state. That's our parasympathetic nervous system taking over, eventually handing control back to the autonomic nervous system.

Stress can come from any source, physical or emotional. Under stress, heart rate is affected and so is HRV. It's maximal at rest and minimal under high stress, so a higher HRV is better. High HRV is desirable because it indicates that the autonomic nervous system is back in control and the heart is in a relaxed state. We measure this by the drift in cycle times between beats. The more relaxed the body, the higher the HRV.

Figure 43 illustrates the heartbeat behavior of an individual at rest (upper plot), and the same individual under physical workload stress (lower plot). The high heartbeat variability in the upper plot indicates a high HRV – a good thing. After the physical stress is removed, it returns to its naturally relaxed, somewhat drifting heartbeat (upper plot).

There are many options to measure HRV and thankfully they require nothing more than wearing a smartwatch or an Oura ring, Whoop wrist strap, or other similar device. The wearable devices do all the tracking for us. There are a few ways to interpret HRV data, evidenced by some different application software, but they all get to a measurement of stress. As with all smart consumer devices, the relative measurements are more relevant than the absolute numbers. Comparing our trends over time is where these devices shine.

Figure 43: Heart Rate Variability (HRV)

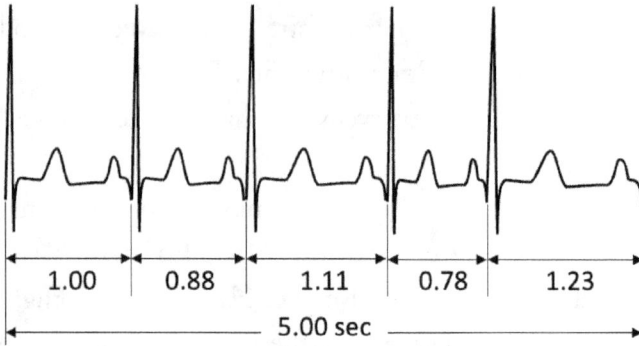

At rest, and under low stress (physical and emotional health), at an average of 1.0 beat/second (60 bpm), frequency drifts freely.

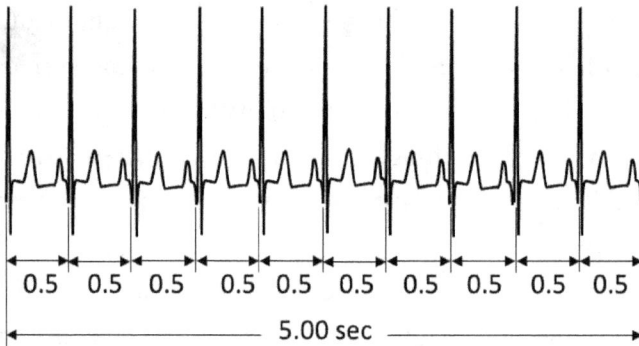

Under stress (elevated heart rate), frequency becomes more precise in response to stress.

GET SMART

Picking up from HRV, the world is getting smarter by the day, based on smart wearable devices. As with all technologies, these are going through some step changes since being introduced more than a decade ago. The GPS-enabled running watch that I wore back in 2010 has come a long way. GPS is more common now, but it's still an energy hog, so these require more frequent charging.

The devices mentioned earlier, along with many more, capture an astonishing amount of data. They aren't as precise as medical-grade devices but they make up for it in accessibility and duration. Like many I suspect, my initial interests were minimal, and wasn't even aware of all that they could do. Thankfully the learning curve with them is short, and we can pick and choose what features catch our interest when we're ready to look into them.

Some of the common features:

- Fitness tracking by activity, duration, frequency, pace, etc.
- Steps per day
- VO2max cardiovascular fitness tracking
- Heart Rate 24/7 throughout activities, rest, and sleep
- Sleep tracking total hours, time at each sleep level, and movement
- Stress via HRV
- Blood oxygen saturation
- Walk, run, bike, swim pace
- Connectivity with many 3rd party health and fitness apps
- Notifications transferred from our smartphone
- Phone; call and answer
- Fall detection
- Emergency SOS notifications

There are many ways to keep health records, from a paper file, to a spreadsheet, to an online app. The best method is the one we're going to keep updated. I'll stress again, the most value is the long-term tracking, and that means something more than tossing it in a paper file. There are few things more disappointing than discovering the signs were there for a few years, and we simply overlooked the trend creeping up on us.

Privacy is always an important consideration, but at some point, without notice, a loved one is likely going to be called upon for help.

Online medical records within our home health system are usually informative, but if an event occurs during a vacation, particularly while traveling outside our country, we've effectively disabled the attending physician(s). At a minimum, travel companions should be equipped with an up-to-date list of medications, diseases, and allergies. Unintended drug combinations can do significant harm, and given the number of medications in circulation, this is not a trivial matter.

Tracking health data can be very rewarding, even though it's not all perfect. It takes a bit of time and organizing, and some biomarkers can be stubborn to get to where we want them. It's never done. Several geographic relocations over the years have required meeting more than my fair share of PCPs. Some are locked into a system that ties their hands, overly focused on productivity and reducing liability. Others are curious and eager to partner. These are the ones who will help us in our quest for continuous learning and proactive health management.

FINAL THOUGHTS

There is always more data we can gather. Our specific health situation and interests will naturally guide us to them, but hopefully, this serves as a constructive foundation for finding a balanced awareness of health. And of course, we should be mindful of not getting consumed in data, such that the data becomes the focus instead of our health. After all, nothing steals health away quicker than stress. It's also important to remind ourselves that data is just information. In health, frequently one plus one doesn't always equal two, and some biomarkers aren't as repeatable as others. Precision medicine is grounded in more data on the individual, enabling more informed decision-making and more reliable outcomes. Our role in the partnership will make a world of difference.

Chapter 16

INVESTING IN WHEALTH

CHANGE IS ABOUT THE only sure thing in our future; invest accordingly.

IMPACT & COMMITMENT

Every financial investment we make contributes to a future purpose, whether it's saving a specific dollar amount from every paycheck for a car, home down payment, trip, retirement plan, or another distant event. We initially view it as a simple binary concept—start now and reap later—something tangible that we can comprehend. It seems far off at the outset, but as we approach our goal, we become more attentive to the balance, realizing it is evolving into something significant.

Measuring our success along the journey, instead of waiting until the end for a door to open, is a gratifying experience. There are measurable milestones that weren't apparent or important to us initially. Perhaps we decide to adjust the plan slightly—an SUV makes more sense than the 2-door coupe we initially envisioned pre-children, or the house needs to be closer to schools. Maybe we want to modify the trip, or we have an opportunity to defer retirement and work three days a week, or perhaps the opposite, and we aim to retire earlier. The journey is never a straight line, or a list of boxes to check, and life may alter the destination, but the value of forward-looking intention is very real. Time spent with successful agers makes this remarkably clear.

Viewing life through a longer lens, coupled with intentional planning, significantly increases our odds of achieving the outcomes we seek. By planning, I don't mean living a scripted life. And by outcomes, I don't just mean the ultimate goal, but the many meaningful milestones along the way. There's a huge difference between putting money away for a rainy day and building toward specific goals.

Rim to Rim

Carol and Carlos stood overlooking the Grand Canyon, a day they had planned for months ahead—a 24-mile hike from the North Rim to the South Rim of the Grand Canyon. Past anniversaries had been marked by dinner, wine, flowers, and chocolate. They were nice, but life was slowly being ruled by routines that lacked intention. They realized that they needed to change the routine before it changed them. This year would be different—very different!

Arriving the afternoon before their trek, they gazed out over the canyon for the first time, standing in awe of its enormous scale. A black speck moved far off in the distance, and another followed closely. Hikers! It was a humbling moment neither felt prepared for. Their time spent training now seemed small. Had they done enough?

At 3:30 AM, standing at the edge, about to take their first step, the mighty canyon features were barely visible under the moonlight. Their headlamps would be their only source of light until sunrise, still hours away.

At mile 6 in Cottonwood Canyon, the sky above showed signs of daylight. Small rock wall features caught the rising sun and lit up like gold. The canyon walls steadily closed in on them as they approached The Box. The granite walls pressed in so close it almost seemed like they could touch both sides. A narrow ribbon of sky shone high above. At mile 16, a curtain seemed to open as the sun suddenly hit the canyon floor, sending the temperature rocketing upward without warning. It had been a warmup to this point. Already on their tired and sore feet for hours, the sun, altitude, and the climb back up were about to test their true preparedness. The 4,000-foot climb up "The Wall" was just ahead, an endless series of nearly 100 switchbacks.

Mile 22.5. The end was now within reach as they paused for their last water refill. A large family dressed in matching bright blue t-shirts emblazoned with "Grandpa's 80th" appeared ahead. They were returning to the South Rim from a shorter down-and-back day hike. In their excitement, the family hadn't noticed that Grandpa had fallen behind, staggering perilously close to the edge of the trail with a sharp drop-off. The effects of altitude and the climb can envelop people in just minutes. Instinctively, Carlos reached out to lead Grandpa to the safety of the wall while Carol went up ahead to notify the family.

Atop the South Rim, Carol and Carlos sat in silence, exhausted beyond anything either of them had ever known. Tears gently trickled down their cheeks as they looked back over the canyon to where their epic day had begun. As they rose awkwardly to their feet, a young boy, about 8 or 9 years old, ran up to them. "Thank you, thank you, thank you! My dad says you saved my Grandpa. He's why we're here."

Carol and Carlos developed a newfound respect and love for life that day. While not every year brings an epic adventure like the Grand Canyon, they commit to undertaking challenging experiences regularly. These endeavors serve as reminders of their past life, and that investing with intention is where real life is discovered.

BEST-BEFORE-DATE COMES HOME

Many aspects of life have a limited time in which they can be fully experienced, and it's often only after recognizing this limitation that we wish we had made different choices.

Nearly every packaged food item we purchase has a *Best Before Date*. While we understand that our health benefits from early intervention before disease, we tend to overlook a similar mindset to our housing. We invest substantial energy in preparing for a newborn to arrive with a well-equipped nursery, gates to block stairways, and plugs for potentially dangerous outlets, but we spend far less effort preparing our living space for life beyond the age of 60. Like food, our homes also have a Best Before Date. In other words, a three-story suburban dream home for a young, abled-bodied family of 4 isn't the ideal home for an elderly couple with limited mobility and desiring community connection without some important upgrades.

Several years ago, I initiated a business to assess the demand for upscale design solutions for retirement-age homeowners. My clients received design solutions that extended the Best Before Date of their homes by 25 years, along with updated aesthetics. We provided what builders ideally should have done during the home's original construction — a residence designed for a lifetime, not just the short window of time with children living at home. Today, many of those clients, some in their 80s and 90s, continue to thrive at home and reach out with questions or expressions of gratitude. It's heartwarming, but I can't help wishing that more of us understood that healthspan is earned, not gifted.

Smart Professionals Aren't Always Smart at Home

A business executive was preparing to retire and insisted on moving their main-floor laundry to an unfinished basement to gain closet storage space. She was heading in the wrong direction. Decluttering and improving accessibility are key principles to aging well at home.

A retired attorney in his mid-70s, who was already dealing with mobility issues, refused to consider functional upgrades to their second-floor ensuite bathroom. His wife had hoped I'd be able to talk sense into him, but he had other plans in mind.

The world is full of interior designers and contractors happy to take $50k for lipstick-on-a-pig projects, but I wisely took a pass on both projects.

Aging well encompasses more than just eating nutritious food, staying engaged, and continuous learning. It involves placing ourselves in a physical environment conducive to success, in a community of people we enjoy, within walking distance to parks, shops, and food. Ryan Fredrick, author of Right Place, Right Time, delves into this masterfully. It also means our home environment supports Forward Flow Design, allowing easy movement through main living spaces and into the outdoors, even on days when we aren't feeling our best. Feeling trapped in our homes should never be a concern, but it happens more easily than we expect.

COST CONUNDRUM

While it's relatively easy to distinguish between investment and cost in near-term personal financial decisions, the line becomes blurred when making money decisions concerning future health. If it were straightforward, issues like life and health insurance would be less complex. Cost is often presented as a barrier to upgrading one's future state, due to inherent uncertainty. Why pay for something we may never use when the funds could be utilized for current needs or tucked away for unforeseen expenses? Home and food are the two areas where this dilemma is most prominent. Let's explore the aspect of home first.

Is a repair bill for a broken furnace or leaky roof a cost or an investment? If deemed a cost, one might opt to go without or delay the expenditure, but this could lead to added collateral costs due to frozen pipes and water damage. A $500 spend that provides an additional 5-7 years of life, likely transitions both cost examples into sound investments.

Consider the earlier example of the attorney who was focused solely on aesthetic upgrades. We like what we know, even when it's a poor choice. In this case, spending money without addressing the tub is a cost and not an investment in functional use. He was still thinking old-school real estate, not realizing converting the tub to a shower would improve both function AND resale.

Modern myth: Homes are required to have a bathtub.

Homes are required to have a shower OR a bathtub. The tub myth is a carryover from the days of tiny metal shower enclosures and Baby Boomers planning to start families. That market now values accessibility and aesthetics.

The attorney's wife later privately shared that her husband's preference was to move into a high-end retirement facility where he could reminisce with his old corporate cronies, and the clock was ticking down on his interest in remaining at home. In contrast, his wife, younger and healthier, had expected to continue living at home for another 15-20 years. His investment mindset focused on a cosmetic facelift, while hers prioritized remaining at home in the community they'd nurtured for 35 years. These standoffs are common. In this case, it reflected a difference in future visions that wouldn't be resolved without some difficult conversations.

FOOD FINANCIALS

With some of the big food confounders out of the way, how does one approach eating for healthspan, and longevity while managing a budget? Focusing on simplicity, quality, variety, and minimizing waste will address many needs. Most of us will naturally land on a healthy balance of carbohydrates, protein, and fat if we're eating a variety of high-quality foods.

It's easy to point to food deserts and the saturation of fast foods in low-income areas, but I've yet to see a compelling case of an inability to eat healthy on a limited budget. A few examples of eating well at a low cost are in Table 3, but there are many more.

Table 3: Tasty Meal Ideas on a Budget

Under $0.50 per serving	Under $0.75 per serving
• Scrambled eggs with rice	• Sweet potato hash
• Roasted sweet potatoes	• Roasted brussel sprouts
• Oatmilk (homemade)	• Chickpea & onions spread
• Zucchini muffins	• Apple coleslaw
• Oatmeal	• Tuna pasta salad
• Granola (homemade)	• Baked beans
• Spicy carrot salad	• Roasted carrots
• Zucchini fritters	• Succotash

Under $1.00 per serving	Under $1.25 per serving
• Kimchi quesadillas	• Frozen organic strawberries
• Baked barley mushrooms	• Frozen organic cherries
• Roasted chicken thighs	• Frozen organic mango
• Pinto bean soup	• Frozen organic blueberries
• Creamed spinach	• Italian wedding soup
• Roasted cauliflower	• Green bean casserole
• Squash soup	• Southwest lentils and rice
• Spiced lentils & vegetables	• Pasta e fagioli
• Vegetable stew	• Kale & pasta salad
• Fresh organic apple	• Tuna casserole

Find more meal ideas by searching online for meals under a specific dollar value.

FRUITFUL EXERCISE

We are familiar with the expression "comparing apples to apples" when making cost and performance comparisons. It's a method of simplifying multiple variables into a very concise list, aiming to provide clarity. However, oversimplification carries its own risks. Strawberries serve as a great example for assessing financial and nutritional value. Let's compare the four options: fresh, frozen, organic, or conventional (with pesticides). We can see in Table 4 that fresh strawberries cost more than frozen, and organic costs more than fresh conventional. It's a $2 or a $0.75 cost to upgrade to avoid the pesticides for fresh and frozen respectively. Which one should we choose? According to the Environmental Working Group, EWG, fresh strawberries have the most pesticide residue of all the foods they test, so in the case of strawberries, organic is a smart choice. From a cost standpoint, fresh strawberries cost almost double that of frozen, especially when factoring in spoilage.

Table 4: Strawberry Pricing Options

Grocer Options	$/lb	Value
1. Fresh strawberries (organic)	$6.99	Fresh, local = optimal but seasonal Fresh, non-local = available year-round
2. Fresh strawberries (conventional)	$4.99	Fresh, local = okay in limited qty, seasonal
3. Frozen strawberries (organic)	$3.74	Available and convenient year-round,, high nutrients, high health benefit
4. Frozen strawberries (conventional)	$2.99	Available and convenient year-round, high nutrients, Limit qty due to health risk

The choice between fresh and frozen partially depends on the intended use. If the strawberries are for a smoothie or to top morning oatmeal or granola, frozen is preferable. Frozen strawberries preserve more flavor because they're allowed to ripen on the plant before being flash-frozen. This also allows the fruit to retain more nutrients compared to fresh foods picked prematurely and trucked long distances. The same rationale applies to several other fruits. I almost always opt for frozen organic, as it is a far better value than fresh, higher in nutrients, more convenient due to a very long freezer shelf life, has no spoilage losses, and supports optimal health. That's a lot of wins!

As with many food choices, there is both a short-term cost and a long-term investment counter-argument. It's not always necessary to buy the most expensive, but it's crucial to weigh the merits. On an annual cost basis, the frozen organic upgrade costs less than a pound of beef. Finding cost offsets without increasing our grocery bill can be achieved by reconsidering high-priced items that we might be better off having less of anyway. The gap in prices for many organic foods, especially packaged ones, is decreasing due to the growing volume of sales and supply, marking a significant change in our food system. Even major food companies are actively transitioning to Regenerative Agriculture (a higher standard of organic) as customer buying habits change and the costs of growing crops in depleted soils from chemical abuse rise.

Anyone who thinks they can't afford to eat healthy costs needs to look at the cost of early onset age-related diseases. There's no financial argument for sacrificing quality. Not everything needs to be organic. The EWG.org lists both the Dirty Dozen (foods to buy organic) and Clean 15 (foods that are low in pesticide residues), helping guide where to invest in organic. There are ways to save money, but sacrificing food quality shouldn't be one of them. One of the most straightforward ways to save is to buy less. Americans are consuming about

25% more calories per day than in 1960. For anyone in that position, a reduction in total calories with a focus on getting healthy, high-fiber calories could cover the cost of eating organic and still save money.

Beef is one of the highest cost-per-calorie foods, so it's not surprising that the industry has worked hard to reduce meat production costs. This accounts for the shift over the decades from grass-fed, pasture-raised livestock to Concentrated Animal Feeding Operations (CAFOs), and cheaper feed (corn after they are weaned instead of grass). About 85% of U.S. beef comes from CAFO feedlots.

Acknowledging the growing public awareness around meat, the industry did what industries do; rebrand a nearly identical product to make it sound healthier, which also allowed them to charge more for it. The result was what we now know as "grass-finished." This refers to cattle offered grass in their final 90 days prior to slaughter. Grass-finished appeals to the gullible consumer who imagines that a 1,000-pound animal can regenerate its muscle cells and transform its health in 90 days. In response to industry marketing behavior, the USDA introduced criteria in 2023 to qualify as grass-fed beef:

"The diet shall be derived solely from forage consisting of grass (annual and perennial), forbs (e.g., legumes, Brassica), browse, or cereal grain crops in the vegetative (pre-grain) state. Animals cannot be fed grain or grain byproducts and must have continuous access to pasture during the growing season."

This serves as another example of the value of digging deeper to understand cost versus investment. Excess consumption of beef presents known health risks, but excessive quantities of low-quality beef for humans present a significantly higher, avoidable risk. Causal health data around this is very clear now. If meat is part of our diet, we need to invest in quality.

THERAPEUTIC DOSE

In the journey of life, there exists a therapeutic dose for everything, but the question of the ideal dose is rarely straightforward. Supplements and specific food items serve as prime examples. We often encounter recommendations that emphasize the health benefits of particular supplements or foods, tempting us to elevate our intake. Those pursuing optimal health are prone to go overboard with things that are deemed beneficial. Vitamin D, for instance, has garnered significant attention, with opinions ranging from it being unnecessary if one spends 15 minutes outdoors daily to advocating mega doses. Some of the considerations:

- Is it sunny or cloudy outside?
- How much skin is exposed?
- Is that inside or outside the tropic latitudes?
- How does UVB-blocking sunscreen play into this?
- Is the gut healthy enough to absorb it properly?

Vitamin D functions as a hormone, operating in tandem with various other biochemical processes in the body. While ensuring an adequate supply is crucial, excess doesn't necessarily equate to better outcomes; in fact, over-supplementation with vitamin D for extended periods can lead to toxicity and negative health outcomes. For individuals spending ample time outdoors and maintaining a high-variety, high-fiber diet, supplementing vitamin D may not offer additional benefits unless blood labs indicate a deficiency. The general guidance for those not outdoors for significant periods suggests a daily intake of around 4,000-5,000 IU for most individuals, but at the end of the day, our blood labs are the definitive guide.

SWEETENERS DOSE

Sugar, the sweet devil, tantalizes our taste buds in many sinful desserts and treats. It has emerged as the nemesis of the Western diet, spreading its influence globally. However, sugar is not a simple entity; it exists in various chemical forms.

We all know that added sugar is bad, but how much can one consume and still be considered part of a healthy diet? Estimates place it at about 25 grams of total added sugar per day. But if only it were that simple. Glucose, sucrose, galactose, fructose, and lactose are all common sugars, and they don't always play nice, especially fructose. Sucrose is a disaccharide consisting of one glucose molecule and one fructose molecule, or 50% glucose and 50% fructose. Of the many forms of sugar available, it is added fructose that's been labeled the devil incarnate, because of how negatively it affects the body. The body deals with glucose and fructose very differently, and while glucose is our primary source of energy, fructose does not contribute to energy or growth. It has no benefit to the body and is damaging. When we read "added sugar" on a label, it's a good bet that it's fructose because it is such a cheap ingredient. Fructose consumption remains rampant, at 23.2 lbs/year per capita, up from zero prior to 1970, as reported by the USDA. That works out to 28.8 grams per day per person ingesting high fructose corn syrup alone. Unfortunately, there's more. The USDA further reports that Americans also consume 50.7 grams of refined cane and beet sugar per day. Those two sources of sugar add up to 3 times the dose the body can metabolically manage.

Natural sugars found in whole foods are rarely an issue because of the fiber that typically is present in these foods. Fiber slows the ingestion rate and attenuates the blood glucose spike response. The sugar question is often posed in the context of desserts or sweet treats. Pairing it with some fiber, or at the end of a meal, is going to work better for us than as a standalone, because it dampens the insulin response. Trying to keep up with the math associated with each sip or bite would break the spirit of the most well-intentioned. The real value is in understanding the concept so that we can apply and manage a balanced intake. It's the villains hiding in plain sight that are often the most problematic. Our lips are the gatekeeper. Is what we are offered friend or foe, investment or cost?

BALANCE FOSTERS RESILIENCE

The therapeutic dose principle extends beyond food and pharmaceuticals, encompassing the Mind, Environment, Diet, Activity, and Community (MEDAC) spectrum. Too much focus on one area can move from an investment in health to a cost. For example, someone compulsively exercising or relying solely on diet as their means of staying "healthy" is not supporting healthspan. Aiming for the right "dose" and considering the benefit to our future self should be our guide. Analogous to sound consoles in recording studios, finding the right balance in various aspects of life allows for individual optimization, adjusting with seasons and age. It's always a moving target. The human body is a dynamic system, and we should welcome the opportunity to continuously tweak the levels to find our sweet spot.

Emphasizing big-picture balance, versus an exhaustive focus on details, greatly simplifies the approach and sets the stage for long-term success and resilience in the face of life's challenges.

When the walls come crashing down

Jim's office was in the hall of one of corporate America's iconic buildings. The view out over the gentle, lush green tree canopy below contrasted the battles being waged within the company. Our once prized flagship business unit was being ejected from the mother ship and tough decisions headlined every meeting agenda. The halls were filled with shuffling feet and glum faces of people consumed in stress and uncertainty. Jim had delayed his retirement to give his successors a fighting chance in the forced venture that was burdened with cost and rife with decades of contractual commitments.

Lean and vibrant, exuding the energy of a 25-year-old, I was beginning to understand why Jim didn't fit the typical classic corporate executive mold. The amusing stories and laughter paused only long enough for a bite of the salad he'd packed for lunch. The work discussion was easy, and in sharp contrast to the hundreds I'd witnessed over the previous months. There's nothing like stress to reveal people's true character. It was refreshing and inspiring, especially given the recent personal tragedy.

Just 2 weeks prior, I had attended a poignant church ceremony where Jim delivered a beautiful, and heartbreaking eulogy to his late wife. His strength left me pondering the source of such uncommon resilience.

Retired, remarried, and moving forward, I occasionally see Jim out running, always smiling, seemingly overflowing with gratitude. When life feels overwhelmingly complicated, and stressful, I think of Jim pulling out his homemade salad, smiling, and making meaningful connections with people despite the walls crashing down around him.

Resilience isn't a stroke of luck, it's nurtured through practice and investment in self. Small persistent investments in self don't just make a difference, they make all the difference. Perhaps, if we're lucky, we too can influence a few innocent observers along the way.

ENVIRONMENT FOR SUCCESS

Fifty years ago, life expectancy was about 10 years less than it is today. That has extended our number of retirement years, but unfortunately, they didn't get plugged in at the start, they got tacked on at the end. In other words, we got 10 more years, but not necessarily 10 more years with the same mobility, capability, and vibrancy. No one told the housing market to do anything different, and so they kept building the same homes they'd been building for decades. It's only very recently that the conversations are happening, which means it will be another decade or more before anything meaningful begins to appear in an already stressed housing inventory. Accommodating the changing needs of these additional years tacked on to retirement will require some very targeted personal planning and actions to support our wealth and healthspan.

Our decisions and plans for where we choose to live grow progressively more important with age. Remaining in place or progressing through a series of places can all work, provided they are well thought through, and we've got the next place chosen a decade or so ahead. Moving in the second half of life requires far more considerations than when we were young. It takes a lot longer to plan and more time to act on it. Years fly by ever quicker and options slip through our fingers.

Beyond age 60, we need to do some critical planning around access to the home. We need to make it accessible beyond our personal needs. It needs to be accessible to others who may be less mobile. Landscaping is the most attractive, and cost-effective, way to eliminate or a least minimize steps to access the home. Done well, it looks like a long overdue upgrade that adds curb appeal and makes entry and exit a breeze.

Average house size has doubled over the last century, but architects and builders haven't kept pace with door sizes, and these become significant barriers to anyone with mobility challenges. Wider (36-inch) doors look and function better, independent of resident ages. The incremental cost of a wider door is about $10, so they're a great investment if new doors are part of a remodel or a new build.

Lifespan homes include a main floor bedroom and bath or a lift to a second floor. Vertical lifts typically cost less than half of an elevator and take up less space. There's nothing wrong with using the stairs, but there will be times when we're not at our best and are better served by taking the lift. Ask anyone who's had foot, knee, or hip surgery. Lifts also eliminate the need and risk of carrying laundry and other bulky items up and down stairs. Injury prevention is fundamental to extending healthspan.

Residential lift. Photo courtesy of Stiltz Homelifts

A forward-looking view of maintenance planning helps maximize our options. Maintenance is one of the first things to slide for seniors who haven't planned well, and home equity slides even faster. Given home equity is what most of us will be relying on in later years, maintaining our primary investment is critical to the financial freedom we're expecting it to deliver. Reverse mortgages are steadily gaining popularity, and again, the equity we can leverage is tied directly to how well the home has been maintained. A yearly maintenance plan goes a long way to ensuring things don't fall off the radar.

From a very practical perspective, as we age, steps are at best a hindrance and at worse a hazard. They also limit our ability to take advantage of technology coming to us at an ever-increasing rate. Soon robots will be performing some of our routine tasks, and the fewer steps to deal with, the more we're going to be able to leverage technology. Looking well down the road, some nursing care is now being provided at home instead of in a facility. That's better for the senior, and it helps address the staffing shortage that will only increase as more Boomers age.

Investment in our homes is critical to improving our chances of optimal outcomes. A forward-looking investment approach that identifies opportunities that map out where we want to be, for how long, and everything we'll need in place to support the plan, will deliver one of the most impactful ROIs.

PROGRESSIVE MINDSET

Life moves faster. We've noticed it every decade of life, and we look forward to it slowing down. It doesn't. As it seemingly speeds up, our opportunities to recover from mistakes grow fewer. We're supposed to have figured it all out by age 40, but ask any 70, 80, or 90-year-old, and they will surely find that laughable. A progressive, forward-looking mindset does a few things for us. It embraces progress over perfection!

Life is progress! The more we can allow that mindset to occupy our thoughts, the more we crowd out the societal noise and negativity with which others seek to burden us.

Forward-looking means we're more than just optimistic, it means we're actively engaged in building a picture of ourselves in a positive setting. While today's view will always occupy the lion's share of our thoughts, a progressive planned approach puts options in front of us early and offers us time to choose between them. Just as the days count down on a 35,000-day life (96 years), so do our options.

Mountain Paradise

Sam ran the general store in a quaint, small town in the Appalachian foothills. His father had run the store, and his grandfather before that. A sign, "If you need it, we have it. If we don't, we'll get it." hung proudly on the wall behind the checkout. The young people had slowly left town and it had grown harder to keep the store staffed. Sam had made the tough decision to close the store, but couldn't bring himself to tell anyone or post a sign. He just stopped ordering inventory and would let it play out.

At first, not much changed. He'd pull stock to the front of the shelf, and things looked pretty much the same. A few close friends and customers had noticed the change in Sam's demeanor and had inquired about his health, wondering if something was wrong. He confided in them about his decision to close the store. Not surprisingly, they started stocking up themselves, and the shelves soon began showing serious signs of low inventory, causing a run on what remained.

Jamie showed up one fall Saturday afternoon, the first Saturday of the month, just like always. Jamie lived over an hour away, deep in the mountains, and had been making the monthly trip for basic supplies for years. Taking a quick loop around the store, Jamie made a beeline for Sam. Several of the staples were gone, and what was left, wasn't fit for use. Jamie was suddenly thrust into a corner without many options. Winter was closing in and life had suddenly taken an unexpected turn. Despite good health and thoughtful planning, it quickly became apparent that the mountain retreat was no longer sustainable. Jamie struggled through the winter, traveling much longer trips for supplies. Making it until spring was the overriding priority. It would be the last at the hundred-acre paradise that had been home since childhood.

Ironically, the next summer found Jamie and Sam sharing a small apartment in the city that looked out toward the mountains. While it would never feel like the mountain home, they still had the memories. And Jamie would finally come to learn about this thing everyone had been talking about since the 1980s: the internet!

PLAN A

Things worked out for Sam and Jamie, nothing like either had planned, but they had their health and were willing to restart their lives in a new location. They were both uncommonly resourceful and willing to adapt, qualities that can't be overstated when longevity is the intention. Both had planned better than most, but both had relied too heavily on Plan A. Plan A is appealing and it's easy. It sounds better than no plan, but life steps in and blindsides us, just like it did for Sam, Jamie, and Jim in the earlier story.

What is Plan A? For most people, it is to keep doing what they've been doing for as long as possible. And when that runs its course; *"We'll cross that bridge when we come to it"* is a common response. Anyone who has lived through coastal hurricanes and flooding inevitably identifies several upgrades that will mitigate the impact of the next storm. As devasting as hurricanes are to property, life events tend to be permanently life-altering. A Plan A mindset is associated with minimal change and a fear of making a bad investment. We all love a sure thing, but aging well acknowledges that change is about the only sure thing. We need to invest early and often.

PLANS B and C

A Whealthspan mindset is a portfolio mindset. If Plan A works out, that's great, but the overwhelming data says it won't. How will that affect my spouse, partner, adult children, grandchildren, etc.? Many people are impacted by our aging outcomes, and it obligates us to devote mind-time to plans B and C. We can't foresee the future, but we can easily envision some scenarios that would likely blow Plan A out of the water in a heartbeat. Major life events come in all shapes and sizes and never at a convenient time. How we respond to them is strongly influenced by our resilience and backup options waiting in the wings.

Getting Options on the Table Early

Angela handles admissions at a popular Continuing Care Retirement Community (CCRC). They have several hundred residents in private cottages, townhomes, apartments, assisted living, and memory care. Her current waitlist is 8 years, and getting on that list requires a significant deposit.

Most people over age 65 don't have a Plan B or C that's 8 months out, let alone 8 years. Those showing up late expecting the shelves to still be stocked will be in for a surprise much bigger than Jamie's. The wait times for getting regular medical appointments are a sure sign that rising demand is already outpacing the supply of medical services. The surge in demand around all things aging over the next 25 years will be unprecedented.

We don't need to plan for every scenario, but making intention-al plans toward living our best life well into our 90s starts decades earlier. It considers our loved ones, provides us with a wonderful goal to work toward, and helps avoid the setbacks that befall others. Plan A is easy. Plans B and C are where the real value resides. Intentional planning here will pay big dividends.

Change happens because life changes. It's about the only thing we can count on and so we benefit immensely by investing across the MEDAC foundations to support our best life.

Chapter 17

REBOOT

IT'S NEVER TOO EARLY and it's never too late is a common message we hear when it comes to making life changes. Despite decades of leading people through the process of change across a spectrum of circumstances, I resist change just like everyone else. Change inevitably involves uncertainty, uncertainty infers risk, and risk infers potential for failure. Life experiences teach us to slow down, assess, and move with caution. The older we are, the more this behavior is entrenched.

Growth involves change and an expectation of effort. Hundreds of millions of people across the globe quit smoking over the last 50 years. They all faced a clear choice between personal health and the habits and communities they found themselves in and chose to make the effort. It often took several attempts, but they eventually got over the hump and never looked back. Beyond the chemical addiction, the physical addiction of that cigarette between their fingers, and the social connections that reinforced their behavior, they opted to take on the hard work of change with very few promises of a better life. All they knew was that it would improve their odds.

Decades later we have the life expectancy data on previous smokers, and it is astounding. Tar-soaked lungs regenerated themselves, and these fortunate people earned their way back to normal life expectancy. Few would have believed that was possible just 20 years ago?

Constant growth is one of the best reasons to get out of bed each morning. Growth can take on many forms, from continuous learning, to extending our influence and impact, to just feeling better about the person inside. Growth is what propels us forward in life to be a better human.

Changing our Whealthspan involves not just doing a few things differently. It requires looking at our lives from other perspectives and acknowledging that some things aren't in alignment with the person we want to be in 5 years, in our later years, and how we want to be remembered. It's normal to get stuck. Life eventually steps in and uproots even the most stubborn of us with one. We have a name for those moments: crises. Proactive changes keep us nimble and on track toward an inviting future.

We are like sailboats. Adjusting course is essential to reaching our destination.

Much of what we've been looking at are the elements of building a personal foundation for growth. Our foundation enables us to go beyond yesterday's expectations and raise the bar. That inevitably involves leaving some things behind, or at least parking them for a considerable time to make space for new opportunities, new approaches, and new solutions. A view of taking a trip can help reduce anxiety around change.

Breaking The Routine

Robin received a call from an old friend. "My partner and I had planned a 6-week tour of Spain, Italy, and Greece but something's come up. Now it's just me. The travel, hotels, and food have all been paid for. It would be almost free for you. I would love for you to come with me. Please say yes."

Six weeks is a long time to turn off daily life and disappear, but what an amazing opportunity. It's long enough to get a true sense of different cultures and habits, away from the distractions that consume seemingly busy lives. Our initial response might be to recoil and think we can't possibly take that much time away from our well-worn daily habits. Stepping on the plane, everything gets very real, and we find it easier than expected to leave daily life behind. For Robin, it was life-changing. By week 4, the travel honeymoon was over, and it was clear that life at home could be so much different. Witnessing how others lived well made it possible to see that the changes so desperately needed weren't nearly as daunting as they seemed before stepping on the plane.

Stepping outside our comfort zone, away from daily rituals, into new places where we can observe healthy, happy habits in action can be one of the most effective ways of finally hitting the reset button. Change requires space, so breaking out of the daily pattern is step one. Cutting the cord to some vices and negative influences seems essential to almost all of us. This is a necessary step to make space in our lives for other doors to open and other hands to reach out and support us. There isn't an intervention coming. It's solely on us to make that first step toward a community that is ready to receive us and lend support in unexpected ways.

It's never the gym that changes a life, rather it's being surrounded by active people that makes the difference. It's never learning to dance, it's the people we dance with. It's never about the food just being healthier, it's about enjoying the exploration and discovery with others that makes it amazing. It's never about the bike, it's where the bike takes us and with whom. Our communities and surroundings help us grow or hold us back, and it's good to look around and assess where we are. Healthy communities surround us. We need only look for them and invite them in. They are notorious for lifting people up, with an *all-tides-rise* philosophy, reducing the uncertainties and risk of failure.

FINDING OUR FLOW

We tend to be careless with words like identity, purpose, and legacy. Taking time to sift through the thoughts of each of them can help to build a framework that will stand the test of time. There are always lots of things we can "do" but how we go about them comes from a place within us. We have to do a lot better than just going through the motions to stay on course toward our long-term goals as the winds of change constantly shift. It's the difference between movement and flow. To find flow, it helps to check in with who we are and what we're really about when everything is stripped away. Are we moving with a supportive community or are we following the masses? Both can create a sense of flow, but where they're headed is likely to be quite different.

Identity: We're told that maintaining our independence is important in life, especially in our later years. We imagine that independence defines our identity, but *interdependence* is where the real value is found. We are social creatures, and it's healthy to need and be needed.

Our identity is what is most at risk as we age. The older we get, the more society tries to marginalize us and strip away our identity. Spending time soaking on who we are, how authentic and connected we are in our relationships, and our ability to express ourselves can pay huge dividends.

Purpose: This gets at our sense of fulfillment and our life's meaning. A sense of contribution and impact is important to all of us, and it isn't measured by anyone's values but our own. As adults, we are quite likely to have more than one purpose, but we need to have clear distinctions between role and purpose. Roles are our responsibilities, tasks, job descriptions etc. Purpose speaks to underlying motivation and meaning. As an example, we say that great songwriters are remembered for having written great songs, but in truth, they are remembered for how their songs made us feel. Creating that experience is a songwriter's purpose, and what keeps them writing.

Legacy: It isn't something we can control but is certainly something we can influence. How would we like to be remembered? In most cases, we are remembered by the emotions we evoke in people. Again, we can't control that, but we can influence it by our behavior. Being authentic and connecting with people in meaningful ways is imperative. Connection needs to be practiced every day and in every interaction. People need to feel important and acknowledged, even if the significance isn't obvious. With practice, it becomes more self-evident.

ALIGNING VALUES

We have all probably overused the term values and diluted its significance. No doubt a more complex and distracted world has made it harder to check in with our values, but connection with them is foundational to realizing the outcomes we envision for ourselves. If we haven't given them dedicated mind time, we risk just going through the motions and falling well short of our potential. James Clear, author of Atomic Habits, offers more than 50 Core Values on his website at jamesclear.com/core-values. James' advice is to select less than 5 core values to focus on. "If everything is a core value, then nothing is really a priority." The better job we do at aligning our small decisions with our values, the easier the big decisions become. It's not rocket science, rather, it is authenticity and rigorous practice.

Adjacent to our personal values are the common values we share with our immediate and extended communities. Common values are what enable communities to come together, some growing into villages, towns, cities, and countries. Collectively we value things like lawful behavior, access to food, home supplies, medical services, etc. The more aligned the values of the people within these organized bodies, the easier it is to understand and accept the small differences, the more that gets accomplished, and the richer the life experiences. We feel safe and supported.

DESTRESSING

Stress comes to us in many flavors and needs constant care.

Clutter is found both in the physical things surrounding us and the felt commitments to those we serve. I've yet to meet anyone truly happier with more stuff underfoot. More stuff carries more burden - a burden to display, clean, show off, find, pay for, fix, justify, etc. Downsizing our material stuff is often one of the most impactful things we can do to ease chronic stress. We hear people talking about downsizing their homes, but often at the root of it is a need to downsize their material possessions.

Decluttering our relationship obligations also goes a long way to shedding stress. A felt need to please too many people or deliver on too many commitments can spill over into how we interact with others. Looking the other person in the eye and focusing solely on listening to what they are saying gets a much more positive reaction than half listening while attempting to multitask. It is core to a mutually gratifying exchange. The genuine hug and the obligatory half-hug send very different messages about how we're willing to engage with someone. Doing fewer things, but doing them well is more effective and more satisfying than trying to do more but falling short on multiple counts. We need to feel good about our capacity to get things done and our competency. It's a dynamic balance that's easy to recognize and manage once we find it.

Stressful events tend to be situational and short-term. Transitional situations may be swiftly addressed or best supported by patience, given time to pass on their own. Patience and intervention both have their place.

Chronic issues run deeper and can push us beyond our ability to resolve on our own. Day by day, these wear us down, eroding our dignity and self-worth, leaving us in a state of chronic stress. When they challenge our values, then we can't afford to be victims. It comes at too high a cost. We need to find a constructive way to get our lives back on track. This may be one of those times in life when we need to let the issue see the light of day and possibly seek help.

Stress can also be environment-induced. Two people in an otherwise healthy relationship can have very different ideas of the ideal place to raise a family or retire. Adult couples can find themselves in partner paralysis; a standoff that can play out over several years, waiting for the other to yield. Place matters a lot. It's easy to get stuck between families in different geographies and lifestyle preferences. No place is perfect, but exploring options and trying them on for size can create pathways to end the stalemate.

Diet frequently contributes to stress. We know from many studies that a poor diet directly induces stress. The chemical additives used in processing and preserving many foods affect us, as do their addictive ingredients. It's impossible to maintain a healthy attitude when we lack nutrients in our diet, and it's hard when families are on different food journeys. Preparing four different meals is a sure sign of unresolved dietary practices. The good news is that dietary stress can be one of the more straightforward to address.

We can all benefit from employing methods to manage stress. Managing stress is a life skill few of us have ever been taught but there are many effective tools and approaches. Finding the ones that work for us can be game-changing. Having a suite of options is better than going all-in on any one of them. Start small and keep expectations low. These all take time to develop our skills and comfort level.

Some active stress management examples:
- Deep breathing

- Exercise and yoga
- Meditation and mindfulness
- Journaling
- Obtaining stronger social support
- Intentioned time management
- Limiting stimulants, depressants, and pharmaceuticals
- Practicing gratitude
- Hobbies
- Improving sleep quantity and quality
- Healthy, nutrient-rich diet

The more objective we can be in evaluating sources of stress, the better our odds of resolving the root cause(s). Maybe we're in the wrong location, but a move to a isn't going to magically address poor lifestyle habits or other stressors. Getting to the root of the stressors, developing coping skills, and putting ourselves in a place for success are the doorways to finding and sustaining more joy.

HORMESIS

Not all stress is bad. Hormetic stresses delivered in healthy doses keep us sharp and aware of our body and mind. Exercise is an excellent example of hormetic stress. A habit of 30-60 minutes of daily exercise elicits small miracles in our mind and body. Inviting positive stressors in manageable doses promotes physical and cognitive resilience. Examples of these positive hormetic stressors include brain exercises, weight training, balancing, fasting, and short-term hot/cold exposures.

The human body requires stress. The question is how much is healthy. The hormesis profile in Figure 44 illustrates exercise stress, but the concept applies to virtually any type of stress. Very few people ever reach their optimal exercise dose. It requires a daily commitment of time. Elite athletes like to play on the far edge of optimal, and risk overtraining, but that requires an immense training load. For the rest of us, a pattern of building up to our optimal hormetic stress provides a positive and sustained health response. A blend of activities and intensities keeps it interesting and challenging, without the need to be overly prescriptive. This is the fun zone, where health becomes very aware and provides ample motivation once we reach this state.

Figure 44: Hormetic Effect of Exercise Activities

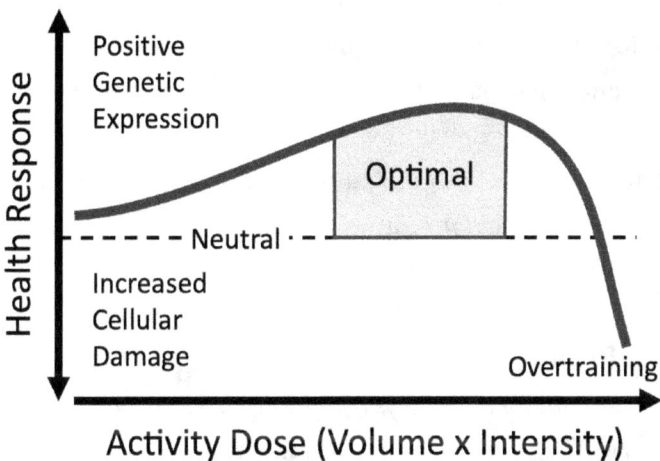

Hormesis stimulates growth and health. An optimal range requires daily, balanced inputs that occasionally challenge our limits and expand our comfort zone.

LIFELONG LEARNING

To be good at anything in life requires knowledge and regular practice. Aging well is no exception. Western society has long portrayed aging as something to be avoided and a liability to Western values. The practice has played a direct role in separating normal, healthy older adults from the mainstream and skewing our perceptions around aging. These stereotypes do us all a disservice and present barriers to experiencing positive aging up close and personal.

Visit, or even better, volunteer at an active senior event or community. Some senior centers are like college campuses, with hundreds of diverse programs, including academic, dance, language, travel, horticulture, technology, music, and arts. Many also feature performing arts for music and drama. The Bernard Osher Foundation has been instrumental in building centers for lifelong learning across the country, with the active participation of 125 colleges and universities and over 100,000 older adult students. A campus setting brings generations together for a rich experience. Teachers are typically experts in their respective fields in community settings of students who choose learning for its own sake. Programs like these are accessible both physically and financially, bringing a wide range of life experiences together in an educational environment. Most of all, they provide opportunities to look into our future and see new activities to challenge ourselves and communities of people waiting for us when it's our time to join them.

Sara's Pivot

What does one do after 35 years, of traveling the world in the mining industry? Why, become a poet of course! Pivots are fascinating moments in our lives, and they come in many forms. They know nothing of chronological time yet are all about timing.

With her formal career behind her, Sara set about exploring words and language in a way she'd never envisioned. It flourished into authoring books, founding a writer's workshop, and becoming a playwright and live actor. A woman of many talents and boundless energy, Sara brought the world to her community, investing in her craft and those looking for guidance and companionship on their journey.

Lifelong learning possibilities are immense and without age restrictions. They are fuel for our curious minds, place us in positive, physical environments, get us out into the world, and place us in supportive communities. They are also doorways to pivot into new and exciting lifestyle habits.

ROLE MODELS

Every medical colleague I know who has a focus on healthy aging, credits an older adult who impacted them early in life, often a grandmother. These people impacted them profoundly, causing them to pursue one of life's most challenging professions. Early role models serve as a far-off beacon, reminding us that there is a great life waiting for us when we finally come of age ourselves one day. These people are examples of purpose, identity, and legacy.

- Eighty-year-old retired accountant Robert McKeague finished Ironman Hawaii in 2005 and inspired me into triathlon. He's still blowing out birthday candles at 98.
- Sister Madonna Buder and I stood in line for coffee together after we'd both completed Ironman Canada. The look on my son's face was priceless. She was 77 at the time. She competed in over 400 events and still going strong at age 93.
- At age 64, Diana Nyad swam the 110 miles from Cuba to Florida. It took 5 attempts before finding success, highlighting her doggedness. She serves as an example that athleticism is about desire and persistence and has little to do with age.
- Julia "Hurricane" Hawkins set the 100-meter world record in the 105+ age group in 2021, broken 2-years later by Naani Rumbai with a time of 45.4 seconds.
- Business mogul Warren Buffett still heads into the office daily at age 93.

- Renowned naturalist and broadcaster, Sir David Attenborough continued to educate and inspire audiences with purposeful documentaries well into his 90s.
- Cicely Tyson, actor and trailblazer, was the oldest person to win a Tony Award for Best Actress at the age of 88, continuing to act well into her 90s.
- Willy Nelson, a unique role model for exercise for positivity, shared his 90th birthday with 17,000 lucky friends and fans, and is still touring and performing.

The examples of credible role models could fill a book. They pivoted at every age, and many pivoted more than once, reminding us that life is not a straight line. Pushing our boundaries and building new opportunities is where new life is discovered.

READY, SET, GO!

For every reason to move forward, there are a hundred more reasons to put it off. The inertia of daily living is often obscured by the thousands of distractions that trick our minds into thinking we are accomplishing more than we are. It's all too easy to feel like we've been extremely busy "making progress" only to find ourselves standing in the same spot we started a week or month ago.

Busy is the enemy of progress.

The digital world has amplified this effect, and we need to adapt and push back. At some point, our world will start shrinking, as a natural phenomenon of aging, so it's crucial to learn this skill early. What constitutes meaningful use of time? What constitutes progress? The answer is most certainly not being a slave to emails, texts, and social media.

Our reasons for change must be our own. No one can tell us the real motivations deep within us, the ones that will resist persistent pressures to slip back into old habits. We all need constant reminders of what is possible, which means placing ourselves in the sphere of others who lead by example. No motivational poster compares to the pull created by being surrounded by seasoned veterans to remind us that speed bumps are only momentary setbacks. The earlier we are in the journey to optimal health, the more nebulous this may seem, but again, look for and reach out to older adults who stand out from the crowd. They'll tell us it only gets easier. Just as a large jigsaw puzzle seems daunting at the start, each piece that's put in place builds more certainty around the life picture we're working toward.

Sustainable progress is measurable, which means there's value in measuring as much as possible about where we are now. When I started running in my forties, I knew that I was slow, but seeing my own progress was more motivating than seeing the longtime athletes trying to hang onto varsity-age versions of themselves. The only person worth comparing ourselves to is the person we were yesterday and the one we want to be tomorrow. There will always be others who are better, stronger, and faster than us. So what!

A lifetime of avoiding hard things catches up with us.

My exposure to disabilities from an early age profoundly influenced my perspective on abilities and attitudes. It rendered a deep respect and appreciation for the things they can do and little attention to what they can't. For us able-bodied people, our focus tends to center on what we can no longer do as well, and we avoid things that take too much effort. The fact that we can't move like we did in our twenties can easily become an excuse not to expend energy on moving now. An "I can't" mentality doesn't serve us, and avoiding hard things catches up with us. That doesn't mean we need to make life unnecessarily difficult, but achieving optimal self involves getting out of our comfort zones and expending some energy. In other words, achieving optimal self involves effort. It's going to feel hard at times. That's the feedback signal that validates our effort is making a difference.

MEDAC EASY START

Throughout the book, I've been consciously dripping the concept of MEDAC. By now the 5 elements might be committed to memory, but if not, here they are again: Mind, Environment, Diet, Activity, and Community. Which of the 5 feels most familiar and most certain? Which one feels least familiar and least comfortable? These 5 foundations work best when they are working together in balance. Out of balance, they are like a table or chair on an uneven floor, persistently rocking.

Where we are in each of these will vary, but what we all have in common is an imbalance. Massive or small imbalance, perfection is never achieved, nor does it need to be. Finding optimal is about continual growth in small ways in many areas. Here are some MEDAC-centered, quick, and easy ways to start building a more stable foundation:

MIND:

Take 2 minutes morning, afternoon, and evening to simply close the eyes while seated and focus on taking deep breaths, feeling a full chest for 5 seconds, and fully exhaling. Many thoughts will come and go, and that's okay. Focus on feedback from the body, things like an expanding ribcage, the building pressure within, the power we feel when filled with air, the sound the air makes running through the nostrils, and the shoulders dropping when the air escapes.

Consider how many moments and minutes each day we currently, actively devote to our health. Celebrate them. Honor ourselves for them.

Why do we choose our favorite MEDAC foundation? Why do we avoid our weakest MEDAC foundation? Should we add more time and commitment, or should we reallocate some of our time? Choose to do one small thing that is realistic and actionable. Make it a promise to ourselves that we can keep, no matter what life throws at us.

Pick an audacious age that we'd like to be doing something spectacular. Soak on that thought for a while. How would it feel? Who might it inspire? We've got lots of time to nurture and shape this one, so think BIG.

ENVIRONMENT:

Visit a nearby park, forest, or natural setting for a walk or hike, away from the trappings of the city and home. Sit with eyes closed and listen intently to the sounds.

Look inside the fridge and cupboards at the foods inside the home. Read the labels. Are they the best quality we can afford? Are there some processed foods we could choose to eliminate? How many fruits and vegetables have we got? How many of them are organic?

Invite an older adult with some physical limitations in for coffee or tea to learn how age-friendly our home really is.

DIET:

Track fiber intake for 5 days. What whole foods would it take to get to a 40-gram/day target? (Ease into it over 3-4 weeks.)

Make a healthy batch dish that provides enough for at least 2 leftover meals during the week (see recipes in the appendix for examples).

Try one new colorful, fiber-rich, whole food.

ACTIVITY: (adjust based on current ability):

Measure walking or running speed for at least 30 continuous minutes and measure the distance. Repeat the activity 3-4 times per week with a friend who's up for the challenge and record the time in a journal. Repeat the measured course weekly for a month. Compare the data over the 4 weeks. Build from there.

Buy some inexpensive resistance bands, and/or do squats and pushups, timed standing on one leg (each leg) 3x per week for 4 weeks. Start easy and build slowly each week. Our muscles will let us know the following day if we pushed too hard or not hard enough. Mild soreness that fades away is a reminder of a balanced effort.

Attend a yoga, tai chi, or mindfulness pilates class with a friend.

COMMUNITY:

Sign up for a special interest class that brings positive-minded people together for meaningful activities, education, and discussions.

Volunteer on 3 separate days at a local senior center and learn firsthand which seniors thrive and why.

Invite neighbors in for a potluck food-tasting event. It's a great way to discover people in the community with shared values around food and health.

There is nothing magical about these examples. The idea is to build our foundation in places we aren't as active as we could be. If it feels like it's on the edge of our comfort zone, that's precisely where we want to be. Start small. Resist overreaching and failing. There are no shortcuts. There will always be ample room to grow, and this is not a race to be won. Steady growth leads to greater confidence in our understanding and abilities.

Most of us will already be strong in some areas. If so, focus on the ones that feel outside our comfort zone. Diversity is the key to building a strong and resilient foundation and makes us more interesting to engage with in social settings.

These suggestions are loosely based on a 4-week plan. Note the word PLAN. There's a lot of power in a pencil and a piece of paper that's kept in view. New habits need help, otherwise we fold back into old habits. Like everything, it takes some time to get results. Keep the plan simple and ideally check off activities as they are completed. We humans love simple rewards – feed ourselves those healthy shots of dopamine.

A helpful organizational plan is to write Mind, Environment, Diet, Activity, and Community across the top of a sheet of paper and add ideas as they come to us. Check them off as we try each one and give the one we enjoyed most, a happy face. Remember that we shouldn't expect everything to be easy. Quite the opposite. It should feel like a healthy challenge, and only practice will lead to improvement.

GROUNDED IN GRATITUDE

Gratitude is a powerful elixir that not only enhances mental well-being but also boosts physical vitality. Numerous studies highlight its role in reducing stress, improving sleep, and enhancing immune function—integral elements of healthy aging. Transforming gratitude into a wellness ritual aligns our thoughts with our innate healing mechanisms. Appreciating the capabilities of our bodies fosters self-compassion, encouraging healthier lifestyle choices and activities that nourish both body and mind. In the tapestry of aging well, gratitude stands as a cornerstone, influencing not only the length but, more importantly, the quality of our years as we savor life's journey with a heart full of thanks.

Gratitude is more than just a platitude. If gratitude feels awkward or it sounds hollow, it might be one of our best places for early focus.

The studies around gratitude consistently reveal that it works. We live better and longer when gratitude is something we practice daily. With practice, we become better grounded and better equipped to transform intentions into outcomes.

In that vein, be thankful for opportunities to fail. It's a sign that we are pushing our boundaries and should be recognized for what it is: growth. Small failures are always filled with positive learning. We're more likely to succeed next time, having learned from the first few attempts. The experience leverages forward into our next opportunity to fail. Soon our attention shifts from failing to improving. Gratitude becomes authentic and second nature.

Finally, allow me to extend my immense gratitude for entertaining the many thoughts and words offered for consideration. May your journey be filled with discovery and opportunities that inspire others and one you'll reflect on with immense happiness and pride for many years.

Let's grow positivity and gratitude together. How can we use this moment to influence others? Who could use a lift? Let's be 5-star advocates for Whealthspan principles.

- One step becomes a million more steps.
- One moment becomes a million more moments.
- One life inspires a million more inspiring lives.

CABBAGE PANCAKES

Serves 4 (6-8 pancakes)

Unlike sweet pancakes, these are a fun and tasty twist on cabbage.

INGREDIENTS:

2	Large eggs
1.5 Tbsp	Soy sauce
1 tsp	Smoked paprika
1 tsp	Tandoori masala
1 tsp	Fresh ground pepper
1/4 C	Ground Flaxseed
1	Carrot, shredded
1/2	Yellow onion, diced
1/4C	Diced red pepper
2 Tbsp	Garlic, diced
1/3	Head cabbage finely sliced

TOPPINGS

1/4 cup	Veganese or mayonnaise
2	Tbsp Kewpie
2 Tbsp	Fresh cilantro, chopped
1	Tbsp Sriracha
1	Tbsp Sesame seeds
2	Green onions, chopped

PREPARATION

1. Preheat oven 350 °F
2. In a large bowl, whisk eggs, soy sauce, smoked paprika, and tandoori masala, pepper seasoning.
3. Gradually add flour, whisking until fully mixed and thickened,
4. Stir in shredded carrots, onion, red pepper, and garlic.

5. Stir in thinly sliced or shredded cabbage (red or white).
6. With a large spoon, scoop mixer and place onto non-stick baking sheet, press flat with spatula.
7. Continue until the baking sheet is full (6 fills a large baking sheet).
8. Press loose cabbage edges toward the pancake so that each is separate.
9. Bake in a 350 °F oven for 15 minutes. Flip and bake another 10 minutes or until desired doneness.
10. While pancakes are baking, mix toppings into a small serving bowl.
11. Serve pancakes hot, with topping.

"HEARTY" GRANOLA

Serves 10-14 meals

This hardy, quick, and convenient heart-healthy fiber and nutrient-rich breakfast has a low glycemic load thanks to the drop in sugar common to grocery options and the numerous complex carbs and healthy fats.

Prep time: 10 minutes, Cook time: 30 minutes

INGREDIENTS (organic whenever possible)
DRY

4C	Sprouted Oats, Gluten Free
1C	Hemp Hearts
2/3C	Chia Seeds
3/4C	Pumpkin Seed
1C	Slivered Almonds
1/2C	Chopped Pecans
1/2C	Chopped Walnuts
1/2C	Shredded Coconut
1/2C	Fresh Ground Flaxseed
1/2C	Sunflower Seed
1/2C	Wheat germ flakes
1/4C	Sesame Seed
3 Tbsp	Cinnamon
1 Tbsp	Nutmeg

WET

1/2C	Extra Virgin Olive Oil
1/2C	100% Pure Maple Syrup

DIRECTIONS

Preheat oven 325°F

Mix dry ingredients in a large bowl

Add wet ingredients and mix well by hand

Spread mixture onto large, lined cookie sheet

Bake 15 minutes, remix with spatula and bake another 15 minutes

Remove from oven after 30 minutes total, set aside to cool completely

Store in airtight container up to 14 days

Serve with favorite fruit and non-cow milk or plain yogurt

NUTTY OATMEAL

Serves 7

Packed with flavor, oatmeal is a minor player in this super-convenient, heart-healthy fiber + nutrient-rich breakfast. Add your favorite fresh or frozen fruit and non-cow milk or plain yogurt to check several healthy boxes that will curb hunger for hours.

Prep time: 5 minutes, Cook time: 12 minutes

INGREDIENTS (organic whenever possible)

1C	Sprouted Oats, Gluten Free
1/2C	Hemp Hearts
1/3C	Chia Seeds
1/2C	Pumpkin Seed
1/2C	Slivered Almonds
1/4C	Chopped Pecans
1/4C	Chopped Walnuts
1/4C	Shredded Coconut
1/4C	Fresh Ground Flaxseed
1/4C	Sunflower Seed
1/4C	Wheat germ flakes
1/4C	Sesame Seed
2 Tbsp	Cinnamon
1 tsp	Nutmeg
3C	Water

DIRECTIONS

Add all ingredients to a 3-quart pot
Cook on medium heat, uncovered until boiled, stirring occasionally

Reduce heat, simmer 10 minutes
Serve with favorite fruit and non-cow milk or plain yogurt
Refrigerate unused oatmeal in an airtight container for up to 7 days
Scoop out and reheat servings as needed

REFERENCES

Chapter 1

1. Australian Museum. (n.d.). How have we changed since our species first appeared? Australian Museum. https://australian.museum/learn/science/human-evolution/how-have-we-changed-since-our-species-first-appeared/
2. Oregon State University. (2011, August). Lasting evolutionary change takes about one million years. Oregon State University. https://today.oregonstate.edu/archives/2011/aug/lasting-evolutionary-change-takes-about-one-million-years#:~:text=Most%20species%20change%20so%20much,evolutionary%20changes%20is%20not%20certain.
3. Verywell Health. (n.d.). Longevity Throughout History. Verywell Health. https://www.verywellhealth.com/longevity-throughout-history-2224054
4. Harvard Health Publishing. (2019). Chocolate and your health: Guilty pleasure or terrific treat? Harvard Health Publishing. https://www.ncbi.nlm.nih.gov/pmc/articles/PMC6592896/
5. Cornell University. (2023, March 3). Wrinkles in time: Experience linked to heartbeat. Cornell University. https://news.cornell.edu/stories/2023/03/wrinkles-time-experience-linked-heartbeat

Chapter 2

1. Administration for Community Living. (n.d.). How much care will you need? Administration for Community Living. https://acl.gov/ltc/basic-needs/how-much-care-will-you-need
2. National Center for Biotechnology Information. (2022). Title of the article. Journal Name, Volume(Issue), Page range. DOI or URL
3. California Association of Health Facilities. (n.d.). Facts and statistics. California Association of Health Facilities. https://www.cahf.org/About/Consumer-Help/Facts-and-Statistics#:~:text=Nursing%20facility%20occupancy%20rates%20in,for%20one%20year%20or%20more.
4. Elder Needs Law. (n.d.). How many older adults will wind up in skilled nursing homes? Elder Needs Law. https://www.elderneedslaw.com/blog/how-many-older-adults-will-wind-up-in-skilled-nursing-homes#:~:text=5%25%20of%20older%20adults%20(aged,with%20three%20or%20more%20conditions.
5. Buena Vida Estates. (n.d.). What long-term care costs and how long you need it. Buena Vida Estates. https://www.buenavidaestates.org/what-long-term-care-costs-and-how-long-you-need-it/#:~:text=A%202019%20report%20from%20HHS,home%20residents%20was%20485%20days.

Chapter 3

1. Genworth. (n.d.). Cost of care trends and insights. Genworth. https://www.genworth.com/aging-and-you/finances/cost-of-care/cost-of-care-trends-and-insights.html
2. Administration for Community Living. (n.d.). How much care will you need? Administration for Community Living. https://acl.gov/ltc/basic-needs/how-much-care-will-you-need
3. Population Reference Bureau. (n.d.). Fact sheet: U.S. dementia trends. Population Reference Bureau. https://www.prb.org/resources/fact-sheet-u-s-dementia-trends/#:~:text=About%203%25%20of%20adults%20ages,adults%20ages%2090%20and%20older.&text=Women%20are%20slightly%20more%20likely,men%20had%20dementia%20in%202019.
4. Project Big Life. (n.d.). Dementia calculator. Project Big Life. https://www.projectbiglife.ca/dementia-calculator
5. Search Logistics. (n.d.). Lottery statistics. Search Logistics. https://www.searchlogistics.com/learn/statistics/lottery-statistics/

6. Federal Reserve Board. (n.d.). Data visualizations. Federal Reserve Board. https://www.fed-eralreserve.gov/econres/scf/dataviz/scf/chart/#series:Net_Worth;demographic:nwcat;popula-tion:all;units:median

7. MarketWatch. (n.d.). Here's exactly how much the average retired household spends each year on everything from housing to clothing. MarketWatch. https://www.marketwatch.com/picks/is-your-retirement-spending-normal-heres-exactly-how-much-the-average-retired-household-spends-each-year-on-everything-from-housing-to-clothing-01669923485

8. Yahoo Finance. (n.d.). How much savings should you have at 70? Yahoo Finance https://finance.yahoo.com/news/much-savings-70-140006145.html

9. Yahoo Finance. (n.d.). How many Americans have $100,000 saved for retirement? Yahoo Finance. https://finance.yahoo.com/news/many-americans-100-000-saved-192658338.html

10. Society for Neuroscience. (n.d.). How the brain changes with age. Society for Neuroscience. https://www.brainfacts.org/thinking-sensing-and-behaving/aging/2019/how-the-brain-changes-with-age-083019

11. Peters R. Ageing and the brain. Postgrad Med J. 2006 Feb;82(964):84-8. doi: 10.1136/pgmj.2005.036665. PMID: 16461469; PMCID: PMC2596698. https://www.ncbi.nlm.nih.gov/pmc/articles/PMC2596698/

12. Yahoo Finance. (n.d.). Here's when your net worth is considered poor in America. Yahoo Finance. https://finance.yahoo.com/news/heres-net-worth-considered-poor-143200526.html

13. CNBC. (n.d.). Average net worth of Americans ages 55 to 64. CNBC. https://www.cnbc.com/select/average-net-worth-of-americans-ages-55-to-64/

14. Forbes Advisor. (n.d.). Long-term care insurance cost. Forbes Advisor. https://www.forbes.com/advisor/life-insurance/long-term-care-insurance-cost/

15. National Center for Biotechnology Information. (2021). Title of the article. Journal Name, Vol-ume(Issue), Page range. DOI or URL

16. Parkinson's Foundation. (n.d.). Statistics. Parkinson's Foundation. https://www.parkinson.org/un-derstanding-parkinsons/statistics

17. CBS News. (n.d.). Social Security, Medicare: Seniors' struggles to pay bills. CBS News. https://www.cbsnews.com/news/social-security-medicare-seniors-more-americans-struggling-to-pay-bills/

18. Federal Reserve Board. (n.d.). Chart comparing data. Federal Reserve Board. https://www.federal-reserve.gov/releases/z1/dataviz/dfa/compare/chart/

19. Federal Reserve Board. (n.d.). Table of net worth distribution. Federal Reserve Board. https://www.federalreserve.gov/releases/z1/dataviz/dfa/distribute/table/#quarter:129;series:Net%20worth;demographic:networth;population:all;units:shares

20. Health System Tracker. (n.d.). How does medical inflation compare to inflation in the rest of the economy? Health System Tracker. https://www.healthsystemtracker.org/brief/how-does-medical-inflation-compare-to-inflation-in-the-rest-of-the-economy/#Annual%20percent%20change%20in%20Consumer%20Price%20Index%20for%20All%20Urban%20Consumers%20(CPI-U),%20January%202001%20-%20June%202023

21. Debt.org. (n.d.). Hospital surgery costs. Debt.org. https://www.debt.org/medical/hospital-sur-gery-costs/

Chapter 4

1. National Center for Biotechnology Information. (2020). Title of the article. Journal Name, Vol-ume(Issue), Page range. DOI or URL

2. Alzheimer Society Canada. (n.d.). Risk factors for dementia. Alzheimer Society Canada. https://alzheimer.ca/en/about-dementia/how-can-i-reduce-risk-dementia/risk-factors-dementia

3. Alzheimer's Association. (n.d.). Genetics. Alzheimer's Association. https://www.alz.org/alzhei-mers-dementia/what-is-alzheimers/causes-and-risk-factors/genetics

4. National Institute on Aging. (n.d.). Alzheimer's disease genetics fact sheet. National Institute on Aging. https://www.nia.nih.gov/health/genetics-and-family-history/alzheimers-disease-genet-ics-fact-sheet

5. Orlando A, Rubin B, Panchal R, Tanner A 2nd, Hudson J, Harken K, Madayag R, Berg G, Bar-Or D. In Patients Over 50 Years, Increased Age Is Associated With Decreased Odds of Documented Loss of Consciousness After a Concussion. Front Neurol. 2020 Jan 31;11:39. doi: 10.3389/fneur.2020.00039. PMID: 32082248; PMCID: PMC7005230. https://www.ncbi.nlm.nih.gov/pmc/articles/PMC7005230/

6. Cook AH, Sridhar J, Ohm D, Rademaker A, Mesulam MM, Weintraub S, Rogalski E. Rates of Cortical Atrophy in Adults 80 Years and Older With Superior vs Average Episodic Memory. JAMA. 2017 Apr 4;317(13):1373-1375. doi: 10.1001/jama.2017.0627. Erratum in: JAMA. 2017 May 9;317(18):1912. PMID: 28384819; PMCID: PMC5847263. https://www.ncbi.nlm.nih.gov/pmc/articles/PMC5847263/

7. Martin GT. Acute brain trauma. Ann R Coll Surg Engl. 2016 Jan;98(1):6-10. doi: 10.1308/rcsann.2016.0003. PMID: 26688392; PMCID: PMC5234377. https://www.ncbi.nlm.nih.gov/pmc/articles/PMC5234377/

8. Nature Neuroscience. (2022). Brain mapping and neuroimaging in dementia. Nature Neuroscience. https://www.nature.com/articles/s41531-022-00410-y

9. Parkinson's Foundation. (n.d.). Incidence of Parkinson's Disease in 2022. Parkinson's Foundation. https://www.parkinson.org/about-us/news/incidence-2022

10. Manly JJ, Jones RN, Langa KM, et al. Estimating the Prevalence of Dementia and Mild Cognitive Impairment in the US: The 2016 Health and Retirement Study Harmonized Cognitive Assessment Protocol Project. JAMA Neurol. 2022;79(12):1242–1249. doi:10.1001/jamaneurol.2022.3543 https://jamanetwork.com/journals/jamaneurology/fullarticle/2797274

11. Parkinson's Foundation. (n.d.). Incidence of Parkinson's Disease in 2022. https://www.parkinson.org/about-us/news/incidence-2022

12. Alzheimer's Association. (n.d.). Causes and risk factors: Genetics. Alzheimer's Association. https://www.alz.org/alzheimers-dementia/what-is-alzheimers/causes-and-risk-factors/genetics

13. Age as the greatest risk factor for Alzheimer's dementia. (n.d.). Alzheimer's & Dementia, 15(7), 965-975. https://doi.org/10.1002/alz.12068

14. National Institute on Aging. (n.d.). Alzheimer's disease genetics fact sheet. https://www.nia.nih.gov/health/genetics-and-family-history/alzheimers-disease-genetics-fact-sheet

15. National Institute on Aging. (n.d.). Study reveals how APOE4 gene may increase risk of dementia. https://www.nia.nih.gov/news/study-reveals-how-apoe4-gene-may-increase-risk-dementia

16. Stanford Medicine. (2022, May). Gene mutation linked to Alzheimer's disease. https://med.stanford.edu/news/all-news/2022/05/gene-mutation-alzheimers.html

17. CBC News. (2022, February 25). Deep sleep, memory and dementia: Second Opinion. CBC. https://www.cbc.ca/news/health/deep-sleep-memory-dementia-second-opinion-1.7030143

18. Neuroscience News. (2022, February 17). Dementia expected to surge. Neuroscience News. https://neurosciencenews.com/dementia-expected-surge-25112/

19. Forbes. (2023, October 1). Study links dementia to oral health: Let's talk oral-brain connection. Forbes. https://www.forbes.com/sites/milletienne/2023/10/01/study-links-dementia-to-oral-health-lets-talk-oral-brain-connection/?sh=60ad75d74a8f

20. NIH Research Matters. (n.d.). Hearing aids may slow cognitive decline in people at high risk. National Institutes of Health. https://www.nih.gov/news-events/nih-research-matters/hearing-aids-slow-cognitive-decline-people-high-risk

21. https://www.nih.gov/news-events/nih-research-matters/hearing-aids-slow-cognitive-decline-people-high-risk

22. Rao RV, Kumar S, Gregory J, Coward C, Okada S, Lipa W, Kelly L, Bredesen DE. ReCODE: A Personalized, Targeted, Multi-Factorial Therapeutic Program for Reversal of Cognitive Decline. Biomedicines. 2021 Sep 29;9(10):1348. doi: 10.3390/biomedicines9101348. PMID: 34680464; PMCID: PMC8533598. https://www.ncbi.nlm.nih.gov/pmc/articles/PMC8533598/

23. Science. (n.d.). The incredible shrinking human brain. Science. https://www.science.org/content/article/incredible-shrinking-human-brain#:~:text=Moreover%2C%20unlike%20the%20gray%20matter,about%206%25%20at%20age%2070.

24. Smolarz, Ana Paula de Souza, et. al., "Effects of Multicomponent Exercise on Functional and Cognitive Parameters of Hypertensive Elderly Women: A Quasi-Experimental Study." Journal of Aging Research, Volume: 2019, DOI: 10.1155/2019/5303761, https://www.ncbi.nlm.nih.gov/pmc/articles/PMC6663540/

25. Comparison of brain images from a young and an elderly participant. (n.d.). ResearchGate. https://www.researchgate.net/figure/Comparison-of-brain-images-from-a-young-and-an-elderly-participant-Brain-images-were_fig1_7921411

Chapter 5

1. Yahoo Finance. (2023, January 26). Retirement in 2023: How much does the average American have saved? Yahoo Finance. https://finance.yahoo.com/news/retirement-2023-much-average-american-120022301.html#:~:text=Investment%20firm%20Vanguard%20analyzed%20data,of%20about%2010%25%20from%202020.

2. Business Insider. (2020, March 30). Investments by age: How Americans are investing in non-retirement accounts. Business Insider. https://www.businessinsider.com/personal-finance/investments-by-age-americans-non-retirement-2020-3

3. Times of Israel. (n.d.). Ahead of annual Memorial Day, 161,400 Holocaust survivors living in Israel. Times of Israel. https://www.timesofisrael.com/ahead-of-annual-memorial-day-161400-holocaust-survivors-living-in-israel/

4. The Motley Fool. (n.d.). Average Retirement Savings: How Do You Compare? The Motley Fool. https://www.fool.com/research/average-retirement-savings/

5. SmartAsset. (n.d.). How Much Retirees Spend on Out-of-Pocket Medical Costs. SmartAsset. https://smartasset.com/retirement/how-much-retirees-spend-on-out-of-pocket-medical-costs

6. Health Care Cost Institute. (n.d.). Privately insured individuals with diabetes have double the out-of-pocket spending on health care than those without diabetes. Health Care Cost Institute. https://healthcostinstitute.org/diabetes-and-insulin/privately-insured-individuals-with-diabetes-have-double-the-out-of-pocket-spending-on-health-care-than-those-without-diabetes#:~:text=Even%20in%20this%20population%20with,%24613).

7. American Diabetes Association. (n.d.). Cost of Diabetes. Diabetes.org. https://diabetes.org/about-us/statistics/cost-diabetes

8. Chua K, Lee JM, Conti RM. Out-of-Pocket Spending for Insulin, Diabetes-Related Supplies, and Other Health Care Services Among Privately Insured US Patients With Type 1 Diabetes. JAMA Intern Med. 2020;180(7):1012–1014. doi:10.1001/jamainternmed.2020.1308 https://jamanetwork.com/journals/jamainternalmedicine/fullarticle/2766588

9. Khan Academy. (n.d.). Signal propagation: The movement of signals between neurons. Khan Academy. https://www.khanacademy.org/test-prep/mcat/organ-systems/neural-synapses/a/signal-propagation-the-movement-of-signals-between-neurons

10. Khan Academy. (n.d.). Introduction to cell signaling. Khan Academy. https://www.khanacademy.org/science/ap-biology/cell-communication-and-cell-cycle/cell-communication/a/introduction-to-cell-signaling#:~:text=Cells%20typically%20communicate%20using%20chemical,released%20into%20the%20extracellular%20space.

11. Nature. (2022). Title of the article. Nature. https://www.nature.com/articles/s41531-022-00410-y

12. BU Today. (2022). Title of the article. BU Today. https://www.bu.edu/articles/2022/why-do-people-live-to-100-and-how/

13. La Jolla Light. (2023, April 19). Love will survive: Holocaust survivor Fanny Krasner Lebovits shares her stories of 100 years of resilience. La Jolla Light. https://www.lajollalight.com/personalities/story/2023-04-19/love-will-survive-holocaust-survivor-fanny-krasner-lebovits-shares-her-stories-of-100-years-of-resilience

Chapter 6

1. PLOS Medicine. (n.d.). Title of the article. PLOS Medicine, Volume(Issue), Page range. DOI. https://journals.plos.org/plosmedicine/article?id=10.1371/journal.pmed.1004212

2. Centers for Disease Control and Prevention. (2020). Title of the document. Centers for Disease Control and Prevention. https://www.cdc.gov/healthyyouth/data/profiles/pdf/2020/cdc-profiles-2020.pdf

3. GlobeNewswire. (2023, July 28). Organic Foods Market to Grow from USD 202.7 billion in 2023 to USD 535.0 billion by 2032 with a compound annual growth rate (CAGR) of 12.90%. GlobeNewswire. https://www.globenewswire.com/news-release/2023/07/28/2713118/0/en/Organic-Foods-Market-to-Grow-from-USD-202-7-billion-in-2023-to-USD-535-0-billion-by-2032-with-a-compound-annual-growth-rate-CAGR-of-12-90.html#:~:text=Market%20Synopsis,period%20(2023%2D2032)

4. Michigan Department of Community Health. (n.d.). Title of the document. Michigan Department of Community Health. https://www.mdch.state.mi.us/osr/InDxMain/Infsum05.asp#:~:text=Historically%2C%20the%20infant%20death%20rate,1%2C000%20live%20births%20in%202010

5. Centers for Disease Control and Prevention. (2008, September 26). Prevalence of overweight and obesity among adults with diagnosed diabetes—United States, 1988-1994 and 1999-2002. MMWR. https://www.cdc.gov/mmwr/preview/mmwrhtml/mm4838a2.htm

6. Centers for Disease Control and Prevention. (n.d.). Chronic diseases. Centers for Disease Control and Prevention. https://www.cdc.gov/chronicdisease/programs-impact/pop/index.htm#:~:text=Chronic%20diseases%20are%20the%20leading,in%20annual%20health%20care%20costs.

7. Raghupathi W, Raghupathi V. An Empirical Study of Chronic Diseases in the United States: A Visual Analytics Approach. Int J Environ Res Public Health. 2018 Mar 1;15(3):431. doi: 10.3390/ijerph15030431. PMID: 29494555; PMCID: PMC5876976. https://www.ncbi.nlm.nih.gov/pmc/articles/PMC5876976/#:~:text=According%20to%20the%20Centers%20for,estimated%20%245300%20per%20person%20annually.

8. U.S. Department of Health & Human Services. (n.d.). Xavier Becerra. U.S. Department of Health & Human Services. https://www.hhs.gov/about/leadership/xavier-becerra.html

9. U.S. Department of Health & Human Services. (n.d.). About HHS. U.S. Department of Health & Human Services. https://www.hhs.gov/about/index.html#:~:text=The%20mission%20of%20the%20U.S.,public%20health%2C%20and%20social%20services.

10. U.S. Department of Health & Human Services. (n.d.). Mission, Values, and Vision. U.S. Department of Health & Human Services. https://www.hhs.gov/about/agencies/asa/foh/about-foh/mission-values-and-vision/index.html

11. Fortune Business Insights. (n.d.). U.S. Non-Alcoholic Beverages Market. Fortune Business Insights. https://www.fortunebusinessinsights.com/u-s-non-alcoholic-beverages-market-107932

12. Centers for Disease Control and Prevention. (2010). National Center for Health Statistics: Health, United States, 2010. Centers for Disease Control and Prevention. https://www.cdc.gov/nchs/data/hus/2010/022.pdf

13. https://www.ncbi.nlm.nih.gov/books/NBK570347/#:~:text=Indeed%2C%20a%20comprehensive%20analysis%20showed,relationship%20between%20mutagenesis%20and%20carcinogenesis.

14. International Agency for Research on Cancer. (n.d.). Agents Classified by the IARC. International Agency for Research on Cancer. https://monographs.iarc.who.int/agents-classified-by-the-iarc/

Chapter 7

1. National Human Genome Research Institute. (n.d.). Genetics glossary. National Human Genome Research Institute. https://www.genome.gov/genetics-glossary

2. Sharma M, Li Y, Stoll ML, Tollefsbol TO. The Epigenetic Connection Between the Gut Microbiome in Obesity and Diabetes. Front Genet. 2020 Jan 15;10:1329. doi: 10.3389/fgene.2019.01329. PMID: 32010189; PMCID: PMC6974692. https://www.ncbi.nlm.nih.gov/pmc/articles/PMC6974692/

3. World Health Organization. (n.d.). Cardiovascular diseases. World Health Organization. https://www.who.int/health-topics/cardiovascular-diseases#tab=tab_1

4. USAFacts. (n.d.). How have US fertility and birth rates changed over time? USAFacts. https://usafacts.org/articles/how-have-us-fertility-and-birth-rates-changed-over-time/
5. United States Census Bureau. (2022, April 12). Fertility rates declined for younger women, increased for older women. United States Census Bureau. https://www.census.gov/library/stories/2022/04/fertility-rates-declined-for-younger-women-increased-for-older-women.html#:~:text=Fertility%20rates%20in%20the%20United,women%20in%20that%20age%20group.
6. University of California, Berkeley. (2021, February 24). Our earliest primate ancestors rapidly spread after dinosaur extinction. University of California, Berkeley. https://news.berkeley.edu/2021/02/24/our-earliest-primate-ancestors-rapidly-spread-after-dinosaur-extinction

Chapter 8

1. Elixir Medical Corporation. (n.d.). Breakthroughs in coronary artery disease history. Elixir Medical Corporation. https://elixirmedical.com/breakthroughs-in-coronary-artery-disease-history/
2. Kandaswamy E, Zuo L. Recent Advances in Treatment of Coronary Artery Disease: Role of Science and Technology. Int J Mol Sci. 2018 Jan 31;19(2):424. doi: 10.3390/ijms19020424. PMID: 29385089; PMCID: PMC5855646. https://www.ncbi.nlm.nih.gov/pmc/articles/PMC5855646/
3. Rodgers JL, Jones J, Bolleddu SI, Vanthenapalli S, Rodgers LE, Shah K, Karia K, Panguluri SK. Cardiovascular Risks Associated with Gender and Aging. J Cardiovasc Dev Dis. 2019 Apr 27;6(2):19. doi: 10.3390/jcdd6020019. PMID: 31035613; PMCID: PMC6616540. https://www.ncbi.nlm.nih.gov/pmc/articles/PMC6616540/
4. Abstract 19074: Prevalence of Age-Advanced Coronary Artery Disease on Coronary CT Angiography
5. Ali M Agha, Jean-Paul Bryant, Maria Marquez, Melissa Kendall, William Sensakovic, Julie Pepe and Jeremy R Burt, 9 Jun 2018 Circulation. 2017;136:A19074, https://www.ahajournals.org/doi/10.1161/circ.136.suppl_1.19074
6. Association Between Family History and Coronary Heart Disease Death Across Long-Term Follow-Up in Men, The Cooper Center Longitudinal Study, Justin M. Bachmann, Benjamin L. Willis, Colby R. Ayers, Amit Khera and Jarett D. Berry, Originally published23 May 012 https://www.ahajournals.org/doi/10.1161/circulationaha.111.065490
7. American Heart Association. (2013). Older Americans and cardiovascular diseases fact sheet. https://professional.heart.org/-/media/phd-files-2/science-news/o/older-americans-and-cardiovascular-diseases-fact-sheet-2013-ucm_319574.pdf?la=en
8. The Athlete's Heart, A Meta-Analysis of Cardiac Structure and Function, Babette M. Pluim, Aeilko H. Zwinderman, Arnoud van der Laarse and Ernst E. van der Wall, Originally published25 Jan 2000 https://doi.org/10.1161/01.CIR.101.3.336 Circulation.
9. Medical News Today. (2023). Is heart disease genetic? Medical News Today. https://www.medicalnewstoday.com/articles/is-heart-disease-genetic#genetic-factors
10. Veljkovic N, Zaric B, Djuric I, Obradovic M, Sudar-Milovanovic E, Radak D, Isenovic ER. Genetic Markers for Coronary Artery Disease. Medicina (Kaunas). 2018 May 28;54(3):36. doi: 10.3390/medicina54030036. PMID: 30344267; PMCID: PMC6122104. https://www.ncbi.nlm.nih.gov/pmc/articles/PMC6122104/
11. Kovalova, S. 2005. What is a "normal" right ventricle? European Heart Journal - Cardiovascular Imaging, 7(4), 293. https://academic.oup.com/ehjcimaging/article/7/4/293/2367119
12. Law MR, Watt HC, Wald NJ. The Underlying Risk of Death After Myocardial Infarction in the Absence of Treatment. Arch Intern Med. 2002;162(21):2405–2410. doi:10.1001/archinte.162.21.2405 https://jamanetwork.com/journals/jamainternalmedicine/fullarticle/214413#:~:text=After%20a%20first%20MI%2C%2036,cumulative%20death%20rate%20of%2070%25.
13. Wilkins, J. T., Li, R. C., Sniderman, A., Chan, C., & Lloyd-Jones, D. M. (2016). Discordance Between Apolipoprotein B and LDL-Cholesterol in Young Adults Predicts Coronary Artery Calcification: The CARDIA Study. Journal of the American College of Cardiology, 67(2), 193-201. Wilkins JT, Li RC, Sniderman A, Chan C, Lloyd-Jones DM. Discordance Between

Apolipoprotein B and LDL-Cholesterol in Young Adults Predicts Coronary Artery Calcification: The CARDIA Study. Journal of the American College of Cardiology 2016;67:193-201.

14. Cromwell, W. C., Otvos, J. D., Keyes, M. J., et al. (2007). LDL particle number and risk of future cardiovascular disease in the Framingham Offspring Study - Implications for LDL management. Journal of Clinical Lipidology, 1, 583-592. https://pubmed.ncbi.nlm.nih.gov/19657464/

15. "Smoking and Cardiovascular Disease." Johns Hopkins Medicine. [https://www.hopkinsmedicine.org/health/conditions-and-diseases/smoking-and-cardiovascular-disease]

16. "Temporal Changes in Intracardiac Flow Patterns Before and After Transcatheter Mitral Valve Repair in Patients With Severe Secondary Mitral Regurgitation: A Cardiac Magnetic Resonance Imaging Study." Circulation: Cardiovascular Imaging. [https://www.ahajournals.org/doi/10.1161/CIRCIMAGING.120.010931?fbclid= IwAR09vOdQkEVaoq1EGhFBIh1eNrF5Qv TuwcWOL-luQsTqi0bstYFDO1sAOyIQ]

17. "Most cardiac arrests happen at home. Here's how to make yours heart-safe." Michigan Medicine Health Lab. [https://www.michiganmedicine.org/health-lab/most-cardiac-arrests-happen-home-heres-how-make-yours-heartsafe]

18. "Cardiac survival rates around 6 percent for those occurring outside of a hospital, says IOM report." National Academies of Sciences, Engineering, and Medicine. [https://www.nationalacademies.org/news/2015/06/cardiac-survival-rates-around-6-percent-for-those-occurring-outside-of-a-hospital-says-iom-report]

19. "Out-of-Hospital Cardiac Arrest: NHLBI Studies Tackle Deadly Public Health Problem." National Heart, Lung, and Blood Institute. [https://www.nhlbi.nih.gov/news/2023/out-hospital-cardiac-arrest-nhlbi-studies-tackle-deadly-public-health-problem#:~:text=Out%2Dof%2Dhospital%20cardiac%20arrest%20claims%20the%20lives%20of%20nearly,Hamlin's%20all%20the%20more%20remarkable.]

20. "Heart Disease Facts." Centers for Disease Control and Prevention. [https://www.cdc.gov/heartdisease/facts.htm]

21. "2019 American Heart Association Focused Update on Advanced Cardiovascular Life Support: Use of Advanced Airways, Vasopressors, and Extracorporeal Cardiopulmonary Resuscitation During Cardiac Arrest: An Update to the American Heart Association Guidelines for Cardiopulmonary Resuscitation and Emergency Cardiovascular Care." Circulation. [https://www.ahajournals.org/doi/epdf/10.1161/CIR.0000000000001123]

22. "Prehospital Advanced Cardiac Life Support for Out-of-Hospital Cardiac Arrest: A Systematic Review and Meta-Analysis." National Center for Biotechnology Information. [https://www.ncbi.nlm.nih.gov/pmc/articles/PMC8520516/]

23. "LDL Cholesterol Test: Understanding Your Results." Quest Diagnostics. [https://www.questdiagnostics.com/healthcare-professionals/clinical-education-center/faq/faq134#accordion-86db772278-item-e9874481e1]

24. "Alcohol Consumption and Cardiovascular Mortality in People With Atrial Fibrillation: The Atherosclerosis Risk in Communities (ARIC) Study." Journal of the American Heart Association. [https://www.ahajournals.org/doi/10.1161/JAHA.122.025858]

25. "CV Event Risk and LDL-C: Framingham Heart Study." LipidLink. [https://www.lipidlink.com/CV-event-risk-and-LDL-C.html]

26. "Exercise and Your Arteries." Harvard Health Publishing. [https://www.health.harvard.edu/heart-health/exercise-and-your-arteries#:~:text=Exercising%20muscles%20need%20more%20blood,use%20oxygen%20to%20generate%20energy.]

27. "Drug Overdose Deaths in the United States, 1999–2019." Centers for Disease Control and Prevention. [https://www.cdc.gov/nchs/products/databriefs/db395.htm]

28. "Premature Heart Disease." Harvard Health Publishing. [https://www.health.harvard.edu/heart-health/premature-heart-disease#:~:text=In%20older%20men%2C%20nearly%20all,about%2080%25%20of%20heart%20attacks.]

29. Pahwa R, Jialal I. "Atherosclerosis." In: StatPearls [Internet]. Treasure Island (FL): StatPearls Publishing; 2023 Jan-. Available from: [https://www.ncbi.nlm.nih.gov/books/NBK507799/]

30. "Stroke Facts." Centers for Disease Control and Prevention. [https://www.cdc.gov/stroke/facts.htm]
31. "Deaths: Final Data for 2019." National Vital Statistics Reports. [https://www.cdc.gov/nchs/data/nvsr/nvsr70/nvsr70-09-508.pdf]
32. "The top 10 causes of death." World Health Organization. [https://www.who.int/news-room/fact-sheets/detail/the-top-10-causes-of-death]
33. "Ischaemic Heart Disease (IHD)." World Health Organization Mortality and Health Statistics. [https://platform.who.int/mortality/themes/theme-details/topics/indicator-groups/indicator-group-details/MDB/ischaemic-heart-disease]
34. "WSO Global Stroke Fact Sheet." World Stroke Organization. [https://www.world-stroke.org/assets/downloads/WSO_Global_Stroke_Fact_Sheet.pdf]
35. "Association Between Marijuana Use and Risk of Stroke: A Mendelian Randomization Study." Scientific Reports. [https://www.nature.com/articles/s41598-023-48602-7]
36. Yankey, B. A., Rothenberg, R., Strasser, S., & Ramsey-White, K. (2022). "Marijuana Use and Cardiovascular Disease Risk: A Review of the Literature." Open Heart, 9(1), e001900. [https://openheart.bmj.com/content/9/1/e001900]
37. "Cannabis Use and Cardiovascular Risk: An Analysis From the National Health and Nutrition Examination Survey." JAMA. [https://jamanetwork.com/journals/jama/fullarticle/2795521]
38. "The Evolving Landscape of Cannabinoid Use in Cardiovascular Care: Implications for Cardiac Structure and Function." Circulation Research. [https://pubmed.ncbi.nlm.nih.gov/36233511/]
39. "Impact of Achieved LDL Cholesterol on Statin Use and Mortality in Patients with Coronary Heart Disease: Insights from the IDEAL (Incremental Decrease in End Points Through Aggressive Lipid Lowering) Trial." Arteriosclerosis, Thrombosis, and Vascular Biology. [https://www.ahajournals.org/doi/10.1161/ATVBAHA.114.303929]
40. "What is the age range for a heart attack?" Medical News Today. [https://www.medicalnewstoday.com/articles/heart-attack-age-range]
41. "Heart Disease and Age." Memorial Hermann Health System. [https://memorialhermann.org/services/specialties/heart-and-vascular/healthy-living/education/heart-disease-and-age#:~:text=While%20the%20average%20age%20for,under%20the%20age%20of%2065.]
42. "Potential Harms from Coronary Artery Calcium Scoring." American Family Physician. [https://www.aafp.org/pubs/afp/issues/2019/1215/p734.html#:~:text=Potential%20harms%20from%20coronary%20artery,misdiagnosis%2C11%20and%20downstream%20testing.]
43. "Safety in X-ray Imaging." RadiologyInfo.org. [https://www.radiologyinfo.org/en/info/safety-xray]
44. "Smoking Rate Hits New Low of 16% in U.S." Gallup. [https://news.gallup.com/poll/237908/smoking-rate-hits-new-low.aspx]
45. Vyas P, Gonsai RN, Meenakshi C, Nanavati MG. "Coronary atherosclerosis in noncardiac deaths: An autopsy study." Journal of Mid-life Health. [https://juniperpublishers.com/jfsci/JFSCI.MS.ID.555843.php]
46. Kissela, B. M., Khoury, J., Kleindorfer, D., et al. (2007). Epidemiology of ischemic stroke in patients with diabetes: the greater Cincinnati/Northern Kentucky Stroke Study. Stroke, 38(2), 419-425. [PDF: https://www.ahajournals.org/doi/pdf/10.1161/STROKEAHA.107.496513]
47. Roberts, M. B., Sloane, R., & Holohan, J. (2004). Influence of Diagnostic Test Interpretation on Medical Decision Making by Primary Care Physicians. JAMA Internal Medicine, 164(8), 864–870. [https://jamanetwork-com.udel.idm.oclc.org/journals/jamainternalmedicine/fullarticle/413914]
48. Nemetz, P. N., Roger, V. L., Ransom, J. E., Bailey, K. R., Edwards, W. D., & Leibson, C. L. (2008). Recent Trends in the Prevalence of Coronary Disease: A Population-Based Autopsy Study of Nonnatural Deaths. Archives of Internal Medicine, 168(3), 264–270. [DOI: 10.1001/archinternmed.2007.79]
49. Schellong, S. M., Porsch, P., Hoffmann, U., et al. (2021). Prevalence of Atrial Fibrillation in Different Stages of Heart Failure: A Systematic Review and Meta-Analysis. Circulation Research. [https://www.ahajournals.org/doi/epdf/10.1161/01.CIR.20.4.527]

50. "Cardiovascular disease risk in patients with multiple sclerosis: a systematic review and meta-analysis." European Journal of Neurology. [https://www.ncbi.nlm.nih.gov/pmc/articles/PMC8654686/]

51. Matthews, J. T., Fahey, A. J., Lund, L. K., et al. (2023). A Randomized Trial of Weight Loss and Exercise in Patients With Heart Failure With Preserved Ejection Fraction: Effects on Exercise Capacity and Quality of Life. Journal of Sports Medicine, 20(1), 38-48. [https://academic.oup.com/jsm/article/20/1/38/6986842]

52. Das A, Durrant D, Salloum FN, Xi L, Kukreja RC. PDE5 inhibitors as therapeutics for heart disease, diabetes and cancer. Pharmacol Ther. 2015 Mar;147:12-21. doi: 10.1016/j.pharmthera.2014.10.003. Epub 2014 Oct 31. PMID: 25444755; PMCID: PMC4494657. https://www.ncbi.nlm.nih.gov/pmc/articles/PMC4494657/

53. Kloner RA, Mitchell M, Emmick JT. Cardiovascular effects of tadalafil. Am J Cardiol. 2003 Nov 6;92(9A):37M-46M. doi: 10.1016/s0002-9149(03)00074-2. PMID: 14609622. https://pubmed.ncbi.nlm.nih.gov/14609622/#:~:text=Across%20all%20studies%2C%20the%20incidence,population%20(0.60%20per%20100%20patient

54. Luo, Y., Wang, Y., Shi, S., et al. (2019). Systematic review with meta-analysis: alcohol consumption and the risk of colorectal adenoma. Scientific Reports, 9(1), 1-10. [https://www.nature.com/articles/s41598-019-42592-1]

55. Xie B, Shi X, Xing Y, Tang Y. Association between atherosclerosis and Alzheimer's disease: A systematic review and meta-analysis. Brain Behav. 2020 Apr;10(4):e01601. doi: 10.1002/brb3.1601. Epub 2020 Mar 11. PMID: 32162494; PMCID: PMC7177569. https://www.ncbi.nlm.nih.gov/pmc/articles/PMC7177569/

Chapter 9

1. "Food Additive Status List." U.S. Food and Drug Administration. [https://www.fda.gov/food/food-additives-petitions/food-additive-status-list]

2. "The National Health and Nutrition Examination Survey (NHANES)." National Center for Biotechnology Information. [https://www.ncbi.nlm.nih.gov/books/NBK216714/]

3. "Deaths: Final Data for 2019." National Vital Statistics Reports. [https://www.cdc.gov/nchs/data/ad/ad347.pdf]

4. "Health, United States, 2018 – Data Finder." National Center for Health Statistics. [https://www.cdc.gov/nchs/data/nhsr/nhsr122-508.pdf]

5. "Prevalence of Diabetes Among Hispanics in Six U.S. Geographic Areas: The Hchs/Sol Results." Journal of Internal Medicine. [https://onlinelibrary.wiley.com/doi/epdf/10.1111/joim.13639]

6. "Autoimmune Diseases." Cleveland Clinic. [https://my.clevelandclinic.org/health/diseases/21624-autoimmune-diseases]

7. "Press Room." American Thyroid Association. [https://www.thyroid.org/media-main/press-room/]

8. "Specialty Crop Block Grant Program." Agricultural Marketing Service - USDA. [https://www.ams.usda.gov/services/grants/scbgp/specialty-crop]

9. "The Troublesome Farming in the U.S." PBS - American Experience. [https://www.pbs.org/wgbh/americanexperience/features/troublesome-farming-us/]

10. "The science of healthy eating; LOOKING TO GIVE YOUR HEALTH A BOOST IN THE NEW YEAR? PROFESSOR TIM SPECTOR CAN HELP YOU REVOLUTIONISE YOUR DIET." Carmarthen Journal [Carmarthen, Wales], 4 Jan. 2023, p. 23. Gale General OneFile, link. gale.com/apps/doc/A732164540/ITOF?u=udel_main&sid=oclc&xid=0546f71a. Accessed 26 Feb. 2024. https://link.gale.com/apps/doc/A732164540/ITOF?u=udel_main&sid=oclc&xid=0546f71a

11. "Food and Nutrition Assistance Programs," United States Department of Agriculture - National Agricultural Statistics Service. [https://www.nass.usda.gov/Publications/Todays_Reports/reports/fnlo0222.pdf]

12. "Your Grandparents Spent More of Their Money on Food Than You Do." NPR - The Salt. [https://www.npr.org/sections/thesalt/2015/03/02/389578089/your-grandparents-spent-more-of-their-money-on-food-than-you-do]

13. "What's on Your Table? How America's Diet Has Changed Over the Decades." Pew Research Center. [https://www.pewresearch.org/short-reads/2016/12/13/whats-on-your-table-how-americas-diet-has-changed-over-the-decades/]

14. "Is the Cyanide in Flaxseeds Destroyed by Cooking?" NutritionFacts.org. [https://nutritionfacts.org/blog/is-the-cyanide-in-flaxseeds-destroyed-by-cooking/?utm_source=NutritionFacts.org&utm_campaign=c4744b83d7-RSS_BLOG_DAILY&utm_medium=email&utm_term=0_40f9e497d1-c4744b83d7-26753945&mc_cid=c4744b83d7&mc_eid=8ce0dc1ed9]

15. "Meat consumption (indicator)." Organisation for Economic Co-operation and Development (OECD) Data. [https://data.oecd.org/agroutput/meat-consumption.htm]

16. "Life expectancy and disparities in survival after a diagnosis of colorectal cancer: A population-based study." PLOS Medicine. [https://journals.plos.org/plosmedicine/article?id=10.1371/journal.pmed.1003889]

17. "Does Diet Soda Raise Blood Sugar A1c?" MedicineNet. [https://www.medicinenet.com/diabetes_does_diet_soda_raise_blood_sugar_a1c/article.htm]

18. "Both diet and regular soda may increase insulin levels." Medical News Today. [https://www.medicalnewstoday.com/articles/both-diet-and-regular-soda-may-increase-insulin-levels#:~:text=A%20recent%20study%20found%20that,diet%20and%20regular%20soft%20drinks.]

19. "Got Dairy? A Look at Dairy Consumption Trends." AEI Ag. [https://aei.ag/2016/05/09/got-dairy-look-dairy-consumption-trends/]

20. "Human exposure to insecticides in the UK general population: Associations with demographic and behavioural factors and implications for future health research." PubMed. [https://pubmed.ncbi.nlm.nih.gov/35876099/#:~:text=Organochlorine%2C%20organophosphate%2C%20synthetic%20pyrethroid%20and,%CE%B4%2D%2C%20and%20%CE%B2%2D]

21. "Beef lags behind chicken in U.S. per capita meat consumption." Farm Progress. [https://www.farmprogress.com/livestock/beef-lags-behind-chicken-in-u-s-per-capita-meat-consumption]

22. "Per Capita Consumption of Poultry and Livestock, 1965 to Estimated 2012, in Pounds." National Chicken Council. [https://www.nationalchickencouncil.org/about-the-industry/statistics/per-capita-consumption-of-poultry-and-livestock-1965-to-estimated-2012-in-pounds/]

23. "Nutrition Guidelines." World Health Organization. [https://www.who.int/publications/i/item/9789240074828]

24. "U.S. Broiler Performance." National Chicken Council. [https://www.nationalchickencouncil.org/about-the-industry/statistics/u-s-broiler-performance/]

25. "Life expectancy at birth, total (years) - Japan, United States." The World Bank. [https://data.worldbank.org/indicator/SP.DYN.LE00.IN?locations=JP-US]

26. "Lifestyle and Chronic Diseases: Application of the World Health Organization (WHO) STEPwise Approach to Chronic Disease Risk Factor Surveillance in Jamaica." PubMed Central. [https://www.ncbi.nlm.nih.gov/pmc/articles/PMC8839931/]

27. "Life: Vegetable Consumption Ranking in the US and Japan." Funalysis. [https://www.funalysis.net/life-vegetable-consumption-ranking-in-the-us-and-japan-with-3-figures-2]

28. "Goat Milk versus Cow Milk: A Comparison." Michigan State University Extension. [https://www.canr.msu.edu/news/goat-milk-versus-cow-milk-a-comparison]

29. "About GE Foods." Center for Food Safety. [https://www.centerforfoodsafety.org/issues/311/ge-foods/about-ge-foods#:~:text=Currently%2C%20up%20to%2092%25%20of,often%20used%20in%20food%20products]

30. "Dairy Goat and Cow Milk Consumption and Their Association with the Odds of Overweight and Obesity Among Children Aged 6–12 Years in Developing Countries." PubMed Central. [https://pubmed.ncbi.nlm.nih.gov/31170989/]

31. "Food & Beverage Manufacturing." Economic Research Service - USDA. [https://www.ers.usda.gov/topics/food-markets-prices/processing-marketing/food-and-beverage-manufacturing/]

32. Donley N. The USA lags behind other agricultural nations in banning harmful pesticides. Environ Health. 2019 Jun 7;18(1):44. doi: 10.1186/s12940-019-0488-0. PMID: 31170989; PMCID: PMC6555703. https://pubmed.ncbi.nlm.nih.gov/31170989/

33. "ABOUT GENETICALLY ENGINEERED FOODS" Center for Food Safety, https://www.centerforfoodsafety.org/issues/311/ge-foods/about-ge-foods#:~:text=Currently%2C%20up%20to%2092%25%20of,often%20used%20in%20food%20products)

34. Finicelli M, Squillaro T, Galderisi U, Peluso G. Polyphenols, the Healthy Brand of Olive Oil: Insights and Perspectives. Nutrients. 2021 Oct 27;13(11):3831. doi: 10.3390/nu13113831. PMID: 34836087; PMCID: PMC8624306. https://www.ncbi.nlm.nih.gov/pmc/articles/PMC8624306/

35. V. Neveu, J. Perez-Jiménez, F. Vos, V. Crespy, L. du Chaffaut, L. Mennen, C. Knox, R. Eisner, J. Cruz, D. Wishart, A. Scalbert, Phenol-Explorer: an online comprehensive database on polyphenol contents in foods, Database, Volume 2010, 2010, bap024, https://doi.org/10.1093/database/bap024

Chapter 10

1. "News & Perspectives on Public Policy: California." Kaiser Permanente. [https://about.kaiser-permanente.org/commitments-and-impact/public-policy/our-impact/news-perspectives-on-public-policy-california]

2. "Who Are Our Health Care Workers?" U.S. Census Bureau. [https://www.census.gov/library/stories/2021/04/who-are-our-health-care-workers.html]

3. "Public acceptability of healthcare services: A comparison of Hong Kong residents' and Mainland Chinese citizens' satisfaction." Nature Scientific Reports. [https://www.nature.com/articles/s41599-018-0201-x]

4. "CDC Childhood Lead Poisoning Prevention Program: A Win-Win Program." Morbidity and Mortality Weekly Report (MMWR). [https://www.cdc.gov/mmwr/preview/mmwrhtml/mm4843a2.htm]

Chapter 11

1. "Glyphosate Exposure Linked to Severe Depression and Cognitive Decline in American Adults - New Study." Sustainable Pulse. [https://sustainablepulse.com/2023/08/29/glyphosate-exposure-linked-to-severe-depression-and-cognitive-decline-in-american-adults-new-study/]

2. "Clinical and environmental exposure factors associated with depressed mood among community-dwelling older adults." Environment International. [https://www.sciencedirect.com/science/article/abs/pii/S001393512301664X]

3. "Impact of Depressive Symptoms on Subclinical Atherosclerosis Measured by Carotid Intima-Media Thickness in Subclinical Vascular Disease in Veterans Study." Circulation: Cardiovascular Imaging. [https://www.ahajournals.org/doi/10.1161/CIRCIMAGING.120.010931?fbclid=IwAR-09vOdQkEVaoq1EGhFBIh1eNrF5Qv TuwcWOLluQsTqi0bstYFDO1sAOyIQ]

4. "History of Flight" National Aeronautics and Space Administration, https://www.grc.nasa.gov/www/k-12/UEET/StudentSite/historyofflight.html

5. Juszczyk G, Mikulska J, Kasperek K, Pietrzak D, Mrozek W, Herbet M. Chronic Stress and Oxidative Stress as Common Factors of the Pathogenesis of Depression and Alzheimer's Disease: The Role of Antioxidants in Prevention and Treatment. Antioxidants (Basel). 2021 Sep 9;10(9):1439. doi: 10.3390/antiox10091439. PMID: 34573069; PMCID: PMC8470444. https://www.ncbi.nlm.nih.gov/pmc/articles/PMC8470444/

6. Eunkyoung Kim, Zhiling Zhao, John Robertson Rzasa, Matthew Glassman, William E. Bentley, Shuo Chen, Deanna L. Kelly, Gregory F. Payne, Association of acute psychosocial stress with oxidative stress: Evidence from serum analysis, Redox Biology, Volume 47, 2021, 102138, ISSN 2213-2317, https://doi.org/10.1016/j.redox.2021.102138.

7. Mackus M, Loo AJV, Garssen J, Kraneveld AD, Scholey A, Verster JC. The Role of Alcohol Metabolism in the Pathology of Alcohol Hangover. J Clin Med. 2020 Oct 25;9(11):3421. doi: 10.3390/jcm9113421. PMID: 33113870; PMCID: PMC7692803. https://www.ncbi.nlm.nih.gov/pmc/articles/PMC7692803/#:~:text=Together%2C%20these%20findings%20suggest%20that,inflammation%20during%20hangover%20are%20associated

8. Cummings JR, Schiestl ET, Tomiyama AJ, Mamtora T, Gearhardt AN. Highly processed food intake and immediate and future emotions in everyday life. Appetite. 2022 Feb 1;169:105868. doi: 10.1016/j.appet.2021.105868. Epub 2021 Dec 13. PMID: 34915102; PMCID: PMC8886797. https://www.ncbi.nlm.nih.gov/pmc/articles/PMC8886797/#:~:text=Overall%2C%20the%20 body%20of%20experimental,sustain%20or%20enhance%20positive%20emotions.

9. Vivana, J., The brain-nutrition connection: Study links ultraprocessed foods to cognitive decline, The Ohio State University, 2023 https://health.osu.edu/health/brain-and-spine/ultraprocessed-foods-linked-to-cognitive-decline#:~:text=The%20brain%2Dnutrition%20connection%3A%20Study%20links%20ultraprocessed%20foods%20to%20cognitive%20decline&text=A%20recent%20study%20suggesting%20a,help%20support%20a%20healthy%20brain.

10. Spalt EW, Curl CL, Allen RW, Cohen M, Adar SD, Stukovsky KH, Avol E, Castro-Diehl C, Nunn C, Mancera-Cuevas K, Kaufman JD. Time-location patterns of a diverse population of older adults: the Multi-Ethnic Study of Atherosclerosis and Air Pollution (MESA Air). J Expo Sci Environ Epidemiol. 2016 Jun;26(4):349-55. doi: 10.1038/jes.2015.29. Epub 2015 Apr 29. Erratum in: J Expo Sci Environ Epidemiol. 2016 Jun;26(4):436. PMID: 25921083; PMCID: PMC4641054. https://www.ncbi.nlm.nih.gov/pmc/articles/PMC4641054/

11. Dorsey ER, Sherer T, Okun MS, Bloem BR. The Emerging Evidence of the Parkinson Pandemic. J Parkinsons Dis. 2018;8(s1):S3-S8. doi: 10.3233/JPD-181474. PMID: 30584159; PMCID: PMC6311367. https://www.ncbi.nlm.nih.gov/pmc/articles/PMC6311367/

12. "How common is Parkinson's disease?" MedicalNewsToday, 2023 https://www.medicalnewstoday.com/articles/how-common-is-parkinsons-disease

13. Muir DCG, Getzinger GJ, McBride M, Ferguson PL. How Many Chemicals in Commerce Have Been Analyzed in Environmental Media? A 50 Year Bibliometric Analysis. Environ Sci Technol. 2023 Jun 27;57(25):9119-9129. doi: 10.1021/acs.est.2c09353. Epub 2023 Jun 15. PMID: 37319372; PMCID: PMC10308830. https://www.ncbi.nlm.nih.gov/pmc/articles/PMC10308830/

14. Enhancing Cardiac Rehabilitation With Stress Management Training, A Randomized, Clinical Efficacy Trial, James A. Blumenthal, Andrew Sherwood, Patrick J. Smith, Lana Watkins, Stephanie Mabe, William E. Kraus, Krista Ingle, Paula Miller and Alan Hinderliter, Originally published21 Mar 2016https://doi.org/10.1161/CIRCULATIONAHA.115.018926Circulation. 2016;133:1341–1350 https://www.ahajournals.org/doi/10.1161/CIRCULATIONAHA.115.018926

15. American College of Cardiology, American Heart Association, & Heart Rhythm Society. (2015). 2015 AHA/ACC/HRS Guideline for the Management of Adult Patients With Supraventricular Tachycardia: A Report of the American College of Cardiology/American Heart Association Task Force on Clinical Practice Guidelines and the Heart Rhythm Society. Circulation, 133(14), e506-e574. https://doi.org/10.1161/CIRCULATIONAHA.115.018926

16. Environmental Protection Agency. (2020, January). Glyphosate Interim Registration Review Decision Case Number 0178 [PDF]. https://www.epa.gov/sites/default/files/2020-01/documents/glyphosate-interim-reg-review-decision-case-num-0178.pdf

17. Vox Media. (2015, January 22). Everything you never wanted to know about poop. Vox. https://www.vox.com/2015/1/22/7871579/poop-feces

18. Zhuang, Z. Q., Shen, L. L., Li, W. W., Fu, X., Zeng, F., Gui, L., ... & Tan, Y. L. (2018). Intestinal Dysbiosis in Alzheimer's Disease. Journal of Alzheimer's Disease, 63(4), 1225-1231. https://content.iospress.com/articles/journal-of-alzheimers-disease/jad230993

19. Finch, Caleb E., & Burstein, Stanley M. (2024, January 1). Dementia in the Ancient Greco-Roman World Was Minimally Mentioned. https://www.verywellhealth.com/cancer-alley-5097197

20. Chen, C. F., & Pascual, M. (2020). US Atlantic Coast Fate of Local 1379: Strategies for Improving Environmental Health Disparities [PDF]. Environmental Science & Technology. https://pubs.acs.org/doi/10.1021/acs.est.9b06379?ref=PDF

21. TILT Research. (2020, August 26). Article of Interest: How Many Chemicals Are in Use Today? https://tiltresearch.org/2020/08/26/article-of-interest-how-many-chemicals-are-in-use-today/

22. Majors, Richard, et al. (2022). Microplastics in Our Environment: Sources, Fate, and Effects. Environmental Science & Technology. https://www.nature.com/articles/s41370-022-00482-1

Chapter 12

1. ResearchGate. (n.d.). The histogram of the bowel movements frequency per week. https://www.researchgate.net/figure/The-histogram-of-the-bowel-movements-frequency-per-week_fig1_344688091

2. González-Torres, S., Martín-Campillo, A., Herrera-Cabezo, J. P., Jiménez-Moleon, J. J., & Martín-Villén, L. (2021). Probiotic Effects on Gut Microbiota: The Impact on Nonalcoholic Fatty Liver Disease. Journal of Clinical Medicine, 10(18), 4051. https://www.ncbi.nlm.nih.gov/pmc/articles/PMC8427160/

3. Centers for Disease Control and Prevention. (2023). High Obesity Program (HOP). https://www.cdc.gov/nccdphp/dnpao/state-local-programs/fundingopp/2023/hop.html

4. American Academy of Child & Adolescent Psychiatry. (n.d.). Children and Watching TV. https://www.aacap.org/AACAP/Families_and_Youth/Facts_for_Families/FFF-Guide/Children-And-Watching-TV-054.aspx

5. National Institutes of Health. (2023, August 24). Highly processed foods form bulk of US youths' diets. https://www.nih.gov/news-events/nih-research-matters/highly-processed-foods-form-bulk-us-youths-diets#:~:text=Results%20were%20published%20on%20August,during%20the%20same%20time%20period.

6. Massa, J., & Sanchez, M. (2023). Sleep and cognitive performance in children with cerebral palsy: A systematic review. Neurology. https://n.neurology.org/content/early/2023/08/09/WNL.0000000000207747

7. https://www.health.harvard.edu/newsletter_article/proton-pump-inhibitors

8. https://www.cdc.gov/healthyschools/foodallergies/index.htm#:~:text=Food%20allergies%20are%20a%20growing,children%20in%20the%20United%20States.&text=That's%201%20in%20013%20children%2C%20or%20about%202%20students%20per%20classroom.

9. https://www.foodallergy.org/resources/facts-and-statistics

10. https://www.jacionline.org/article/S0091-6749(20)31587-6/fulltext

11. Allergen Bureau. (n.d.). Study finds surprising number of people living with multiple food allergies. https://allergenbureau.net/study-finds-surprising-number-of-people-living-with-multiple-food-allergies/

12. Dixon, B. E., & Haggstrom, D. A. (2019). Health Information Exchange Participation and Health Outcomes: A Systematic Review and Meta-Analysis. Journal of Medical Internet Research, 21(12), e15924. https://www.ncbi.nlm.nih.gov/pmc/articles/PMC6324316/

13. Boyman, O., Kaegi, C., & Akdis, M. (2018). Bavarian-Made Preparations for the Common Cold Have No Effect on Upper Respiratory Tract Infections: A Randomized Controlled Trial. Frontiers in Immunology, 9, 2939. https://www.frontiersin.org/articles/10.3389/fimmu.2018.02939/full

14. USAFacts. (n.d.). How many people in the United States suffer from allergies? https://usafacts.org/articles/how-many-people-in-the-united-states-suffer-from-allergies/

15. Cedars-Sinai. (n.d.). Autoimmune Diseases on the Rise: What to Know. https://www.cedars-sinai.org/newsroom/beverly-hills-courier-autoimmune-diseases-on-the-rise--what-to-know/

16. Autoimmune Institute. (n.d.). Autoimmunity on the Rise. https://www.autoimmuneinstitute.org/articles/about-autoimmune/autoimmunity-on-the-rise/

17. MedlinePlus. (n.d.). ANA - Antinuclear Antibody Test. https://medlineplus.gov/lab-tests/ana-anti-nuclear-antibody-test/

18. National Institutes of Health. (n.d.). Autoimmunity May Be Rising in the United States. https://www.nih.gov/news-events/news-releases/autoimmunity-may-be-rising-united-states

19. Leonard, J. (2020, October 7). Most common medications: Uses and side effects. Medical News Today. https://www.medicalnewstoday.com/articles/most-common-medications#lisinopril

20. National Institute of Diabetes and Digestive and Kidney Diseases. (n.d.). Overweight & Obesity Statistics. https://www.niddk.nih.gov/health-information/health-statistics/

overweight-obesity#:~:text=the%20above%20table-,Nearly%201%20in%203%20adults%20
(30.7%25)%20are%20overweight.,9.2%25)%20have%20severe%20obesity.%20have%20se-
vere%20obesity.)

21. Vargason, T., Booth, J., & Ward, W. (2018). Eating Disorders. [Updated 2021 Jan 15]. In: Stat-
Pearls [Internet]. Treasure Island (FL): StatPearls Publishing. https://www.ncbi.nlm.nih.gov/pmc/
articles/PMC5872693/

22. Zhu, Y., Li, X., Zhu, J., & Zhang, Z. (2022). Environment-driven changes in the gut microbiome contribute to obesity-associated liver tumorigenesis. Nature Communications, 13(1), 1259.
https://www.nature.com/articles/s41467-022-31502-1

23. Hernández, M. A., & Cano, P. (2015). Seasonal influences on the gut microbiome of the lizard
Sceloporus mucronatus. PLoS One, 10(1), e0111678. https://www.ncbi.nlm.nih.gov/pmc/articles/
PMC4281373/

24. Qin, C., Liu, L., Sun, D., et al. (2021). Relationship between sleep duration and the development
of hypertension in adults: A systematic review and meta-analysis. Molecular Nutrition & Food
Research, 65(1), e2001133. https://onlinelibrary.wiley.com/doi/full/10.1002/mnfr.202001133

25. Rostami, K., Kasravi, F., & Rostami-Nejad, M. (2021). Microbiota and Obesity: Is There Any
Association? [Updated 2021 May 25]. In: StatPearls [Internet]. Treasure Island (FL): StatPearls
Publishing. https://www.ncbi.nlm.nih.gov/pmc/articles/PMC9146949/

26. Centers for Disease Control and Prevention. (n.d.). Adult Obesity Prevalence Maps. https://www.
cdc.gov/obesity/data/prevalence-maps.html

27. National Institute of Diabetes and Digestive and Kidney Diseases. (n.d.). Overweight & Obesity
Statistics. https://www.niddk.nih.gov/health-information/health-statistics/overweight-obesity

28. National Safety Council. (n.d.). Crashes by Time of Day and Day of Week. https://injuryfacts.nsc.
org/motor-vehicle/overview/crashes-by-time-of-day-and-day-of-week/

29. Bureau of Transportation Statistics. (n.d.). National Household Travel Survey: Daily Travel Quick
Facts. https://www.bts.gov/statistical-products/surveys/national-household-travel-survey-daily-trav-
el-quick-facts

Chapter 13

1. United States Department of Agriculture. (n.d.). DRI Calculator for Healthcare Professionals.
https://www.nal.usda.gov/human-nutrition-and-food-safety/dri-calculator/results

2. United States Department of Agriculture, FoodData Central. (n.d.). FoodData Central. https://
fdc.nal.usda.gov/index.html

3. Liebermann, A. (2019, August 21). Pioneering Work in Organics Pays Off for Grimmway Farms.
Organic Grower. https://organicgrower.info/article/pioneering-work-in-organics-pays-off-for-grim-
mway-farms/

4. Li, Y., He, Y., Qi, L., et al. (2023). A meta-analysis of energy intake and body weight in
Chinese adults. Appetite, 169, 105478. https://www.sciencedirect.com/science/article/pii/
S0002916523233298#:~:text=Population%20characteristics&text=Among%20the%20partici-
pants%20who%20were,2073%20kcal%2Fd%20in%202000.

5. Scully, M. (2022, July 21). Charlottesville ranks 14th on 'Most Restaurants per Capita' list. I Love
Cville. https://ilovecville.com/charlottesville-ranks-14th-on-most-restaurants-per-capita-list/

6. Johnson, J., & Patel, N. (2021, October 5). Prevalence of Persistent Low Back Pain in U.S.
Adults. Medscape. https://www.medscape.com/viewarticle/995045?src=soc_lk_share&form=fpf

7. Emeka, P., & Osie, M. (2019). Comparative Analysis of Phytochemical Composition and Antioxidant Activities of the Leaves of Five Varieties of Vigna unguiculata (L.) Walp. Antioxidants, 8(8),
284. https://www.ncbi.nlm.nih.gov/pmc/articles/PMC6680489/#:~:text=The%20decreasing%20
order%20of%20total,%C2%B1%2012.44%20mg%20GAE%2Fg

8. Glycemic Index Foundation. (n.d.). Glycemic Index Chart. https://glycemic-index.net/glyce-
mic-index-chart/

9. United States Department of Agriculture, National Agricultural Statistics Service. (n.d.). Cattle
On Feed. https://www.nass.usda.gov/Surveys/Guide_to_NASS_Surveys/Cattle_On_Feed/index.

php#:~:text=Feedlots%20with%201%2C000%20or%20more,1%2C000%20head%20or%20 more%20capacity.

10. Chang, J. J., Lu, Y. H., & Wang, M. L. (2019). Nutritional management for inflammatory bowel disease and associated symptoms. Pediatric Gastroenterology, Hepatology & Nutrition, 22(1), 1-14. doi:10.5223/pghn.2019.22.1.1. https://pubmed.ncbi.nlm.nih.gov/30638909/

11. Ju, S. Y., & Lee, J. Y. (2015). Stomach cancer prevalence and risk factors in Korea. Gut and Liver, 9(5), 615-622. doi:10.5009/gnl14120. https://pubmed.ncbi.nlm.nih.gov/25552267/

12. Monteiro, C. A., Cannon, G., Moubarac, J. C., Levy, R. B., Louzada, M. L., & Jaime, P. C. (2013). The UN Decade of Nutrition, the NOVA food classification and the trouble with ul-tra-processing. Public Health Nutrition, 21(1), 5-17. doi:10.1017/S1368980017000234. https:// www.sciencedirect.com/science/article/pii/S0261561423003631

13. Park, S., & Bae, J. H. (2013). Probiotics for weight loss: A systematic review and meta-analysis. Nutrition Research, 33(9), 711-721. doi:10.1016/j.nutres.2013.05.007. https://pubmed.ncbi.nlm. nih.gov/24309174/

14. Sareen, S., & Kumari, S. (2013). Associations between nutrition, physical activity, obesity, and glycemic load with health-related quality of life among rural and urban Central-Eastern Europe-an adolescents. Acta Universitatis Sapientiae, Food and Nutrition, 6(1), 123-146. doi:10.2478/ journal-content-2013-0008. https://understandingag.com/nutritional-comparisons-be-tween-grass-fed-beef-and-conventional-grain-fed-beef/

15. Wojtala, J., Boniecka, I., Nowak, P., Rytel, L., & Zdybel, J. (2015). Influence of glycemic index of breakfast on energy intake at subsequent meal among healthy people: A meta-analysis. Nutrients, 7(5), 3449-3459. doi:10.3390/nu7053449. https://www.rootsofchange.org/wp-content/uploads/ Nutrient-Density-Data-Report-Sample.pdf

16. Fatemeh Ramezani, Farzad Pourghazi, Maysa Eslami, Maryam Gholami, Nami Mohammadian Khonsari, Hanieh-Sadat Ejtahed, Bagher Larijani, Mostafa Qorbani, Dietary fiber intake and all-cause and cause-specific mortality: An updated systematic review and meta-analysis of prospec-tive cohort studies, Clinical Nutrition, Volume 43, Issue 1, 2024, Pages 65-83, ISSN 0261-5614, https://doi.org/10.1016/j.clnu.2023.11.005.

Chapter 14

1. Kaiser Permanente. (n.d.). Regular Exercise Benefits Both Mind and Body: A Psychia-trist Explains. https://mydoctor.kaiserpermanente.org/mas/news/regular-exercise-bene-fits-both-mind-and-body-a-psychiatrist-explains-1903986

2. Cleveland Clinic. (n.d.). Dopamine. https://my.clevelandclinic.org/health/articles/22581-dopa-mine

3. Lopes, D., & Gallagher, M. (2020). Norepinephrine: From Basic Functions to Neurological Disorders. In Neurotransmitters in Brain Functions and Disorders (pp. 63-82). Academ-ic Press. doi:10.1016/B978-0-12-818701-1.00005-6. https://www.ncbi.nlm.nih.gov/books/ NBK540977/#:~:text=First%20identified%20in%20the%201940s,cognitive%20func-tion%2C%20and%20stress%20reactions.

4. Sperber, C., Cushing, C. C., & Klingman, K. J. (2021). Dopamine, Reward, and Motivation in Psychosis: A Review of Behavioral and Neuroimaging Research. Brain, 144(8), 2243-2258. doi:10.1093/brain/awab161. https://academic.oup.com/brain/article/144/8/2243/6174120

5. Stubbs, B., Koyanagi, A., Veronese, N., Vancampfort, D., Solmi, M., Gaughran, F., ... & Fornaro, M. (2021). Physical activity and loneliness among adults aged ≥50 years in six low-and middle-in-come countries. Aging & mental health, 25(10), 1806-1812. doi:10.1080/13607863.2020.18852 95. https://pubmed.ncbi.nlm.nih.gov/37332638/

6. Opel, N., Redlich, R., Kaehler, C., Grotegerd, D., Dohm, K., Heindel, W., ... & Dannlowski, U. (2019). Hippocampal atrophy in major depression: a function of childhood maltreatment rather than diagnosis?. Neuropsychopharmacology, 44(10), 1870-1876. doi:10.1038/s41386-019-0418-2. https://www.ncbi.nlm.nih.gov/pmc/articles/PMC6862425/

7. Morais, V. A., Silva-Correia, J., Barbosa, M. A., & Costa, B. M. (2019). BDNF levels are increased two weeks after a single intravenous infusion of autologous bone marrow mesenchymal stem cells in Alzheimer's disease patients. Scientific Reports, 9(1), 1-10. doi:10.1038/s41598-019-40040-8. https://www.nature.com/articles/s41598-019-40040-8#:~:text=BDNF%20levels%20are%20increased%20two,less%20characterized%20after%20chronic%20exercise.

8. Gomez-Pinilla, F. (2011). The combined effects of exercise and foods in preventing neurological and cognitive disorders. Preventive Medicine, 52(Suppl 1), S75-S80. doi:10.1016/j.ypmed.2011.01.025. https://pubmed.ncbi.nlm.nih.gov/33949164/

9. Hendriks, S. A., Dall, C. H., Granholm, A. C., & Fickling, S. D. (2021). A 10-week aerobic exercise intervention improves hippocampal function in predementia Alzheimer's disease: A randomized controlled trial. Alzheimer's & Dementia, 17, e052145. doi:10.1002/alz.052145. https://alz-journals.onlinelibrary.wiley.com/doi/abs/10.1002/alz.052145

10. Passos, G. S., Santana, M. G., Santos, P. C., Oliveira, A. V., Dias, R., & Medeiros, A. R. (2017). Can exercise affect hippocampal volume and function in the healthy aged? Evidence from animal studies. Frontiers in aging neuroscience, 9, 3. doi:10.3389/fnagi.2017.00003. https://www.ncbi.nlm.nih.gov/pmc/articles/PMC5463976/

11. Atzori, C., & Villari, A. (2012). Nitric oxide and geriatrics: Implications in diagnostics and treatment of the elderly. Reviews in the Neurosciences, 23(5-6), 615-623. doi:10.1515/revneuro-2012-0044. https://www.researchgate.net/publication/229072659_Nitric_oxide_and_geriatrics_Implications_in_diagnostics_and_treatment_of_the_elderly

12. Ahmadian, M., & Rostami, M. (2021). Nitric oxide supplementation improves cardiac health, enhances performance during exercise, and delays fatigue in moderately trained individuals: Nitric oxide supplementation. Integrative Medicine Research, 100814. doi:10.1016/j.imr.2021.100814. https://www.ncbi.nlm.nih.gov/pmc/articles/PMC9710401/

13. No author. (n.d.). Continuous vs. Intermittent Exercise: Does it Matter?. Zing Bars. https://zingbars.com/blogs/blog/continuous-vs-intermittent-exercise-does-it-matter

14. University of Basel. (2022, August 15). Exercise not only prevents but also reverses diabetes. ScienceDaily. https://www.sciencedaily.com/releases/2022/08/220815085707.htm

15. Alzheimer's Society. (n.d.). Physical exercise. Alzheimer's Society. https://www.alzheimers.org.uk/about-dementia/risk-factors-and-prevention/physical-exercise

16. Negative Splits. Fellrnr. https://fellrnr.com/wiki/Negative_Splits

17. Springer. (2022, November 29). Short and long sleep durations associated with increased mortality. Neuroscience News. https://neurosciencenews.com/sleep-mortality-22551/

18. Holsinger, T., Barker, W. W., & Harwood, D. G. (2023). Association Between Sleep Duration and Cognitive Decline. JAMA Neurology, 80(5), 582–588. doi:10.1001/jamaneurol.2022.4880. https://jamanetwork.com/journals/jamaneurology/fullarticle/2813439

19. Piedmont Healthcare. (n.d.). How exercise helps balance hormones. Piedmont Healthcare. https://www.piedmont.org/living-real-change/how-exercise-helps-balance-hormones

20. World Health Organization. (n.d.). Physical activity. World Health Organization. https://www.who.int/news-room/fact-sheets/detail/physical-activity

21. Nilsson, P. M., Emdin, C. A., & Kahan, T. (2023). Low physical activity levels and risk of incident cardiovascular disease events. Atherosclerosis, 350, 95–103. doi:10.1016/j.atherosclerosis.2022.12.023. https://www.atherosclerosis-journal.com/article/S0021-9150(23)05221-8/fulltext

22. Williams, A., 2021, "Nutritional comparisons between grass-fed beef and conventional grain-fed beef." Understanding Ag. https://understandingag.com/nutritional-comparisons-between-grass-fed-beef-and-conventional-grain-fed-beef/

23. Getting Good Sleep Could Add Years to Your Life - Neuroscience News. https://neurosciencenews.com/sleep-mortality-22551/

Chapter 15:

1. Li, C., Ford, E. S., Zhao, G., & Mokdad, A. H. (2020). Prevalence and trends of high fasting plasma glucose among U.S. adults: National Health and Nutrition Examination

Surveys, 1999–2012. JAMA Internal Medicine, 175(12), 1962–1964. doi:10.1001/jamaint-ernmed.2015.4100. https://jamanetwork.com/journals/jamainternalmedicine/fullarticle/2765245

2. Shanmugam, S. (2021). Exercise, blood sugar, and diabetes. StatPearls Publishing. https://www.ncbi.nlm.nih.gov/books/NBK566165/

3. The Public Library of Science (PLoS). (2021). Continuous glucose monitoring system and the ISO 15197:2013 criteria for the accuracy of blood glucose monitoring systems in type 1 diabetes. PLOS ONE, 16(5), e0251462. doi:10.1371/journal.pone.0251462. https://www.ncbi.nlm.nih.gov/pmc/articles/PMC9666953/

4. Mayo Clinic Laboratories. (n.d.). Blood Glucose. Cleveland Clinic. https://my.clevelandclinic.org/health/diagnostics/12363-blood-glucose-test#:~:text=Venous%20blood%20glucose%20tests%20are,of%20your%20baseline%20blood%20suga

5. Thomas, M. C. (2021). Using Home Continuous Glucose Monitoring for Hypoglycemia Detection. The Diabetes Educator, 47(2), 151–155. doi:10.1177/0145721721989055. https://www.ncbi.nlm.nih.gov/pmc/articles/PMC7576954/#:~:text=ISO15197%3A2003%20standards%20for%20blood,when%20below%2075%20mg%2FdL.

6. Christman, J. W. (2020). Clinical methods: The history, physical, and laboratory examinations (3rd ed.). Butterworths. https://www.ncbi.nlm.nih.gov/pmc/articles/PMC7235902/

7. Cleveland Clinic. (n.d.). Blood Glucose Test. https://my.clevelandclinic.org/health/diagnostics/12363-blood-glucose-test#:~:text=Venous%20blood%20glucose%20tests%20are,of%20your%20baseline%20blood%20sugar

8. Hristov, A. D., Rizzo, J. A., Ata, A., et al. (2020). Age, Sex, and Comorbidity as Risk Factors for Mortality in COVID-19 Patients: A Systematic Review and Meta-Analysis. PubMed Central. https://www.ncbi.nlm.nih.gov/pmc/articles/PMC7356999/

9. National Human Genome Research Institute. (n.d.). Polygenic Risk Scores. Genome.gov. https://www.genome.gov/Health/Genomics-and-Medicine/Polygenic-risk-scores

10. DeCamp, M., Ramadugu, K., Hoffman, M. D., et al. (2021). Telehealth and the COVID-19 Pandemic: Are We Ready to Make Telemedicine Primary? PubMed Central. https://www.ncbi.nlm.nih.gov/pmc/articles/PMC8615896/

11. Vigo, D. E., Thornicroft, G., & Atun, R. (2021). Estimating the true global burden of mental illness. PubMed Central. https://www.ncbi.nlm.nih.gov/pmc/articles/PMC9955360/#:~:text=The%20autonomic%20nervous%20system%20(ANS)%20modulates%20HR.,and%20increases%20HRV%20%5B42%5D.

12. Jochelson, K. (2020). Suicide in the UK: statistics and trends. PubMed. https://www.ncbi.nlm.nih.gov/pmc/articles/PMC7583712/

13. Sickle Cell Disease Association of America. (n.d.). What Is Sickle Cell Disease? PubMed. https://www.ncbi.nlm.nih.gov/books/NBK132148/#:~:text=For%20each%20state%2C%20a%20small,sickle%20cell%20disease%2C%20and%20hypothyroidism.

14. Dhana, K., Evans, D. A., Rajan, K. B., et al. (2020). Healthy lifestyle and the risk of Alzheimer dementia: Findings from 2 longitudinal studies. PubMed. https://pubmed.ncbi.nlm.nih.gov/32554763/#:~:text=Compared%20to%20participants%20with%200,to%205%20healthy%20lifestyle%20factors.

15. Centers for Disease Control and Prevention. (n.d.). FastStats - Deaths and Mortality. CDC. https://www.cdc.gov/nchs/fastats/deaths.htm

16. National Research Council (US) and Institute of Medicine (US) Committee on Health and Behavior: Research, Practice, and Policy. (2001). Health and Behavior: The Interplay of Biological, Behavioral, and Societal Influences. PubMed. https://www.ncbi.nlm.nih.gov/books/NBK1116/

17. Huang, J., Zhang, Y., & Chen, K. (2006). Multiobjective optimization of integrated water supply and wastewater treatment systems. Computers & Chemical Engineering, 31(7), 718-730. https://doi.org/10.1016/j.compchemeng.2006.01.015

18. Sampson, E. L., Muniz-Terrera, G., Davis, D. H. J., & Briggs, R. (2017). How exactly does a healthy lifestyle help prevent dementia? Medical News Today. https://www.medicalnewstoday.com/articles/how-exactly-does-a-healthy-lifestyle-help-prevent-dementia

19. Kong, H., & Zhou, J. (2012). Use of biochar derived from swine manure to improve soil quality and increase crop yield. Journal of Soil and Water Conservation, 67(5), 321-331. https://www.ncbi.nlm.nih.gov/pmc/articles/PMC3419206/

20. Gilroy, K. (2019). Meet hearables: The next revolutionary medical devices. Medical Device Online. https://www.meddeviceonline.com/doc/meet-hearables-the-next-revolutionary-medical-devices-0001

21. Dzaye, O., Razavi, A., Dardari, Z., et al. (2021). Modeling the Recommended Age for Initiating Coronary Artery Calcium Testing Among At-Risk Young Adults. Journal of the American College of Cardiology, 78(16), 1573–1583. https://doi.org/10.1016/j.jacc.2021.08.019

22. Zhang, J., Jia, Y., Qin, Y., et al. (2015). Impacts of nitrogen addition on soil ammonia-oxidizing microbial communities in a wheat maize rotation system. Applied Soil Ecology, 86, 16-24. https://www.ncbi.nlm.nih.gov/pmc/articles/PMC4581900/

Chapter 16

1. The Barbecue Lab. (n.d.). Healthy Eating Statistics. https://thebarbecuelab.com/healthy-eating-statistics/#:~:text=93%25%20of%20Americans%20want%20to,say%20they%20eat%20healthy%20ALWAYS.

2. Livingston, G. (2021). COVID Calories: 100 Million Americans Are Eating 18,000 More Calories. Psychology Today. https://www.psychologytoday.com/us/blog/never-binge-again/202105/covid-calories-100-million-americans-are-eating-18000-more-calories

3. US Department of Agriculture. (2023, March 17). What is grass-fed meat? AskUSDA. https://ask.usda.gov/s/article/What-is-grass-fed-meat#:~:text=Mar%2017%2C%202023&text=The%20diet%20shall%20be%20derived,pasture%20during%20the%20growing%20season.

4. US Department of Agriculture, Economic Research Service. (n.d.). Sugar and Sweeteners Yearbook Tables. USDA ERS. https://www.ers.usda.gov/data-products/sugar-and-sweeteners-yearbook-tables/

5. Harvard T.H. Chan School of Public Health. (n.d.). Added Sugar in the Diet. The Nutrition Source. https://www.hsph.harvard.edu/nutritionsource/carbohydrates/added-sugar-in-the-diet/#:~:text=The%20AHA%20suggests%20a%20stricter,of%20sugar)%20for%20most%20men%20for%20most%20men).

6. US Department of Agriculture. (2013, January 28). What's Your Beef: Prime, Choice, or Select? USDA Blog. https://www.usda.gov/media/blog/2013/01/28/whats-your-beef-prime-choice-or-select

7. US Department of Agriculture. (n.d.). What do beef grades mean? AskUSDA. https://ask.usda.gov/s/article/What-do-beef-grades-mean